A
National
Policy
for the
Environment

NEPA and Its Aftermath

RICHARD A. LIROFF is a Project
Associate for the Environmental Law
Institute, a unique nonprofit national
research center engaged in interdisciplinary education, research, and
publishing.

A
National
Policy
for the
Environment

NEPA and Its Aftermath

Richard A. Liroff

INDIANA UNIVERSITY PRESS
Bloomington · London

Chapter 3 originally appeared, in somewhat different form, in the August 1973 issue of *Environmental Law Reporter*. It is reprinted from *Environmental Law Reporter* with the permission of the copyright holder, the Environmental Law Institute.

Portions of Chapter 4 appeared in the Winter 1972 issue of *Loyola University of Chicago Law Journal*, and are reprinted with the permission of Fred B. Rothman and Company.

Portions of Chapter 4 also appeared in Stuart Nagel (ed.) *Environmental Politics*, copyright 1974 by Praeger Publishers Inc., and are reprinted with the permission of Praeger Publishers Inc.

Table 4–5 is used with the permission of The Conference Board.

Published in Canada by Fitzhenry & Whiteside Limited, Don Mills, Ontario

Manufactured in the United States of America

Library of Congress Cataloging in Publication Data
Liroff, Richard A
    A national policy for the environment.
    Bibliography
    Includes index.
    1. Environmental law—United States. 2. Environmental policy—United States. I. Title.
KF3775.L5 344'.73'046 75–28910
ISBN 0–253–33973–1   1 2 3 4 5 80 79 78 77 76

For my family and friends,
all trustees of the environment
for the generations to come

Contents

Tables

Acknowledgments

Many organizations and individuals supported preparation of this book. Thanks are due to the Woodrow Wilson National Fellowship Foundation and to the Brookings Institution for their financial assistance. Several congressional aides and many administrators in the Washington and regional offices of federal agencies patiently endured hours of questioning. Special thanks to Dan Mazmanian of Pomona College, who waded through and bluntly critiqued the earliest versions of several chapters. Similarly, Paul Friesema of Northwestern University offered tough criticism and much helpful advice. Lynton Caldwell of Indiana University furnished a useful assessment of a later draft. The Environmental Law Institute provided a congenial atmosphere in which to complete the manuscript. I owe a deep debt of gratitude to my colleagues there, who fully appreciated the importance I attached to completing this work. Peter Crane, former associate editor of *Environmental Law Reporter*, and Timothy Atkeson, former general counsel of the Council on Environmental Quality, contributed numerous helpful editorial suggestions prior to publication of an earlier version of Chapter 3. For their camaraderie and for their rapid typing of the manuscript, I thank Edith Dimond, Van Fitzgerald, Kristin Gehring and Keith Stanford. While all these organizations and individuals contributed to this work, as its author, I of course bear sole responsibility for its factual accuracy and for the analyses presented.

Most of the research reported here was conducted several years ago. The major issues arising during NEPA's first years are examined. While many significant developments through mid–1975 are noted, the major "second-generation" NEPA issues will have to be reserved for detailed treatment in "Son of 'NEPA and Its Aftermath'."

Richard A. Liroff

Washington, D.C.

A
National
Policy
for the
Environment

NEPA and Its Aftermath

1

Introduction

And the Lord spake unto Moses, "There is both good news and bad news. The good news is that plagues shall smite your Egyptian oppressors. The Nile shall be turned to blood. Frogs and locusts shall cover the fields, and gnats and flies shall infest the Pharaoh's people. Their cattle shall die and rot in the pastures, and hail and darkness shall visit punishment upon the land of Egypt. Then will I lead the children of Israel forth, parting the waters of the Red Sea so that they may cross, and thereafter strewing the desert with manna so that they may eat."

And Moses said, "O Lord, that's wonderful; but tell me, what's the bad news?"

And the Lord God replied, "It will be up to you, Moses, to write the environmental impact statement." [1]

That story appeared in *Playboy* in early 1975, and refers to an environmental impact statement required by the National Environmental Policy Act of 1969 (NEPA).[2] Not every law enacted by Congress produces contemporary revisions of biblical history, especially those published in *Playboy*. What is it about NEPA that is so special?

NEPA is the most sweeping environmental law ever enacted by a United States Congress. It was signed into law on January

1, 1970—President Nixon's first major executive action of the new decade. The law contains three principal provisions. First, it establishes environmental quality as a leading national priority by stating a national policy for the environment. Second, it makes environmental protection part of the mandate of all federal agencies, establishing procedures for incorporation of environmental concerns into agency decision making. Third, it establishes a Council on Environmental Quality in the executive office of the president to oversee and coordinate all federal environmental efforts.

Some of NEPA's impacts are readily measurable. For example, millions of dollars have been spent by federal agencies to prepare the environmental impact statements. Also, citizen activists have brought successful NEPA-based lawsuits that temporarily halted a variety of federal agency actions—from the granting of permission for construction of the trans-Alaskan pipeline to the granting of a federal charter for operation of a bank in Woodstock, Vermont.

As is any bold departure, NEPA has been praised and damned. One environmentalist stated that "it has done more to preserve and protect the environment than all of the previous environmental protection measures combined." Senator Henry Jackson, the leading architect of the Act, described it as making "fundamental and far-reaching changes at all points in the federal decision-making process which touch on environmental questions." [3]

Other commentators have been less charitable. A member of the Federal Power Commission, for example, characterized NEPA as a "paper monster." Life under the law had "approached chaos," claimed the *Oil and Gas Journal* in 1972, while the federal bureaucracy was reported as feeling that the statute was "the most annoying and troublesome law to be passed in years." [4]

NEPA's broad language has been in large measure responsible both for the statute's enormous impact and for the passions aroused in its support and opposition. It has been characterized as "almost constitutional" in its breadth and lack of specificity. One federal judge wrote that its meaning is "more uncertain" than most statutes because of the generality of its phrasing, while a second justice commented that it is "so broad yet opaque, that it will take even longer than usual to fully comprehend its import."[5]

The controversies stemming from this broad law have been the consequence of a system of governance in which piecemeal, incremental decision making predominates. This study traces the interactions of legislative, administrative, and judicial decision makers operating within this system over approximately five years—one year of legislative consideration of NEPA and four years of its implementation. The questions addressed include: What were Congress' expectations when it enacted NEPA? How was the law implemented by administrative agencies and interpreted by the courts, and how did the early pattern of conflict over it coincide or diverge from congressional expectations? Finally, how did Congress respond to the unanticipated consequences of its initial enthusiasm for environmental protection legislation?

NEPA was enacted when public interest in the quality of the environment was rising. The Santa Barbara oil spill had just occurred, the Cuyahoga River had caught fire, and the news was laden with stories of environmental trauma. Clearly a gesture of congressional concern was in order. For many legislators, undoubtedly, a vote for NEPA was symbolic—akin to a vote for motherhood and apple pie. Little did they realize, however, that in voting to enact NEPA, they were placing a potent weapon in the hands of citizen activists.

The impact of NEPA was probably greater than that expected by many congressmen, and the pattern of conflict over its implementation probably assumed a form far different from that which they anticipated. The absence of clear criteria within the law by which the legal adequacy of a decision could be adjudged, the limited policy coordinating influence of the Council on Environmental Quality (CEQ) established by the statute, and the opportunity NEPA provided for judicial review of agency decisions all encouraged the enforcement and definition of the law's requirements through judicial rather than administrative processes. Environmental groups acted as surrogates for CEQ through their litigation, playing a considerable oversight role that was beyond the Council's capabilities. The courts' role in providing a substantial degree of citizen access to agency decision making produced a reaction against NEPA in certain segments of Congress. Legislation was proposed for limiting court jurisdiction and exempting administrative actions from NEPA's provisions.

The message of this study is that Congress did not really enact a national environmental policy when it passed NEPA. Rather, it enacted only a statement of national environmental policy. The policy that actually followed NEPA's passage was the sum of all federal agency actions that had an environmental impact. Those actions, and their impacts, were shaped by CEQ's interpretation of NEPA, by the agencies' own procedural guidelines, by the litigation initiated by environmental activists, and by the response of Congress to judicial decisions resulting from the environmentalists' lawsuits. The process of interaction by which the de facto environmental policy emerged can be represented by the modest graphic model that provides the organizational backbone of this study. (See Figure I)

Chapter 2 focuses on NEPA's genesis in Congress. The Act's path through Congress is traced and its proponents' expectations and opponents' fears are examined. The interest groups most likely to be affected by NEPA showed little interest. The principal disputes over the bill were jurisdictional and involved only a few congressmen and senators, and hardly any attention was devoted to the bill's implications for judicial oversight of administrative decision making. Only two congressmen were alert to the possibility that NEPA might become a powerful tool

Figure I—Relationships Among Key Actors in Implementation of NEPA*

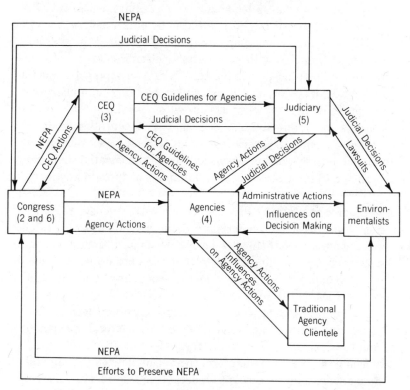

*All possible linkages are not shown. The numbers represent the principal chapters in which the key actors are examined.

for environmentalists, and they were outmaneuvered in conference committee and not heeded on the House floor.

Chapter 3 describes the role of the CEQ, established as a policy coordination body by Title II of NEPA. The CEQ had few resources to persuade a reluctant agency to comply with the Act. Its presidential advisory relationship was fragile, its budget was reviewed by a potentially hostile committee, it had few rewards to offer potential constituents, and it had no sanctions to impose. CEQ's inability to produce executive agency action consonant with what it deemed to be the requirements of NEPA produced a flurry of lawsuits initiated by citizen activists.

NEPA's broad language and CEQ's limited power left executive agencies with considerable discretion to decide for themselves how best to implement NEPA. Chapter 4 explores alternative ways of measuring and explaining administrative response. It begins with a survey of pertinent theoretical writings on administrative behavior. The central portion of chapter 4 examines several measures of the agencies' behavior, and the closing portion draws on the administrative behavior literature to suggest possible explanations of the administrative response measured.

Environmentalists' dissatisfaction with agency response, their desire to see an elaboration upon NEPA's broadly stated requirements, and their viewing NEPA as an ultimate weapon to use against on-going projects that they hitherto had unsuccessfully opposed—all combined to push many vital decisions about NEPA's meaning into the courts. NEPA's enactment at a time when the courts were increasingly opening their doors to "public interest groups" also spurred this lateral movement from the executive to the judiciary.

The first portion of chapter 5 focuses on how environmentalists managed to gain access to federal courtrooms. It focuses on both the funding of environmental litigation and on the lowering of courtroom entry barriers. The succeeding section of the chapter explores a major force—judicial annoyance with abuse of agency discretion—underlying the generally positive courtroom reception given environmentalists. The courts could seek to foreclose abuse by checking and structuring the exercise of discretion.[6]

The concluding portion of chapter 5 describes and analyzes NEPA litigation involving water resource development projects. That litigation provides a microcosmic view of NEPA's treatment by the judiciary.[7] There was a definite trend in judicial decision making, with decisions hardest on the agencies coming in 1971 and 1972 and courts showing considerable moderation, for the most part, by the end of 1973. Some courts were not as demanding as others, but there were enough tough decisions so that agencies could no longer blithely ignore NEPA.

Chapter 6 examines the congressional reaction to NEPA and citizen suits that was prompted by the judicial activism of late 1971 and early 1972. A major portion of the effort to amend NEPA evolved from some congressional committees' discontent with the statute's impact on programs that hitherto had been immune to challenge because of the fraternal relationship between the committees and certain administrative agencies. Environmental groups played a far different role in the 1972 struggle over NEPA from the one they played during NEPA's enactment. Their active role was in large measure a result of their recognition of NEPA's importance, a recognition not manifested at the time NEPA was enacted. Environmentalists realized that whatever success they enjoyed in bringing pressure to bear on agencies through the use of the courts would be diminished by congressional actions that would undercut the statute.

The closing chapter examines parallels between the institutional relationships affecting NEPA implementation and those that influence the implementation of other broad "social policy" laws. It notes the suggestions that have been made for the preparation of impact statements assessing the social, economic, and institutional impacts of agency decisions, and it describes some of the outstanding issues in environmental impact assessment.

2

Legislative
History
of NEPA

Since its enactment NEPA has been the focus of considerable controversy. In view of the character of the Act that is not surprising. A law that declares a sweeping national environmental policy where none existed, provides a statutory mandate for all federal agencies to consider the environmental impact of their actions, and establishes an environmental policy coordinating body in the office of the president must be considered a major piece of legislation of the sort likely to engender broad conflict.

Despite its broad implications, NEPA was not a highly controversial item of legislation in 1969. Congressional deliberations concerning NEPA were not the subject of substantial news coverage. Nor could lobbyists for environmental and resource development interests be seen busily visiting congressional offices and hearing rooms. NEPA was not even passed on a roll call vote, and in this respect, its final passage stood in marked contrast to that of earlier, more limited environmental legislation.

Interest group publications showed little interest in NEPA.

Readers of the 1969 newsletters of the Izaak Walton League, the Sierra Club, and the National Wildlife Federation were aware of NEPA's existence, but the coverage was more a travelogue of the bill's movements than an exposition of its ramifications. Similarly, readers of *Mining Congress Journal*, a publication presenting the viewpoint of natural resource developers, were merely provided a straightforward, factual account of the bill's progress.

Although the expected array of lobby groups paid little attention to NEPA, the bill was nevertheless the focus of considerable conflict among key legislators in both the Senate and the House. In the Senate, the bill was subjected to tough, protracted bargaining sessions between Senator Henry Jackson, chairman of the Interior Committee and NEPA's chief architect, and Senator Edmund Muskie, chairman of the Air and Water Pollution Subcommittee of the Senate Public Works Committee. While the Senators' disagreements were largely based on jurisdictional jealousies, they derived as well from a fundamental difference in outlook concerning the manner in which protection for environmental values should be provided in federal decision making.

In the House, the NEPA bill, authored by Representative John Dingell and cosponsored by all but one member of the Fisheries and Wildlife Conservation Subcommittee of the Merchant Marine and Fisheries Committee, ran into a roadblock in the Rules Committee. A rule establishing the boundaries of debate was required from the Rules Committee prior to the bill's consideration on the floor. Objection to the granting of a rule was raised by Representative Wayne Aspinall, the chairman of the House Interior Committee. Aspinall was noted for his support of exploitation of the natural resources found on public lands. He was concerned about the bill for jurisdictional reasons, and was ill at ease over the vagueness of its language. The price of a rule from the Rules Committee was modification of the bill with an amendment by Aspinall that would have gutted it. The

House Interior Committee chairman, however, was outmaneuvered in conference and his amendment deleted from the final version of NEPA.

The Final Version: NEPA's Provisions

The law eventually enacted contained three principal sections: a statement of national environmental policy, provisions for implementation of the policy by federal agencies, and provisions establishing a Council on Environmental Quality in the executive office of the president.

Section 101 of Title I establishes a national policy for the environment.[1] It commits the federal government to use all practicable means, consistent with other policy considerations, to make the most judicious use of the nation's resources. The policy has as its genesis a concern with the profound environmental impact of "population growth, high-density urbanization, industrial expansion, resource exploitation, and . . . technological advances."

Section 102 has been the most controversial section of the Act. It requires all federal agencies to develop information on the ecological consequences of their actions and to weigh these impacts in their policy making. They are charged with the responsibility to implement the established national environmental policy "to the fullest extent possible."

Section 102(2)(C) mandates the preparation of a "detailed" environmental statement to accompany "proposals for legislation and other major Federal actions significantly affecting the quality of the human environment." The statement is to be comprised of five parts, describing:

1. The environmental impact of the proposed action.
2. Any adverse environmental effects that cannot be avoided should the proposal be implemented.

3. Alternatives to the proposed action.
4. The relationship between local short-term uses of man's environment and the maintenance and enhancement of long-term productivity.
5. Any irreversible and irretrievable commitments of resources that would be involved in the proposed action should it be implemented.

The statement is to be circulated among government agencies for comment, and is to accompany the proposal through the agency's review processes.

Section 103 requires agencies to review their statutory authority, rules, regulations, and policies to determine whether they present obstacles to full compliance with NEPA. Agencies are ordered to report any statutory conflicts to the president by July 1, 1971, along with recommendations for their elimination.

Section 104 states, in part, that nothing in NEPA is to affect the statutory obligations of agencies to comply with environmental criteria or standards. Finally, Section 105 indicates that the policies and goals of the Act are supplementary to those set forth in agencies' existing authorizations.

Section 102's impact statement provisions developed from the realization that most of the adverse environmental impacts of the growth processes mentioned in Section 101 were by-products of actions that had been taken without consideration of their environmental consequences. This was particularly true with respect to the activities of public works agencies. Roads and dams were built and mineral exploration rights granted, often with little concern for their environmental impact. While some of the responsible agencies had statutory environmental obligations to which they gave little weight, many other agencies had no obligation whatsoever to consider their actions' environmental consequences. By making environmental quality the responsibility of all agencies, NEPA's authors hoped to insure that most if not all of the adverse environmental consequences of government action would be anticipated and weighed by federal agencies.[2]

Title II of NEPA establishes the Council on Environmental Quality and details its responsibilities. It provides, among other things, for an annual environmental quality report to the president and to the Congress.[3] The institutional change embodied in Title II represented an idea whose time had finally come; as early as 1936, a presidential advisory committee had recommended establishing a National Resources Planning Board in the executive office of the president.[4]

The desire to reorganize government to enable it to deal more effectively with increasingly evident environmental problems was manifested in diverse executive and legislative actions in the 1960s. Executive branch studies were commissioned, and many proposals were made for establishing new departments, new executive office advisory councils and new legislative committees.[5] The principal congressional proposals for executive and legislative reorganization, however, were never reported favorably from committee.

The movement for development of a national environmental policy gained momentum in 1968 when the Subcommittee on Science, Research and Development of the House Committee on Science and Astronautics published a report on managing the environment.[6] A joint House-Senate colloquium was convened to discuss a national environmental policy and a "Congressional White Paper" on a national environmental policy, based on the colloquium, was published shortly thereafter.[7]

In the early 1960s, public concern with the environment had remained at a relatively low level. While by 1969 approximately 50 percent of the public had developed some interest in preserving environmental quality, Senator Jackson's sponsorship of NEPA led rather than followed public opinion.[8] However, NEPA's passage by the entire Congress four months before the first nationwide Earth Day undoubtedly was made easier by congressional awareness of the heightened public interest in the environment.

NEPA in the Senate

The Senate version of NEPA, S.1075, was introduced by Senator Jackson on February 18, 1969.[9] It contained a preamble and two titles. The preamble stated the goals of the legislation, and while not a statement of national environmental policy, it expressed in abbreviated form some of the environmental goals enacted as national policy ten months later. Title I authorized the secretary of the interior to conduct ecological research while Title II established a Council on Environmental Quality to advise the president and to prepare an annual environmental report. Senator Jackson conducted hearings on his bill on April 16, 1969, indicating that he regarded the introduced version of S.1075 as a "working paper." [10] At the hearings, many witnesses expressed support for a source of ecological advice within the executive branch and independent of the cabinet departments. Moreover, because environmental responsibilities were lodged within scores of subdepartmental agencies, many desired to centralize responsibility for oversight of environmentally impacting programs.[11]

Some witnesses also proposed granting of a stop-order power to the Council, enabling it to halt, at least temporarily, environmentally harmful actions undertaken by federal agencies.[12] That idea was given intensive consideration at staff level and was the subject of discussions between the staff and Senator Jackson. However, there was little discussion of the proposition by the full committee, for it was felt that such a substantial veto power should not be given to appointed officials.

Other witnesses suggested granting the Council some independence from the president. Michael McCloskey of the Sierra Club spoke of staggered terms for Council members,[13] while

Representative Henry Reuss proposed giving them statutory six-year terms. Those proposals were not incorporated into S.1075.

Professor Lynton Caldwell's testimony before the Jackson committee was one of several crucial turning points in NEPA's history.[14] Caldwell had served as a consultant to the committee and had prepared a report to it on a national environmental policy. He contended that a statement of national environmental policy, such as one Jackson was considering for S.1075, would be meaningless unless it was implemented through some "action-forcing mechanism." The committee staff had been contemplating a need for such a mechanism and the Caldwell testimony lent new impetus to their considerations.

Caldwell suggested that federal agencies, in preparing action proposals, should develop an evaluation of the proposals' effect upon the environment. He clearly contemplated an important oversight role for the Bureau of the Budget (BOB), arguing in particular that it should be authorized to scrutinize the environmental impact of proposals for public works projects. In a complementary manner, the licensing procedures of independent regulatory agencies would include requirements for the evaluation of environmental impacts.

Senator Jackson sought a bill that would give all agencies responsibility for considering environmental impacts. Desirous of avoiding an agency-by-agency recodification of federal statutes, he felt that delegating some discretionary power to the BOB to make policy judgments on environmental grounds would prompt many agencies to incorporate environmental considerations into their decision making.[15]

Following the hearings, Senator Jackson amended S.1075.[16] All references to the secretary of the interior were deleted from Title I. Section 101(a) became a lengthy statement of environmental policy and Section 101(b) embodied congressional recognition that "each person has a fundamental and inalienable right to a healthful environment."

Section 103 became an explicit statement that the function

of the proposed law was to expand the existing authority of executive agencies:

> The policies and goals set forth in this Act are amendatory and supplementary to, but shall not be considered to repeal, the existing mandates and authorizations of Federal agencies.

Section 102 of Title I was the new action-forcing provision. It was the precursor of the Section 102 enacted into law, and it included a requirement for development of environmental impact findings by executive agencies.[17] The environmental impact findings requirement had been drafted by William Van Ness and Daniel Dreyfus, special counsel and professional staff member respectively of the Senate Interior Committee. Dreyfus had worked for federal water resource development agencies, and he felt it was important to key environmental considerations into the "decision documents" that accompanied water resource development proposals. A short statement of environmental findings would be designed to accompany the proposals through agency decision making, through the BOB, and to Congress. The findings of environmental impact were to be an added element in the budget review process. Their absence would provide a budget examiner with an additional reason for challenging a proposed agency expenditure. "The idea was to make them [the agencies] do something which they couldn't escape doing, and to make them pay if they didn't." [18] The requirement for findings was also designed to assure that specific individuals within agencies were identified as being responsible for both approval of particular projects and investigation of their environmental consequences.

Section 102's drafters were particularly concerned about the need for an evaluation of alternatives. In their committee experience, they had been struck by the absence of alternative choices in the administrative proposals presented to legislators. They were aware of the use within the executive branch of program budget (PPBS) documents, which laid out alternative options for decision makers, and they felt that for sound managerial reasons, Congress should have similar material. It was hoped that the statements of environmental findings, with their discussions of alternatives, would serve this purpose. The findings requirement was also designed to prod agencies into giving greater weight to those courses of action, among a broad spectrum of alternative actions, that would be least environmentally harmful. Hopefully, agency decision making would be improved; fewer environmentally controversial decisions would be made because ecologically injurious projects would be denied serious consideration in their early stages.

On June 18, 1969, the Senate Interior Committee unanimously reported out S.1075, as amended. At the request of the BOB, which had submitted some revisions to the bill, the committee reconsidered its action, made some additional changes, and again reported S.1075 out.[19]

THE MUSKIE-JACKSON COMPROMISE

On June 12, 1969, Senator Muskie, with forty cosponsors, introduced S.2391, an amendment to the omnibus water pollution control bill being considered by his committee.[20] As introduced, S.2391 provided for establishment of an Office of Environmental Quality in the executive office of the president. Its introduction was the first indication on the public record of senate concern about the jurisdictional implications of the Jackson proposal. Senator Muskie feared that S.1075 would debilitate existing environmental protection programs over which his Air and Water Pollution Subcommittee had jurisdiction.

At the heart of the disagreement between Senators Muskie and Jackson, two of the Senate's strongest advocates of environmental protection, was a fundamental difference over the conduct of environmental policy. Senator Jackson's view was that with enactment of NEPA, mission-oriented public works agencies would internalize environmental values as they began to develop evaluations of projects' environmental impacts. But Senator Muskie and the Public Works Committee staff harbored grave misgivings about the self-enforcement qualities of NEPA's action-forcing provisions. They believed that some form of external policing mechanism was needed; the mission-oriented agencies could not be trusted to consider seriously the environmental consequences of their actions and the requirement for environmental findings provided but the narrowest basis for outside review. In Senator Muskie's view, external policing could be provided by federal water and air pollution control agencies, for whose reviews provision had to be made.

After protracted negotiations, Senators Muskie and Jackson agreed to a revised version of S.1075. It was presented to the Senate on October 8, 1969, during a discussion of Senator Muskie's water pollution control bill.[21] As part of the compromise, Senator Jackson urged conference committee adoption of the revised version of S.1075 to which he had just agreed, rather than adoption of the Interior Committee version that had passed the Senate on July 10.

By October 8, considerable adjustments had been made in Section 102 to ease the fears of Senator Muskie. First, the mandate for environmental findings was changed to a requirement for a "detailed statement" of environmental impact.[22] In addition, prior to preparing the statement, agencies would be required to consult with and obtain the comments of other federal agencies possessing expertise about any environmental impact involved. That was an obvious reference to the air and water pollution control agencies. Copies of the statements, and comments received, would be circulated to federal, state and local agencies, to the president, to a Board of Environmental Quality Advisors (BEQA), and to the public. The statement would also accompany the proposal through all agency review processes. The compromise also strengthened the role of the BEQA. Senator Jackson's S.1075 had required agencies to develop methods for weighing unquantified environmental values in their decision making.[23] The compromise version required the approval by the Board of proposed agency methods.[24]

A new Section 103 was added to the bill. It provided that the preparation of environmental impact statements would not affect the statutory obligations of federal agencies to comply with water quality criteria or standards, or to act in accordance with the environmental quality certifications of state or federal pollution control agencies.[25] This provision, too, was designed to assure a continued important role for the environmental protection agencies then in existence.

The legislative compromise ordered the establishment of two executive office entities, the BEQA and the Office of Environmental Quality (OEQ). The former was provided for in Senator Jackson's revised bill and the latter in Senator Muskie's. That arrangement displeased Senator Gordon Allott, ranking member of Senator Jackson's committee, who was the only senator to express discontent with the Muskie-Jackson compromise.[26] Allott was dismayed that these bodies were established in addition to the interagency Environmental Quality Committee, which had been established by the president in May 1969.[27] In Senator Allott's view, it was not desirable to have three environmental policy bodies in the executive office of the president. Senator Allott, however, did not express any misgivings whatsoever regarding the action-forcing processes to which Senators Muskie and Jackson had agreed.

NEPA in the House

While the Senate weighed S.1075, the House considered its own version of NEPA. House consideration in the 91st Congress began with Representative John Dingell's introduction of H.R.6750.[28] H.R.6750 was drafted as an amendment to the Fish and Wildlife Coordination Act, over which Representative Dingell's Subcommittee on Fisheries and Wildlife Conservation of the Committee on Merchant Marine and Fisheries had jurisdiction. Modeled after the Full Employment Act of 1946, which established the Council of Economic Advisors, H.R.6750 contained a brief statement of environmental policy and established a Council on Environmental Quality within the executive office of the president. It also mandated the preparation of an annual environmental quality report that was to be submitted to the president and to Congress. It did not contain any provisions requiring the preparation of environmental findings or environmental impact statements.

The Dingell proposal for a Council on Environmental Quality had been introduced in the 90th Congress.[29] After referral to the House Interior Committee it was re-referred to the Subcommittee on Science, Research and Development of the House Committee on Science and Astronautics. The Subcommittee did not report the bill, believing that Congress should establish a permanent presidential council of environmental advisors only if interagency environmental coordination efforts were unsuccessful.[30]

Representative Dingell convened his subcommittee for hearings on H.R.6750 in May and June 1969. In the course of the hearings, President Nixon issued an executive order establishing an interagency Environmental Quality Council.[31] The Council was composed of the vice-president, the secretaries of those departments most directly concerned with environmental matters, and various representatives from executive office agencies. Staff assistance was to be provided by the Office of Science and Technology. The interagency council would have broad responsibility for coordinating federal environmental policy in much the same way as Representative Dingell's proposed CEQ.

The President had been reviewing a draft of his executive order as early as February 1969. Senator Jackson let his dislike of the proposal be known and persuaded the administration to postpone final issuance of the order at least until his April hearing on S.1075.[32] After the S.1075 hearing, additional negotiations between Senator Jackson and the White House delayed the order until May, in the midst of Representative Dingell's hearings.[33]

The issuance of the order laid the groundwork for a confrontation between the Dingell subcommittee and Dr. Lee DuBridge, director of the president's Office of Science and Technology, concerning the relative merits of a presidentially established interagency environmental council, as compared to an independent statutory council within the executive office.[34]

Dingell's hard questioning of DuBridge underscored the following weaknesses of the interagency council:

1. It could be eliminated at the whim of the president.[35]
2. It would be staffed by Office of Science and Technology personnel having competing concerns for their time.
3. It would be a part-time operation because of conflicting demands on the departmental secretaries and their representatives.
4. It would be under no obligation to report annually to Congress.

The limitations inherent to the decision making of the interagency council deeply concerned committee witnesses. Most felt that an interagency council would have less independence from congressional and clientele demands than a statutorily established CEQ; it would be less free to produce telling critiques of agency policies.[36] Moreover, several thought that a norm of noncriticism would prevail at most of its meetings. In the words of Charles Callison of the National Audubon Society:

There is a natural human tendency by the members of such an interagency council to be good fellows, have a meeting and decide we will run our program in our department and you run yours and we will take a quick look at these programs and then perhaps make a few adjustments but they never really come to grips with the genuine problems that have arisen in these programs.[37]

In sum, a statutory CEQ was seen as a catalyst for substantial administrative change. Perhaps because a statutory CEQ was seen as stronger than an interagency council, little mention was made of the pressures likely to be placed on the proposed CEQ to force it to be part of a loyal administration team. It might be expected to adhere, for the most part, to an executive environmental program that had been developed following interagency negotiations.

Witnesses placed primary emphasis on the CEQ's roles as environmental advisor, as forecaster of long-term trends, and as source of public information. But attention was also paid to giving the Council some form of "stop-order" power for ongoing projects and actions. Exercise of the stop-order power would function to lay a controversial action before the president or Congress for review. Subcommittee Counsel Ned Everett asked several witnesses for their views on granting the Council stop-order power, and virtually all supported the notion.[38]

In executive session, however, consideration of stop-order power was "put on the back burner." [39] First, the subcommittee was wary of writing changes into the bill that might endanger its passage. Second, the bill had originally been modeled after the Full Employment Act, and the subcommittee wanted to "pretty much leave it that way." [40]

Congressman Dingell's H.R.6750 did not contain any environmental findings or statement requirements. However, between the third and fourth sessions of the hearings, Congressman Nedzi introduced H.R.12143, which contained findings provisions, and this bill was referred to the Dingell subcommittee.[41] The introduction of H.R.12143 was an obvious ploy to establish jurisdiction for Dingell's subcommittee over the NEPA bill that would be coming to the House from the Senate. But scant attention was paid the Nedzi bill by any of the subcommittee's witnesses. Two executive agencies submitted comments on it, but neither written comment addressed the environmental findings provision.[42]

In executive session the Dingell subcommittee designed a

slightly revised bill, H.R.12549. Similar to H.R.6750, it contained no environmental findings or statement provisions. The bill was reported by the full Merchant Marine and Fisheries Committee on July 11, 1969, but did not reach the House floor until September 23. The delay was caused by the specific opposition of Representative Aspinall to the bill's broad language.

A CEQ bill had been introduced into Congressman Aspinall's Interior Committee in the preceding session of Congress, but no action had been taken.[43] CEQ bills also had been introduced in the first session of the 91st Congress,[44] but hearings were never held because the Committee was involved with other matters, particularly water resource development projects in the Columbia River Basin.[45]

Some of Aspinall's qualms about the bill from Congressman Dingell's subcommittee were embodied in his August 7 statement before the Rules Committee, through which the bill had to pass to reach the House floor. Essentially, Congressman Aspinall was concerned about the bill's jurisdictional implications for both the legislative and executive branches. He argued that "environment" was too broad and too generalized a subject for treatment in a single piece of legislation from one committee. He believed that existing laws and institutions, if administered properly, could be brought to bear on many of the environmental problems that motivated the bill. Furthermore, because the President had already established an advisory environmental council, he felt that the law's passage would "dilute the effectiveness of the Executive." [46]

In his statement, Congressman Aspinall denied seeking jurisdiction over the bill. He sought to call attention, however, to the jurisdictional problems it raised, for he recognized that the bill would impact resource-development programs overseen by his committee. He observed, furthermore, that his committee would be prohibited from attending the conference on H.R.12549 and S.1075, even though S.1075 had been reported from his committee's counterpart in the Senate, Senator Jackson's Interior Committee.

Congressman Aspinall was greatly concerned about the bill's potentially sweeping impact on executive agencies. He was not quite sure what its effects would be, but he felt uneasy nevertheless. In his view, two changes were needed. First, it should stand on its own rather than be part of the fish and wildlife law over which Congressman Dingell's subcommittee had jurisdiction. Second, it needed a specific provision indicating that the authority of existing agencies would not be changed. Such a provision would assure a continued preeminent role for those congressional committees supporting agencies' traditional missions. Agencies would examine their policies, propose changes consonant with the new environmental policy, and then offer legislative recommendations that would be reviewed by each oversight committee.

Strategically blocked by Aspinall, who had considerable influence in the Rules Committee, Dingell accepted the Interior Committee chairman's proposed amendments. The amendments were offered when the bill was reported to the House on September 23.[47] The first principal amendment deleted any reference in the bill to the Fish and Wildlife Coordination Act. The second added the following provision:

Nothing in this Act shall increase, decrease, or change any responsibility or authority of any Federal official or agency created by other provision of law.[48]

The second amendment effectively gutted the intent of Dingell's bill. It stood in marked contrast to the provision in Jackson's S.1075 specifying the following:

The policies and goals set forth in this Act are amendatory and supplementary to, but shall not be considered to repeal, the existing mandates and authorizations of Federal agencies.[49]

With the exception of the Aspinall amendments, no significant changes were made on the House floor. Most of the representatives supported the measure; only one spoke in opposition to it.[50] Significantly, an attempt by Congressman Daddario to add environmental impact findings provisions to the law was ruled out of order at Aspinall's request.[51]

With House passage of H.R.12549, the only roll call vote on NEPA was recorded. The vote was 372 to 15, with 43 abstentions.[52] Those opposing the bill were conservative representatives, primarily from the South and Midwest. Among them were two members of the Appropriations Committee subcommittee that would ultimately oversee the CEQ's budget, Chairman Jamie Whitten and Congressman William Scherle.

NEPA in Conference

Representing the Senate in the conference committee were Senators Jackson, Church, Nelson, Allott, and Jordan, all members of the Interior Committee. Representing the House were the chairman and ranking member of the Merchant Marine and Fisheries Committee, Representatives Garmatz and Mailliard respectively, and John Dingell. Also on the House delegation were Congressmen Aspinall and Saylor, chairman and ranking member respectively of the Interior Committee. The unusual conference procedure of joint House committee representation was part of the Dingell-Aspinall agreement. It marked the first time in Aspinall's memory that representatives of two different House committees sat in the same conference.

The conference considered three bills—H.R.12549, S.1075 as originally passed by the Senate, and S.1075 as modified by the Muskie-Jackson compromise. There were also three viewpoints represented at the conference—that of the Senate conferees controlled by Jackson; that of the House conferees, Saylor included, in agreement with Dingell; and that of Aspinall.

In conference, Jackson was willing to delete the environmental council provisions in order to retain the action-forcing provisions of Title I. Dingell's objective, in contrast, was to obtain a CEQ, and he was willing to discard S.1075's Title I in exchange. Later in the conference, Dingell altered his goal. Aspinall did not seriously object to a CEQ but, as indicated, he had reservations about the sweep of the entire bill.

Aspinall stood alone. He foresaw Section 102 of S.1075 as providing a "new handle for environmentalists," [53] and was concerned about the administrative cost of program delays. He was not quite sure what the exact impact would be, but he nevertheless sought to limit it. "His concern was more a matter of principle than a fear of specific consequences . . . . He didn't know what the consequences would be." [54] One staff proponent of Section 102 acknowledges that he was "one of the few individuals smart enough to see the possibility of procedural delay deriving from the general provisions of Section 102." [55]

Aspinall's staff advisor was taken aback by events at the conference. The conference was one of the few he had attended in which the House representatives' opening statements indicated a preference for the Senate language. [56] On the Senate side, Jackson was in complete control. In the view of one staffer, Senators Jordan and Allott, who tended to favor natural resource exploitation of the public lands, just "hadn't taken a close look at the bill." [57]

The two primary issues at the conference were Jackson's provision asserting every citizen's "right" to a clean environment, [58] and the scope of the requirements of Section 102 in Title I of S.1075. The environmental rights provision was deleted out of fear of its implications for future legal decisions. [59]

The changes written into S.1075's Title I are the portions of the conference committee compromise that are of greatest interest. The changes in language were not absolutely required. Conference decisions are reported if a majority of the conferees of each house approve them, and Congressman Dingell and Senator Jackson controlled the requisite votes. The language, nevertheless, was altered to accommodate Congressman Aspinall.

First, the requirement was dropped that agencies' procedures for evaluating unquantified environmental values must be reviewed and approved by the CEQ. The agencies were required by the compromise merely to consult with the CEQ when developing procedures.[60]

The second major change involved a shifting of the phrase "to the fullest extent possible." In the Muskie-Jackson version of S.1075, the phrase was placed at the beginning of Section 102 as follows:

> The Congress authorizes and directs that the policies, regulations and public laws of the United States, to the fullest extent possible, be interpreted and administered in accordance with the policies set forth in this Act, and that all agencies of the Federal Government-- . . . .[61]

It then served to modify only the clause concerning the "policies, regulations and public laws," and did not modify the responsibilities of the federal agencies listed in subsections (a) through (f) following the two hyphens.[62] The conference committee, at Aspinall's suggestion, shifted the location of the words so that they modified both the "policies, regulations and public laws" clause and the language following the hyphens in all of Section 102's subsections. The altered language, which was enacted into law, was:

> The Congress authorizes and directs that, to the fullest extent possible: (1) the policies, regulations, and public laws of the United States shall be interpreted and administered in accordance with the policies set forth in this Act and (2) all agencies of the Federal Government shall-- . . . .[63]

The Senate conferees agreed to this phrase shift in exchange for the deletion of Aspinall's limiting amendment to the Dingell version of NEPA. The agreement on the compromise language was embodied in House Report 91-765, the conference report on NEPA. Reported to the Senate and House on December 17, the brief document, signed by all the conferees, stated the compromise language without interpretation.[64]

While there was an agreement in conference as to NEPA's language, the interpretations of the agreed language by Aspinall on the one hand, and by Jackson and Dingell on the other, were totally different. Aspinall thought the language merely embodied the intention of his limiting amendment to the Dingell bill, to whose deletion he had agreed. He understood the words "to the fullest extent possible" in Section 102, in conjunction with Sections 103 and 105,[65] to mean that, as far as they could under existing authority, agencies would comply with the NEPA procedures. If agencies reviewed their authority and found they were unable to comply, then no compliance was necessary. Congress, by establishing a deadline for a review of agency authority, would allow the agencies to study the impact of NEPA on their programs and to develop changes in their authority needed to permit compliance. That procedure would also assure that proposed changes would be reviewed in an orderly manner by the legislative committees overseeing agency activities.

Senator Jackson's interpretation, however, was considerably different. It was embodied in the "Statement of Managers on the Part of the House," which accompanied the conference report to the House and Senate floors.[66] The statement had been written principally by the Senator's staff, and had been coordinated with Dingell and his staff. The statement's language indicated that unless an agency's authorization explicitly excluded environmental impact from its deliberations, it was automatically given an environmental mandate. The language "to the fullest extent possible" was to be interpreted as follows:

It is the intent of the conferees that the provision "to the fullest extent possible" shall not be used by any Federal agency as a means

of avoiding compliance with the directives set out in Section
102 . . . . no agency shall utilize an excessively narrow construction of its existing statutory authorizations to avoid compliance.[67]

Similar language broadly construing NEPA was placed in the
House Managers' discussion of Sections 103 and 105 of NEPA.[68]
The unwritten message, of course, was that Wayne Aspinall had
been outmaneuvered in the conference. Understandably, he
refused to sign the "Statement."

Passage of the Conference Report

When the conference report was brought to the House floor,
Aspinall tried to recover. In his remarks before the full House,
he contended that "the statement of [the] managers, in certain
respects, does not accurately interpret the language in the
conference report." [69] He argued that there was no language in
NEPA to support some of the House managers' interpretations.[70]

House debate on the conference report was brief; it occupies
only six pages in the *Congressional Record*. The only dissenting
voice was that of Representative William Harsha, a member of
the Public Works Committee. While raising the questions of
committee jurisdiction that had been present throughout consideration of NEPA, he also made some prophetic remarks:

I must warn the Members that they should be on guard against
the ramifications of a measure that is so loose and ambiguous as
this . . . . this is a major revision of the administrative functions of
the U. S. Government . . . .
The impact of S.1075, if it becomes law, I am convinced, would be
so wide sweeping as to involve every branch of the Government,
every committee of Congress, every agency, and every program of
the Nation.[71]

Noting that the members of Congress were anxious to adjourn for Christmas, Harsha urged that Congress delay action until January. His warnings were unheeded and the House passed the conference report.

In the Senate, the conference report was approved on December 20, 1969. Debate was brief and consisted principally of lengthy speeches by Jackson and Muskie on the implications of NEPA's enactment for the activities of environmentally protective agencies like the Federal Water Quality Administration. They failed, unfortunately, to describe unambiguously how NEPA should apply to environmentally protective agencies, and this failure fostered considerable controversy in later years concerning NEPA's applicability to the Environmental Protection Agency (EPA). The only dissent noted was the undetailed comment by Gordon Allott, ranking Republican on the Interior Committee, that he regarded only the conference committee report, and not necessarily Senator Jackson's interpretation of it, as legally binding.[72] NEPA passed the Senate without a roll call vote.

Overview—Consideration of NEPA's Judicial Impact

In the light of subsequent events, it is noteworthy that in only one place in the entire legislative history of the law were NEPA's implications for judicial review of agency action examined.[73] This discussion focused on Jackson's environmental rights proviso, which was deleted. Aspinall, in all his comments, never mentioned the judicial implications of the environmental impact statement. Jackson recognized that litigation might result from the law, but he did not anticipate the volume of litigation that was ultimately to ensue.[74] Judicial review of environmental impact statements, which ultimately proved to be the most important role for the courts, was never discussed.

One reason for the lack of discussion of judicial review may

lie in the genesis of the environmental impact analysis requirement. Jackson, for his part, had devoted little effort to developing a legislative record on the provision for environmental
findings. Perhaps he believed that little work on this point was
necessary because, in his view, environmental findings were
management tools, largely internal to the federal bureaucracy.
When the findings provision was changed to a statement
provision late in NEPA's legislative history, many of the
requirements remained unspecified; for example, the impacts to
be evaluated, the alternatives to be discussed, and the timing of
statement preparation. The change from a findings to a statement obligation had considerable implications for judicial review, establishing as it did a unique document the scope of
whose review by the courts had never been defined.[75]

Another possible reason for the lack of concern with the
courts stemmed from the relative youthfulness of the environmental law movement. At the time of NEPA's consideration,
environmental lawyers had not become a significant force in
administrative politics. Several indicators serve to portray the
low level of environmentalist legal action. Table 2-1 reports the

Table 2-1

LAWSUITS CITED IN THE LAND AND NATURAL RESOURCES DIVISION
SECTION OF THE U.S. ATTORNEY GENERAL'S ANNUAL REPORTS,
FY68–FY71

Year	Total Cases Cited	Citizen Environmental Lawsuits Cited	Proportion of Citizen Environmental Lawsuits to All Cases Cited (in percent)
FY68	6	0	0
FY69	50	3	6
FY70	60	13	22
FY71	78	23	29

Sources: Annual Reports of the Attorney-General, FY68 through FY71.

number of cases cited in the annual reports of the Justice Department's Land and Natural Resources Division, which handled most citizen-initiated environmental lawsuits at that time.[76] The number of citizen environmental lawsuits cited for FY68 and FY69 was quite low, indicating that they did not merit much attention from the division. In the succeeding two years, the number of citizen suits cited increased appreciably, and by FY71, such suits were approximately 29 percent of all the cases cited in the division report.

Environmental group statistics mirror the Justice Department figures. A review of Sierra Club litigation in the January 1971 issue of the *Sierra Club Bulletin* described forty-six state and federal cases participated in by the club.[77] Of the twenty-three cases litigated in the federal courts, the citations indicate that most were initiated in 1969 and 1970.

Institutional indicators can also be used to describe the low level of development of environmental law in the 1969–1970 period. It was not until 1970 and 1971, for example, that two "environmental law" journals and two "environmental law" reporting services were founded.[78] Public interest environmental law groups were also a relatively recent phenomenon.[79]

Litigation over the location of highways, another measure of environmentalists' use of the courts, provides further confirming evidence. Most, though not all, highway location suits are brought for environmental reasons, and most are brought by environmental groups. The figures in Table 2-2 describe the volume of highway litigation from 1966 to 1972. The figures in column 1 show the number of highway location cases brought in which plaintiffs complained about violation of highway and relocation statutes. The number of cases brought between 1966 and 1969 was quite low and barely exceeded the total number of such cases brought in 1970 alone. The 1970 figure shows a marked upward climb in highway litigation, and the plaintiffs' complaints did not even mention noncompliance with the newly

Table 2–2

HIGHWAY LOCATION LITIGATION, 1966 TO 1972

Year	Type of Case* 1	2	3	Yearly Total
1966	1	. . .	. . .	1
1967	4	. . .	. . .	4
1968	3	. . .	. . .	3
1969	6	. . .	. . .	6
1970	11	1	5	17
1971	5	4	18	27
1972	2**	8**	38**	48**

Source: "Hearings on S.3589 and S.3590 before the Subcomm. on Roads of the Senate Comm. on Public Works," 92d Cong., 2d Sess. 910–911 (1972).
* Type 1 cases are those in which plaintiffs' complaints concern violation only of highway and relocation statutes. Type 2 cases are those charging only noncompliance with NEPA. Type 3 cases are those in which plaintiffs charge noncompliance with both NEPA and highway or relocation statutes.
** Figures for 1972 are extrapolations of six-month figures presented in the hearings cited above.

enacted NEPA. The total number of highway location cases in the years 1966 through 1969 is far lower than the total number of such cases in the years 1970 through 1972; the former constitute only 19 percent of the latter. The decline in the number of lawsuits charging noncompliance solely with highway and relocation statutes (indicated in column 1) and the marked increase in the number of lawsuits charging noncompliance with highway statutes, relocation statutes, and NEPA (indicated in column 3), reflects in part NEPA's encompassing the environmental provisions of earlier highway legislation.

Closing Observations

The conclusion is obvious: Congress failed to examine the consequences of NEPA. As several Congressional staff members who were involved in NEPA's development said:

If we had waited another year, we would have developed legislation which wasn't so drastic in terms of program effect.

If Congress had appreciated what the law would do, it would not have passed. They would have seen it as screwing public works . . . . The timing of the bill complicated the way it worked. Had it passed a year earlier or later, things would have been far different.

If Congress had known what it was doing, it would not have passed the law.[80]

The failure to recognize the implications of the law was not unique to Congress. Environmental groups, resource developers, and even the press paid little attention to the Act. Though NEPA had not been subjected to lengthy floor debate or to intense lobbying by interest groups and the White House, its legislative history contained a major theme: all federal agencies had an affirmative responsibility to integrate environmental considerations into their decision making.[81]

3

The Council on
Environmental
Quality

The Council on Environmental Quality (CEQ) was established in Title II of NEPA to serve as the guardian of environmental concerns within the executive branch. It was given the functions of advising the president, monitoring other agencies' compliance with NEPA, and providing information to the public on environmental matters.[1]

CEQ compiled for itself a record impressive in many respects during its first years of existence. The quality of its staff and of its publications, notably its annual reports, was widely acknowledged. The Council prepared a comprehensive legislative program, much of which the President adopted and forwarded to Congress in annual environmental messages. Moreover, CEQ was instrumental in elevating its role from that of passive observation of the NEPA process to one of more active involvement in both defining adequate agency procedural compliance and reviewing impact statements. Its guidelines interpreting NEPA were frequently employed by the courts in halting projects authorized by other governmental units.

In some areas, on the other hand, CEQ's success was less marked. In part, this may be traced to the difficulty of performing simultaneously the several roles assigned to the Council by NEPA. Although nominally the primary authority within the executive branch on environmental affairs, CEQ constantly competed with other agencies and advisors who placed a far lower priority on environmental concerns. CEQ might have mobilized public support on individual issues, but at the risk of jeopardizing its confidential relationship with the White House, under a President known for his dislike of public discord within his administration. CEQ's behind-the-scenes approach, however, caused the Council sometimes to appear less than altogether zealous and effective in defense of the environment. Consequently the Council was eclipsed by the greater public exposure of the Environmental Protection Agency and the courts.

The CEQ as Overseer of the NEPA Process

NEPA assigned a multitude of duties to CEQ, but it did not clearly delegate to it responsibility for developing guidelines for agency implementation of the statute's procedures. Support for a strong CEQ oversight role could nevertheless be found in NEPA, for such responsibility could arguably fall within the Council review activities sanctioned by Title II. However, legislative history could also be cited that implied a major role in impact statement oversight and coordination for the Office of Management and Budget (OMB).[2] The lack of clear delegation of oversight responsibility provided the Council with an opportunity to carve out for itself an imaginative oversight role.

Executive order 11514, issued March 5, 1970,[3] elaborated CEQ's responsibilities under NEPA. Drafted at OMB with input from CEQ, the order provided the first public indication that primary responsibility for guiding the environmental impact statement process was to be vested in CEQ and not in OMB.[4] CEQ, which sought the authority and met no resistance from OMB,[5] fulfilled its oversight obligation by issuing procedural guidelines for preparation of environmental impact statements, issuing supplementary memoranda describing the NEPA process' requirements, and reviewing environmental impact statements.

CEQ GUIDELINES

When Congress enacted NEPA, it did not elaborate on the requirements of the impact statement process, and thus gave considerable latitude to CEQ for developing procedural guidelines. The Council had to interpret such terms as "adverse environmental effects," "major action," "significant effect," and "long term productivity and short term use." Those terms had to be defined in such a manner that guidelines could readily be applied to the many federal programs having environmental impact.

CEQ Interim Guidelines. The Council's initial "interim" guidelines were released on April 30, 1970.[6] Prepared in consultation with the staffs of Senator Jackson and Representative Dingell, the guidelines added significant details to the statutorily mandated environmental impact statement. For example, they required federal agencies to establish their own separate procedures for implementing the requirements of NEPA and executive order 11514. They also established a requirement for "draft" and "final" statements, in order to assure that action-initiating agencies would give other agencies and the public a detailed basis for comment prior to making the final decision on a proposed action.[7] Furthermore, the guidelines stressed the early, detailed evaluation of alternatives to proposed actions in order to avoid the premature foreclosure of other policy options that might have less detrimental environmental impacts.[8]

In three ways, however, the guidelines were as vague as NEPA itself. They provided little detailed guidance for the kinds of actions requiring statements, gave scant direction with respect to statement content, and left somewhat ambiguous the matter of NEPA's applicability to ongoing projects.[9] While one could perhaps fault the Council for the generality of the interim guidelines, criticism would have to be tempered with the recognition that the Council was in many instances feeling its way, attempting to write directions applicable to a diverse range of agency activities. As NEPA itself had with one sentence given all federal agencies an environmental mandate,[10] the CEQ guidelines, without action-by-action details, provided impact statement preparation procedures for "all major federal actions significantly affecting the . . . environment." The guidelines assigned to agencies the obligation to define for themselves the specific manner in which, consonant with the broad CEQ interpretation, NEPA should be implemented.

CEQ Revised Guidelines. Following a series of meetings with agencies to ascertain their experiences with NEPA, and after solicitation of public comment and extensive oversight hearings held by Dingell's subcommittee,[11] the Council moved to revise its guidelines. New guidelines were published in April 1971.[12] They were accompanied by a memorandum in which CEQ Chairman Russell Train called the agencies' attention to those sections of the revised guidelines that discussed public access to environmental statements. Train also quoted at length from one judicial decision and referred to two others, all of which indicated that adequate compliance with Section 102(2)(C) would be required by the courts.[13] CEQ promulgated a second major revision of its guidelines in August 1973.[14]

The CEQ guidelines reflected three themes that were present in congressional consideration of NEPA. First, evaluation of environmental impact is the responsibility of all agencies.[15] Second, environmental impact evaluation should be an explicit component of choice processes at all levels of agency review.[16] Third, outside commentators should play an important role in environmental review, and provision must be made for their

timely intervention in administrative decision-making processes.[17] The guidelines also expanded on the implicit goal of
NEPA's architects: that the public should be provided information concerning the rationale underlying agency choices of
action.[18]

CEQ Memos. Between the issuance of revised guidelines in
April 1971, and the publication of proposed revisions in May
1973, CEQ continued to meet informally with agencies to elicit
their views regarding problems of NEPA implementation. It
also relied on a series of memoranda to elaborate upon agency
responsibilities.

One memo, circulated in July 1971, was devoted to a
description of the Calvert Cliffs decision of the District of
Columbia Circuit Court of Appeals.[19] In its opinion the court
stated that the Atomic Energy Commission's procedural interpretation of NEPA had made a mockery of the Act. CEQ's
lengthy discussion of the case is a further indication of the
prime role the courts played in interpreting NEPA's requirements and in assuring agency compliance with the law.[20]

Another memorandum described CEQ's impatience with
delays in agencies' developing procedural guidelines for implementing NEPA. Chairman Train noted that "Continued failure
of any agency to establish . . . procedures can only attract
unfavorable Congressional and public comment and possible
legal difficulties." [21]

In late 1971 CEQ issued two general memoranda to agencies
as background information for joint agency and CEQ procedural
review sessions. One memorandum provided a lengthy summa-
tion of key court decisions, abstracting eight topics for special
emphasis.[22] The second addressed itself to matters that CEQ felt
must be discussed in agency guidelines.[23] That memorandum
was a major supplement to the revised guidelines of April 1971,
dealing with such issues as identification of agency actions likely
to require a NEPA statement; timing of impact statement
preparation; the role of the NEPA statement in the decision-

making process; development of agency commenting procedures; and provision for public information. Like the preceding
guidelines, it elaborated upon the congressional intent expressed
in NEPA's legislative history.

Five months later, CEQ circulated another major addendum
to its published guidelines.[24] In a memorandum to agency NEPA
coordinators and general counsels, CEQ General Counsel Timothy Atkeson forwarded ten recommendations for improvements
in agency NEPA procedures. The memorandum discussed the
agencies' duty to prepare statements that would disclose the full
range of environmental impacts; balance the advantages and
disadvantages of a proposed action; and consider both opposing
views and reasonable alternatives to a proposed action. It also
discussed various procedural matters, and emphasized the informed involvement of outside commentators as early as possible in the formulation of environmental decisions.

The format of the May 1972 memorandum differed from that
of the previous memoranda in that it made specific recommendations to the agencies regarding the implementation of NEPA.
Some have suggested that the change of format was an
immediate response to criticism of CEQ's coordinating efforts by
the General Accounting Office, for the memorandum was
prepared just before the public issuance of a GAO report.[25] The
memorandum, however, appeared at a time of year when one
might expect CEQ to revise its guidelines, and although its
content may have been influenced by the GAO report, it was in
fact a direct product of the CEQ's desire to revise its guidelines
and the Council's concern for the OMB "quality of life" review
process through which any formal guideline revision would have
to pass.

In the OMB quality of life review, proposed agency rules and
regulations pertaining to the "quality of life" were subjected to
the same review process to which agency legislative proposals
were subjected; that is, they were submitted to OMB, which
provided copies to other executive agencies for comment. The

process assured a unified administration stance once draft proposals were made public.[26]

Traditionally, agencies with rule-making powers published any proposed rule changes in the *Federal Register*. After a suitable delay for outside comments, the agencies responded to the submitted comments and published final regulations. In instances where environmentally protective regulations were weakened between the publication of a strong initial proposal and a milder final one, the administration was subjected to the criticism that it had buckled under to the interest of polluters and their defenders within the government. The OMB quality of life review process, begun in October 1971, saved the administration some embarrassment by giving agencies likely to oppose strict environmental safeguards, such as the Commerce Department, ample opportunity to express their reservations prior to the publication of draft agency proposals.

During early 1972, when CEQ was considering revising its guidelines, the beginnings of a congressional backlash against NEPA were evident. That backlash was coupled with expressions of increased concern about possible energy shortages. CEQ feared that if it attempted to revise its guidelines, incorporating into them the many court interpretations of NEPA that had been issued in the preceding year, the guidelines that would ultimately emerge from the review process might be even weaker than those the Council had promulgated in 1971. To avoid this possibility, while at the same time prodding the agencies to implement NEPA more fully, the CEQ resorted to the use of a memorandum containing specific recommendations. The memorandum was not subject to the quality of life review.

Cumulatively, the CEQ memoranda provide interesting insight into the NEPA implementation process. Their lengthy discussion of court decisions underscores the considerable role that the courts played in defining NEPA's requirements. They also indicate that the CEQ had apparently encountered some difficulty in obtaining administrative procedural compliance with the law and that its only ultimate sanction was to suggest that agencies would be subject to adverse publicity and legal action should noncompliance continue.

REVIEW OF IMPACT STATEMENTS BY CEQ

Structure of Statement Review. NEPA did not require the CEQ to review impact statements, but merely stated that the Council was to receive them when they were forwarded to the president and to the public.[27] Moreover, Congress did not intend for the Council to become involved in the daily decision making of federal agencies.[28] Nevertheless, the review of impact statements was useful in identifying general areas of weakness in agency impact statement procedures. Furthermore, despite the legislative history of the statute, impact statement review also provided a means for CEQ to become involved in an environmentally partisan manner in debates within the federal government concerning the wisdom of individual project proposals.

Although it reviewed impact statements, the Council did not regard that function as its principal means of shaping federal environmental policy. Mindful of its limited manpower and political resources, the Council made such analysis a subordinate means of policy oversight, placing its primary emphasis on reforming agency decision making to ensure both the early consideration of environmental factors and the maximum involvement of the public.

Process of Statement Review. Impact statements on over 4,000 major federal actions had been forwarded to CEQ through April 1973.[29] Because the CEQ staff was small, detailed review of each statement was impossible. Some environmentalists nevertheless found direct contact with CEQ staff examiners a functional means of influencing individual agency actions. The examiners searched in particular for full disclosure of environmental impacts and for adequate discussion of alternative actions and their environmental consequences. Should a project or statement have proved deficient, the CEQ might have attempted to obtain modifications. The decision to seek such remedial action, of course, required a calculation of political costs and benefits by CEQ. Should the Council have wished to complain about a project or statement deficiency, contact by phone or letter was initiated by the concerned impact evaluation staff examiner with the "NEPA liaison" of the agency in question. If satisfaction was not obtained at this level, a letter might then have been sent by the CEQ staff director to a departmental assistant secretary. If no affirmative agency action resulted from the second contact, a letter to the departmental secretary was prepared for the CEQ chairman's signature. If any of those initiatives failed, CEQ had the option of seeking relief through the presidential domestic council staff.

CEQ'S PUBLIC COMMENTS ON AGENCY COMPLIANCE WITH NEPA

CEQ's reliance on memoranda and other forms of informal communication was consistent with its reluctance to condemn agencies publicly for not complying with NEPA. That reticence was best exemplified by the following colloquy between Chairman Train and Representative Paul McCloskey at the first NEPA oversight session held by Dingell's subcommittee:

MR. McCLOSKEY: Could you give us a list in declining order of cooperative attitudes of the Federal agencies that have been reluctant to comply with the act as you would interpret it?
MR. TRAIN: I would hope you wouldn't press that question, Mr. McCloskey. Our effort is to elicit their cooperation and it seems to me that kind of characterization would perhaps be tailor-made to result in no cooperation. . . . Performance has not been as good in all cases as we would like. I would rather focus on the actual performance, rather than on such subjective factors as cooperative attitude.[30]

CEQ's policy of refraining from public criticism of federal agencies was also reflected in Council publications. In its second annual report, CEQ observed that environmental statements were often written to justify decisions previously made rather than to provide a mechanism for critical review of such decisions; that consideration of alternatives was often inadequate; and that agencies frequently defined their mission so narrowly as to neglect their responsibility to protect the environment. In rendering those judgments, however, CEQ did not single out any agencies for individual criticism, although it mentioned by name several agencies that had taken positive action to implement NEPA's environmental goals.[31] An analysis of the CEQ's second annual report prepared by a member of Congressman Dingell's subcommittee staff recognized the CEQ's reluctance to admonish specific agencies. After discussing some of the specific problems concerning the Department of Interior's proposed NEPA regulations, Dingell's staff member bluntly added: "CEQ is known to be unhappy about this—why didn't they say so?" [32]

OFFICIAL CRITIQUES OF CEQ OVERSIGHT ACTIVITIES

GAO Report—May 1972. The General Accounting Office (GAO), the investigatory arm of Congress, released a report in May 1972 that questioned the adequacy of CEQ's oversight efforts.[33] In discussing CEQ's processes for reviewing agency procedures and impact statements, GAO stated that CEQ's practice of assisting federal agencies generally and informally, and relying on the agencies themselves to resolve specific issues, would "not result in the most uniform and systematic implementation of [NEPA]." [34] GAO contended that it had been advised by CEQ that while the Council was placing greater emphasis on review of impact statements than on procedural review, it expected eventually to place greater emphasis on review of procedures when the overall quality of impact statements improved.[35] GAO evidently misunderstood CEQ's priorities, for in fact CEQ had been placing primary emphasis on procedural review. Nevertheless, GAO concluded that the Council's coordinating efforts needed improvement:

> . . . the Council should do more toward reviewing agency procedures and providing the agencies with specific advice and formal guidance so that problems in agency procedures are adequately and timely resolved.[36]

Oversight Hearings. In December 1970, Congressman Dingell's subcommittee held the first of a series of oversight hearings on the administration of NEPA. Dingell sought to learn the agencies' attitudes toward NEPA while prodding them towards fulfillment of NEPA's goal of full disclosure.[37] CEQ Chairman Train was the first witness at the hearings, and Dingell made it clear to him that he was dissatisfied with at least one CEQ interpretation of NEPA.

CEQ had incurred Dingell's displeasure by contending that the release of a draft environmental statement to the public was not required by NEPA. In a letter to the Congressman, Train had argued that NEPA requires only a "detailed" environmental statement to be made public. CEQ interpreted the final statement, not the draft statement, as being this statutorily required "detailed" statement. Since according to this logic a draft statement was merely an administratively devised requirement, agencies were not legally obligated to release it.[38]

In response, Dingell commented that NEPA "literally drips language which makes clear that it is the intent of Congress that . . . information should reach the public at the earliest possible moment." [39] He stated that under CEQ's existing interim guidelines, an agency could release a draft statement, agency review comments upon it, and a final statement all on the same day it planned to undertake a particular action.[40] Such a procedure would negate the possibility of mobilizing public opinion against a proposed project.

In reality, NEPA cannot fairly be said to "literally drip

language" emphasizing the importance of having information reach the public at the earliest possible moment. An emphasis on public participation was not well developed in NEPA's legislative history, although it was quite evident in executive order 11514.[41] Increased public involvement may have been in the minds of Jackson and Dingell when they promoted NEPA, but it was not a theme developed in explicit fashion in legislative documents pertaining to the Act.[42]

Dingell's overstatement notwithstanding, Train conceded that the Congressman's hypothetical case of an agency railroading a proposal through was a possibility under the Council's interpretation of NEPA. But, he argued, if the subcommittee wanted to ensure that railroading would not occur, then it should ask Congress to write into law a requirement for public release of draft statements.[43] In reply, Dingell suggested that CEQ had sufficient authority under executive order 11514 to initiate a requirement for release of draft environmental statements. He added, "I would suggest to you, Mr. Train, that it would be well for you to give this committee full information as to how you propose to change your guidelines so that this Executive order is carried out." [44]

CEQ's initial stance in this controversy was a temporary exception to its general attitude of encouraging citizen participation in decision making. Its revised guidelines, issued four months later, responded to Dingell's concern over the withholding of draft statements and also ordered a moratorium period between an agency's release of the final statement and the occurrence of final agency action.

Presidential Advisor or Public Ombudsman?

When first established, CEQ was designed primarily to be an advisor to the president. It was not to become involved in the day-to-day decision making of federal agencies but it was to provide a general evaluation of federal programs and to recommend, when appropriate, changes in program direction. While emphasizing the advisory role, NEPA's architects anticipated a second role for the Council, that of environmental ombudsman. CEQ was intended to be the body within the government to which citizens could turn for objective information on the state of the environment.[45] This role was elaborated upon in executive order 11514, which granted the Council the power to convene public hearings on matters of environmental significance.[46]

The job of environmental ombudsman was not to be envied. Professor Lynton Caldwell pointed out at the Senate hearings on NEPA that the Council would be required to make a number of tough, potentially unpopular environmental assessments. In his view, "service on . . . a Council would probably preclude a future political career." [47]

In setting up the two roles for the Council, Congress was interested in establishing both an advisory and a public voice independent of parochial agency and departmental positions. One representative who recognized the potential conflict between CEQ's dependent advisory role and independent public role was Congressman Henry Reuss. Apprehensive over the loss of public independence that might result from CEQ's advisory relationship to the president, Reuss suggested that CEQ members be given staggered six-year terms.[48] This idea was rejected by Jackson and his staff, who felt that the staggered term might give Council members some additional independence, but at the risk of affecting adversely their ability to influence the president; a member serving a six-year term spanning two administrations might become an outcast within the executive office during the latter part of his term.

NEPA and executive order 11514 thus established a role conflict for CEQ. On the one hand the Council was directed to advise the president confidentially concerning ongoing federal programs although it was not to interfere in agencies' daily decision making. On the other hand, it was supposed to be a source of public information on environmental problems. The Council had to choose. It could be restrained in its public information activities and in its public involvement in environmental controversies, in order to assure its continued welcome at the White House; or it could publicly reveal its views on a broad range of issues and face the possibility of being removed from effective participation in the formation of White House policy.

By the outset of the December 1970 Dingell subcommittee oversight hearings, CEQ's dilemma had become apparent. Chairman Train, in indicating to Dingell that CEQ should not make public its comments on environmental impact statements, observed:

> I think, gentlemen, to be very honest about it, there is a major dilemma here . . . . We cannot be, in a sense, the public ombudsman on environment and at the same time be the confidential advisors to the President on the development of policy. It is just an impossibility to fill both these roles.[49]

Congressman John Dellenback, a member of the Dingell subcommittee, emphatically disagreed with the Council's view. Choosing to ignore the language of the Senate report on S.1075 that supported Train's view, he argued that NEPA did not create an office of confidential advisor to the president, whose staff could withhold information from Congress.[50]

Dellenback's remarks notwithstanding, by June 1971 the subcommittee appeared to have resigned itself to acceptance of CEQ's interpretation of its role. In a report critical of CEQ in several respects, the committee did not attack CEQ for keeping its views confidential, but merely noted Train's point of view.[51]

Recognition of the administrative pragmatism of the CEQ position was also embodied in a staff memo prepared for the Dingell subcommittee minority:

> It [the Council] cannot be expected to wash the administration's
> environmental dirty linen in public as some people would have it do.
> Otherwise, it probably would lose the confidence and support of the
> White House . . . .[52]

The consequences of CEQ's initial choice become apparent on examination of the controversy over the trans-Alaskan pipeline. In 1970, the granting of right-of-way permits for the line was enjoined until such time as draft and final environmental impact statements were prepared by the Interior Department.[53] The draft statement produced by the Interior Department in early 1971 was roundly criticized by federal and citizen commentators, and the final environmental statement issued in March 1972 met with similar criticism. Following release of the final statement, pipeline critics sought public hearings to discuss the new information contained in the statement. The critics were joined in their plea by 82 members of the House of Representatives, but no department sponsored hearings were held.[54]

While the Interior Department had spent nine million dollars on its environmental study, the mere magnitude of its investment was no assurance that the evaluation would not be biased towards approval of the oil companies' proposed pipeline route. In light of the unwillingness of the Interior Department to subject itself to potentially embarrassing criticism at departmentally sponsored public hearings, CEQ could have assumed responsibility for airing the pros and cons of the departmental evaluation by convening hearings of its own. But it did not do so, perhaps because it recognized the intensity of the administration's commitment to the trans-Alaskan route.

Although CEQ's advisory role placed evident limitations on its ability to speak out publicly on issues of environmental significance, the constraints on the Council did not originate solely within the executive branch. While the Dingell subcommittee exhorted CEQ to compel strict adherence to NEPA's requirements, the Council also had to be responsive to another subcommittee with quite a different viewpoint. CEQ's budget, along with that of the Environmental Protection Agency was, until early 1975, reviewed by the House Appropriations Committee Subcommittee on Agriculture, Environmental and Consumer Protection, chaired by Representative Jamie Whitten.[55] Whitten, a conservative Mississippi Democrat and author of a propesticides book entitled *That We May Live*,[56] voted against establishing CEQ. His view of CEQ is indicated in his remarks before the Twenty-Sixth National Convention of the National Association of Conservation Districts:

> . . . I must preside over the annual funding request of the Council on Environmental Quality and the Environmental Protection Agency. It is a disturbing assignment. I didn't seek it, but it's there. I have frequently pointed out they are no longer satisfied to protect and improve our environment but are opposed to change.
>
> They represent, under the guise of the public interest, a narrowest of constituencies—a tiny fringe of viewpoint which is against development and not really sure about people.[57]

CEQ's first two appearances before the Whitten subcommittee were devoid of rancor. The FY1972 appropriations hearing, which marked the first appearance of CEQ before the subcommittee, served to demonstrate the subcommittee's ignorance of the Council's activities. At the end of the hearing, Chairman Whitten observed that the Council had received "kid-glove treatment," but that the questions might be more pointed in the future, after specific actions were taken by CEQ.[58] The subcommittee allocated the full sum requested by the Council.[59] For FY73, the subcommittee again allotted CEQ's full request, although funds for eight professional staff positions were ultimately impounded by OMB.[60]

For FY74, the Appropriations Committee report on the CEQ appropriations contained language ordering CEQ to conduct research that would emphasize the costs, rather than the benefits, of environmental pollution control. Included among these studies were examinations of (1) the economic impact on consumers of government action to restrict or ban chemicals, (2) the impact of environmental standards and regulations on energy consumption, including increased dependence on foreign sources of energy, and (3) the extent to which American industry is moving to foreign countries because of environmental considerations.[61] Dingell objected on the House floor to these research requirements, noting that the mandated studies might duplicate the work of other agencies, and were somewhat outside the expertise of CEQ. He insisted that if the studies were to be done, his subcommittee would have to be consulted on their design.[62]

CEQ's obligation to undertake the studies was reduced considerably by the conference committee appropriation report, which suggested in vague language that CEQ and the Appropriations Committee reach an accommodation on the subjects of CEQ research.[63]

The subcommittee manifested no overt hostility towards CEQ in the appropriations hearings, but it was a group CEQ knew it could not afford to antagonize. Former CEQ member Robert Cahn observed in a resignation interview that it was "absolutely ridiculous" to have the budgets of CEQ and EPA reviewed by the Whitten subcommittee.[64]

THE CEQ AS PRESIDENTIAL ADVISOR

The essence of giving advice to a president rests in competing successfully with many others who seek his attention and confidence. A study of the Council of Economic Advisors [CEA] underscores the uncertainties and rivalries that characterize the relationships of the president and his advisors. In *Economic Advice and Presidential Leadership: The Council of Economic Advisors*, Edward Flash concluded that the relationship between CEA and the president is moved more by the president's acceptance of CEA than by his dependence upon it, and it is more personal than institutional.[65] The president relies on CEA for advice and CEA derives strength from its presidential affiliation, but this interdependence is asymmetric. For while the president is CEA's only source of strength, the president need not depend solely upon CEA for economic advice.

Because it has no constituency of its own, CEA has always sold its views rather than prescribed them; it lacks the power to impose its will on others. Its advice and methods of operation have always been circumscribed, its involvement in policy problems taking the form of "opportunistic accommodation rather than forceful impingement." [66] Its operations have been determined less by what the president wants it to do than by what he does not object to its doing.[67]

The CEA relates not only to the president, but to the Congress as well. While it does not reveal to Congress the advice it has provided the president, it does furnish discussion and analysis of the president's economic program as ultimately formulated. But this role places the CEA in an awkward position, for the line between explanation and defense of policy is quite narrow.[68]

The characteristics that Flash attributed to the CEA's presidential relationship would seem to apply in some measure as well to the CEQ's. That is not surprising, for CEQ was explicitly modeled after CEA. Nevertheless, CEQ can be distinguished from CEA in two principal ways.

First, CEQ has a stronger legal basis for consulting with agencies, because executive order 11514 assigned CEQ oversight responsibilities for the environmental impact statement process. That process has no procedural counterpart in the legislation that established CEA.

Second, CEQ has a larger natural constituency, comprised of numerous active environmental groups, often intensely concerned with specific issues of federal environmental policy. However, in its early years of existence, the Council's choice of an advisory relationship with the president both limited its ability to take public actions that might mobilize its supporters and bred distrust among environmentalists suspicious of the administration's commitment to environmental values. Environmental lawyer Joseph Sax commented in 1970 that the Council's role

> will in essence be that of a spokesman for the administration, rather than—as had been widely hoped—a spokesman for the public, openly expressing views which might at times be at odds with the administration's position and thereby using its prestige and public constituency as leverage to induce the administration to adopt sounder environmental policies.[69]

In 1972, environmentalist Anthony Roisman accused the Council of "dereliction of duty." CEQ, he said, "was created by NEPA to act as a technical consultant to federal agencies to assist them in complying with NEPA [but] has instead become a chief spokesman for amending NEPA and has been notably devoid of any constructive suggestions for administrative solutions to the problems of federal agencies." [70]

The Council's problems were aggravated in 1972 by congressional and administrative efforts to modify NEPA. CEQ, having taken the position that some modifications of NEPA were necessary in order to preserve the statute from large scale assault, found itself under attack from environmentalists who opposed any amendment of the statute. At the end of 1972, environmental lobbyist Joseph Browder wrote in *Nixon and the Environment* that Council members had become

> salesmen for White House programs to erode water pollution legislation, delay regulation of strip mining, speed up construction of environmentally unsound power plants, whitewash destructive Agriculture Department stream channelization policies, and even weaken the National Environmental Policy Act.[71]

Browder may have overstated his case, but his views were symptomatic of the constituency problems that confronted CEQ. Such problems derived from the Council's position as advisor to the president. To preserve its entry to executive level deliberations, the Council had to be a "team player." It adopted the view that it could not trumpet its policy triumphs, nor adopt tough public adversary stances concerning particular agency projects. In the words of one staff member, it adopted the view that more could be achieved through the use of "molasses" than through the use of "vinegar," for it viewed private encouragement as more functional than public castigation in promoting environmental consciousness on the part of federal agencies.[72]

By drafting proposed legislation and shepherding it through the executive clearance process, the Council had a degree of success in influencing executive environmental policy. But because most of its impact was a function of behind-the-scenes advising, the Council was not always credited for its achievements. Furthermore, since the legislative proposals it supported publicly were the end product of negotiations with executive agencies having a lesser commitment to environmental protection, CEQ was often compared unfavorably to legislators who introduced legislation that was perceived as being stricter than the administration proposals that CEQ had to defend.

In promoting environmental policy concerns within the executive branch, CEQ had to overcome considerable obstacles. First, because many environmental problems were the by-products of the actions of mission-oriented agencies, many of CEQ's recommendations for reducing adverse environmental impacts necessarily had to challenge the manner in which existing agencies performed their missions. Compared to the mission agencies whose actions it wished to challenge, CEQ could muster few resources, in the form of clientele and congressional supporters, to support its point of view.

Second, many of the programs that CEQ was likely to advocate, especially those dealing with water pollution, required massive federal expenditures. Such proposals had to compete for the federal dollar with other programs that conferred much greater political benefits on their backers. OMB realized this too.

Third, societal awareness of environmental problems was a relatively new phenomenon. It is reasonable to suppose that the environmental concern and value orientation of CEQ was not shared by all individuals within the executive office. For executive decision makers, increases in rates of unemployment or inflation were undoubtedly far more immediately disturbing than rising levels of air or water pollution. Furthermore, to the extent that knowledge is a basis of power, for those policy areas in which the state of the art in environmental evaluation was not well developed, the basis for CEQ's policy expertise was reduced and its influence thereby lessened.

CEQ in the White House Policy Environment: A Structural View. Although CEQ was designed to advise the president on environmental matters, the occasions for personal contact between the three-man Council and President Nixon were few. (Of course as Watergate illustrated, a lack of direct contact between the President and his titular advisors was the rule rather than the exception.) In its first three years, the Council met only twice with the President, both times on the occasion of the presentation of the annual CEQ report. Russell Train's contacts with the President, however, were somewhat more frequent, particularly in connection with his work on international conventions and bilateral agreements.

The Council, in its routine work, was three steps removed from President Nixon during his first term. Its primary conduit to him was John Whitaker, the presidential assistant principally responsible for environmental matters. Whitaker, in turn, reported to John Ehrlichman, then director of the domestic council staff, and Ehrlichman reported directly to the President.

Whitaker was generally considered by the Council staff to be an equitable administrator. One staff member described him as "very fair . . . . He generally would give a ruling which the parties would regard as a fair application of the President's priorities in the situation."[73] In those instances where the Council was unhappy with a Whitaker decision, it had the option of contacting Ehrlichman directly, and it ultimately could write a memo specifically directed to the President's attention. But writing directly to the President was a last resort, for the Council had little political leverage within the White House.

In 1974 President Nixon resigned and was replaced by Gerald Ford. The Ford White House was far more open than the Nixon White House, and Russell Train's successor as CEQ Chairman, Russell Peterson, was personally consulted by President Ford on a number of occasions.

CEQ in the White House Policy Environment: A Process View. At CEQ's inception in early 1970, considerable executive level concern existed for environmental matters. Indeed, there was a sense of urgency in the President's first annual message on the environment: "The time has come when we can wait no longer to repair the damage already done, and to establish new criteria to guide us in the future." [74] The sense of urgency was present as well in the President's message six months later accompanying the CEQ's first annual report:

> Unless we arrest the depredations that have been inflicted so carelessly on our natural systems—which exist in an intricate set of balances—we face the prospect of ecological disaster.[75]

In his introduction to the first CEQ report, the President summarized his environmentally protective actions of the first six months of 1970. These included executive orders and legislative proposals dealing with marine pollution and a reorganization plan for improving environmental management. During the latter half of 1970, the administration undertook additional environmentally protective actions, many of which involved CEQ. However, as a new entity operating under severe budget and staff constraints,[76] CEQ, in the words of one newspaper correspondent, was "overruled, unheeded or unconsulted (in one degree or another)" on a number of major federal environmental actions.[77]

CEQ's influence in the White House became most evident to

the general public in early 1971 when, at its behest, the President terminated construction of the controversial Cross-Florida Barge Canal.[78] This decision, based in part on information developed by private environmental groups, suggests the important added access to executive decision making provided to such groups by CEQ. Whatever satisfaction environmental activists derived from the President's action on the Canal, however, was quickly dissipated. Within six months, President Nixon presided at opening ceremonies for the equally controversial Tennessee-Tombigbee Waterway.[79]

Early 1971 was marked by many executive initiatives designed to protect the environment.[80] CEQ staff interviewed in 1972 and 1973 consider the period the high-water mark of CEQ legislative success. But by summer 1971, the administration's attitude concerning environmental problems had changed markedly. Troubled by national economic problems and, perhaps, by industry complaints that the country was moving too far and too fast on environmental matters, the administration consciously began to moderate its environmental rhetoric. By the time of the second annual CEQ report, the new tone was evident. In his introduction to the report, the President stated that attention had to be paid to the economic impacts of environmental quality decisions:

> The effects of such decisions on our domestic economic concerns—jobs, prices, foreign competition—require explicit and rigorous analyses to permit us to maintain a healthy economy while we seek a healthy environment. . . . It is simplistic to seek ecological perfection at the cost of bankrupting the very tax-paying enterprises which must pay for the social advances the nation seeks.[81]

Because 1972 was an election year, consideration of CEQ's initiatives within the White House was undoubtedly colored by electoral factors; the Council had much less success than in 1971 in clearing its legislative proposals for the President's environmental message. The Council made numerous suggestions for legislation, but these were pared down by OMB, on grounds that many proposals were unnecessary since a large number of the administration's 1970 and 1971 proposals were still bogged down in Congress. One Council staffer interviewed diminished the importance of electoral factors, however, contending that although many CEQ proposals did not survive the clearance process, they tended to be lower priority items that had not received as much staff attention as the more successful, high priority projects.

The year 1972 was also marked by controversy over "censorship" of CEQ's third annual report. When the report was issued, three chapters that the Council had proposed for inclusion had been deleted. The ensuing uproar produced an unusual arrangement in which newsmen were permitted to examine drafts of the excised chapters at CEQ's offices.[82]

The deleted chapters had apparently required considerable revision. When word came from John Whitaker and OMB that this was so, CEQ assented and asked that publication be delayed accordingly. The Council argued that excision of the chapters would be misinterpreted by the public, but its request for delay was denied.

In general, while most of the chapters in the annual reports have been well received and have been viewed as objective environmental studies, the chapters on federal activities have tended to be laudatory reports on various administration environmental actions. Nevertheless, the censorship controversy represents another episode in the life of CEQ that sheds light on the lack of realism in the Dingell subcommittee's view of the CEQ it proposed. By establishing CEQ in the executive office of the president, the subcommittee must have known that the annual report would be subjected to executive review procedures. It appears, therefore, that the subcommittee was unduly optimistic when, in its discussion of the annual CEQ report, it emphasized the importance of a frank appraisal in the annual report of environmental conditions, even if there should be disagreement over the appraisals within the government:

The stakes are too high, and the consequences of inaction are too apparent, for the report of the Council to be anything less than the best that each member of the Council can produce; if honest disagreement occurs within the Council, your committee would hope that this would not be smothered in an attempt to show consensus where no consensus actually exists.[83]

CEQ as a "Team Player." The Cross-Florida Barge Canal termination decision of 1971 suggests the considerable impact a "team-playing" CEQ could have within the White House. The delaying of the Tocks Island Dam project, the secretary of transportation's decision against the controversial Minarets Road in California, and the promulgation of an executive order governing predator control all reflected favorably upon the Council's influence. Two other incidents, however, suggest how CEQ could be overruled when its goals conflicted with those of other, more influential, White House advisors. In the President's third annual environmental message, the Council had included a proposal for a presidential directive forbidding issuance of permits for dredging and filling of coastal wetlands unless developers could show cause why they could not build elsewhere. The proposal was apparently dropped by OMB at the insistence of the Commerce Department. Environmentalists within the administration believed that the department's opposition derived from its concern that the burden imposed by the directive would be too hard for developers to bear, and that the order would be unfair to businesses that might need wetlands for development.[84]

A second example of the CEQ's limited influence within the White House can be traced to a controversy over clearcutting in the national forests.[85] In January 1972, the Council drafted a proposed executive order governing clearcutting in the national forests. The executive order was routinely circulated through the executive branch for comments of executive agencies. The Commerce Department, in turn, contacted representatives of the timber industry to obtain their views. The industry became concerned when it learned that clearcutting would be banned in areas of "scenic beauty." It feared the judicial impact of this proviso, seeing it as an invitation for groups and individuals opposed to clearcutting to obstruct proposed federal timber sales while a determination of scenic beauty was made.

Alarmed, the industry requested a meeting with administration officials. Following two meetings of high administration officials, CEQ decided not to ask President Nixon to sign the executive order. That decision was undoubtedly influenced by the opposition of many western governors and most western Congressmen. Newspaper reports indicated that executive branch officials were concerned about the order's impact on timber company profits, timber supplies, and support for Republican candidates in an election year.[86]

It may be suggested that CEQ's influence within the executive branch diminished because of decreased administration interest in environmental matters and increased concern with inflationary pressures and energy supplies. Such a conclusion, however, is uncertain. To be sure, in 1973 new administration environmental initiatives did not seem to flow as quickly as once they did. However, some concern for environmental impacts developed in the federal bureaucracy, and was accompanied by the recognition that CEQ was a useful source within the executive branch for guidance and information concerning environmental decision making. CEQ, in its advisory capacity, was perhaps in a better position to promote environmental considerations than if it itself were a line environmental protection agency. It was viewed within the administration as an executive branch staff organization working to improve agency procedures. The environmentalists who worked within mission-oriented agencies and waged internal fights to improve decision making often found the Council a welcome source of aid and comfort outside their agencies, yet within the executive branch.

CEQ and the Public

PROMOTION OF CITIZEN ACCESS TO GOVERNMENT

In its role as coordinator of federal environmental policy, CEQ used guidelines, memoranda, and informal meetings to promote compliance with NEPA. While the Council felt that those techniques were useful, it had few resources to persuade a reluctant agency to comply with the Act. Its presidential advisory relationship was fragile, its budget was reviewed by a potentially hostile committee, it had few rewards to offer potential constituents, and it had no sanctions to impose. Consequently citizen activists were key allies of the Council in promoting NEPA compliance.

The Council repeatedly spoke in glowing terms of the important role citizen environmentalists could play in assuring environmentally sound administrative decision making. In its first annual report, it devoted a full chapter to citizen participation.[87] In its second report, the Council stated that citizen litigation had speeded court definition of the requirements of federal environmental protection statutes, had forced greater sensitivity to environmental considerations in both public and private sector decision making, and had educated lawmakers and the public as to the need for new environmental legislation.[88]

The Council's third annual report echoed the second, noting that "citizen lawsuits continue to provide a check on agency compliance with NEPA and to resolve important questions about its interpretation." [89] It added, moreover, that, "The willingness of citizens to sue to vindicate NEPA and the vigilance of the courts in enforcing the Act help to ensure that the agencies take their new tasks seriously." [90]

CEQ had reservations concerning some court interpretations of NEPA, and opposed general federal legislation permitting class action environmental lawsuits "for any unreasonable impairment of the environment." [91] It nevertheless had much to owe citizen legal initiatives and it supported broad citizen standing to litigate under NEPA and citizen suit clauses to enforce federal environmental legislation. In particular, it pushed for the inclusion of citizen suit provisions in administration sponsored water pollution, noise control, and toxic substances bills.

The Council also recognized the importance of public interest environmental law firms when it advocated retention of the firms' tax-exempt privileges under the Internal Revenue Code. In response to an announcement that the Internal Revenue Service (IRS) was reconsidering its policy concerning the deductibility of contributions to public interest law firms, CEQ Chairman Train spoke out strongly on the firms' behalf. He noted that private litigation had been an important supplement to and reinforcement for government environmental protection programs and that a change in the firms' status would "seriously curtail" their litigation efforts.[92] CEQ's ardent support for the firms, a public action unusual for a Council opting for a quiet advisory role, appears to have played an important part in IRS' reversal of its initial decision to revoke the firms' tax exempt status.[93]

The Council also endorsed legislation permitting tax-exempt environmental groups to spend up to 20 percent of their funds in lobbying activities. Under existing IRS regulations, such groups can lose their tax-exempt status if a "substantial part" of their activities consists of "carrying on propaganda or attempting to influence legislation."[94] Because of the vagueness of the term "substantial," organizations are often unsure of the precise limits placed on their actions. In his testimony before the House Ways and Means Committee that the existing IRS regulations "have the practical effect of discriminating against [tax-exempt organizations]," CEQ Chairman Train observed that unlike the financially strapped public interest groups, businesses and administrative agencies have "open access" to the Congress.[95]

CEQ's inability to bring about executive agency action consonant with what it deemed to be the requirements of the Act produced a flurry of lawsuits initiated by citizen activists. The CEQ staff more often than not cheered judicial decisions construing NEPA, but not all court decisions favoring environmentalist plaintiffs coincided with CEQ's view of the statute. While some decisions construing NEPA drew heavily on CEQ's guidelines, a few decisions directly contradicted the Council's interpretation of agency obligations under NEPA.[96]

Of particular interest at this juncture are those four suits in which the absence of administrative regulations for implementing NEPA, or the promulgation of regulations insufficiently implementing NEPA, led to court decisions faulting agencies for their lack of procedural compliance with the Act. These decisions favorable to environmentalists were the end product of recalcitrant agencies' noncompliance with an Act whose general message was clear: environmental considerations would have to be weighed at all stages of agency decision making, and agencies would have the affirmative responsibility to evaluate the environmental consequences of their activities. In all four instances, environmentalist lawsuits were a vital supplement to CEQ efforts to promote implementation of NEPA.

Calvert Cliffs' Coordinating Committee v. *Atomic Energy Commission.*[97] The Calvert Cliffs case was brought by a coalition of major environmental organizations who prior to the suit had unsuccessfully petitioned the Atomic Energy Commission (AEC) to revise its proposed guidelines for implementing NEPA. In their lawsuit the environmentalists included four major allegations concerning the AEC's implementing regulations. First, they contended that the AEC refused to review independently the nonradiological water quality impact of nuclear power plant operations upon which state or federal pollution control agencies had already passed judgment. Second, they opposed the AEC's refusal to require its review boards to examine nonradiological environmental factors, unless such factors were raised by outside intervenors or AEC staff members. Third, they contested the AEC's refusal to consider nonradiological factors in the licensing for construction of those power plants for which public hearing notices had been published in the *Federal Register* before March 4, 1971. Fourth, they attacked the AEC's absolute refusal to consider retrofitting, construction halts, or alteration of plans for nuclear facilities that had been granted construction permits, but not operating permits, prior to NEPA's enactment.

Taken together, the AEC regulations ran counter to the letter and spirit of NEPA: they delayed implementation of the Act, unduly limited the number of projects to which the Act applied, and ignored the requirement that environmental factors must be considered throughout the entire decision-making process. The Court of Appeals for the District of Columbia Circuit, in overturning the regulations in July 1971, stated that the Commission's "crabbed interpretation" of NEPA "made a mockery of the Act." [98]

That condemnation of the AEC stands in sharp contrast to the CEQ's uncritical public position regarding the Commission's rules and regulations. The Council's public acquiescence to the Commission's actions was undoubtedly influenced by the AEC's concession in its Section 103 statement[99] that nothing in the Atomic Energy Act of 1954 precluded Commission compliance with NEPA. If the Commission had taken the position that the 1954 Act did preclude compliance, and would therefore require modification, this contention might have precipitated a serious conflict between supporters of NEPA and the congressional Joint Committee on Atomic Energy.

At the Dingell subcommittee oversight hearings, prior to the Calvert Cliffs decision, Chairman Train called the AEC's actions under NEPA "responsive developments." [100] He stated, in addition, that the AEC was doing "an exceedingly good job" of meeting procedural requirements.[101] One month earlier, CEQ member Dr. Gordon J. MacDonald had described the AEC's impact statements as "the most complete, the best thought out, and the most sophisticated of any agency." [102]

Although the Council publicly acquiesced to the Commission's rules, it was not completely pleased with three of the four rules called into question in Calvert Cliffs.[103] The Council agreed with the AEC's contention that the Commission could accept at face value the water quality certifications isued by water pollution control agencies, but it felt that the Commission should not absolutely refuse to consider retrofitting, construction halts, and alteration of plans for plants granted construction permits, but not operating permits, prior to NEPA's enactment. The Council would also have liked to see the rules take effect earlier than March 1971.

The Council also raised the question of the consideration of environmental matters by the licensing boards. Although making mention of it, CEQ did not press the AEC as vigorously on this matter as it did on the retrofitting of nuclear plants. Definition of the role of the licensing boards was part of the larger issue of merging regulatory agencies' obligations under NEPA with their obligations under the Administrative Procedure Act,[104] a matter with which the CEQ was still wrestling at the time the AEC's pre–Calvert Cliffs regulations were published in final form in December 1970. By December 1970, CEQ had largely concluded that, given the general air of uncertainty as to the specific procedural requirements of NEPA, the AEC rules were probably the best that they could expect from the Commission, and they did not have any "serious objections." [105]

The AEC later conceded that until the time of the Calvert Cliffs decision it had not done much to implement NEPA.[106] The citizen-initiated suit left a major mark on the Commission and positively influenced its relations with CEQ. As one CEQ staffer noted:

After the decision, the change in attitude was remarkable. They came in within days . . . and said, "Help us draft some regulations that will let us get on with our work." . . . Internally, one of the things the *Calvert Cliffs'* decision did was to make the AEC pay attention to the Council whereas to a large extent it didn't beforehand.[107]

After Calvert Cliffs was decided, CEQ declined to reveal whether it had commented negatively to the AEC at the time the Commission was promulgating its regulations. At a hearing on the Calvert Cliffs decision before the Senate Interior Committee, Senator Gravel asked Chairman Train why it took a court "to find out an error of this magnitude," when CEQ had been specifically established to monitor NEPA. Chairman Train merely replied that the Council thought that it was making "constant progress" in its discussions of NEPA with the AEC.[108] At the conclusion of the hearing, Senator Jackson submitted pointedly written questions to CEQ concerning its views of the AEC's procedures before Calvert Cliffs, but CEQ merely responded with generalities, restating Chairman Train's and Dr. MacDonald's previous comments.[109]

Greene County Planning Board v. *Federal Power Commission.*[110] A second test of agency regulations implementing NEPA was *Greene County Planning Board* v. *Federal Power Commission.* In Greene County, the 2d Circuit ordered the Federal Power Commission (FPC) to prepare its own draft environmental impact statements for circulation to agencies and the public. Prior to the decision, the routine FPC practice was to circulate for comment the draft environmental statements prepared by applicants for Commission licenses. In ordering the Commission to assume responsibility for draft impact statement preparation, the Greene County court observed that statements prepared by applicants were likely to be comprised of "self-serving" assumptions. The court observed that the impact statement, which was the subject of the litigation, had described a 35 mile transmission line, built in a 150 foot wide corridor, as having "no significant adverse impact on the environment." [111]

Prior to Greene County, the CEQ had privately expressed to the FPC its dissatisfaction with the Commission's regulations implementing NEPA. In a November 28, 1970, memorandum to Gordon Gooch, general counsel of the Federal Power Commission, CEQ General Counsel Timothy Atkeson stated CEQ's desire to see Commission-drafted impact statements, noting that the Council needed "the independent objectivity of a draft statement prepared by [FPC] staff." Atkeson added that if the Commission itself did not prepare a statement, there was no way of knowing whether the discussion of alternatives in the impact statement was adequate. [112]

In discussions with CEQ in December 1970, the FPC forcefully argued against assuming responsibility for preparation of a draft environmental impact statement. CEQ, in response, felt that the FPC argument was "entitled to a hearing," although it disagreed with the agency's contention. [113] In its revised guidelines of April 1971, the CEQ inserted language that permitted the FPC to continue its practice of relying upon the applicants' environmental impact statements. [114] By December 1971, when CEQ met again with the FPC, the Greene County litigation had begun, and CEQ told the FPC that it felt the Commission would lose the case. When the FPC lost at the circuit level, it requested the solicitor general to appeal the case to the Supreme Court. CEQ advised the solicitor general that the appeal, if taken, would be unsuccessful. Ultimately, the Supreme Court declined to review the circuit court decision.

Ely v. *Velde.* [115] in *Ely* v. *Velde*, environmentalists challenged the failure of the Justice Department's Law Enforcement Assistance Administration (LEAA) to comply with NEPA. The suit was brought because LEAA contended that it did not have to prepare an environmental impact statement for its law enforcement assistance grants to states. The agency argued that it was obligated by the Safe Streets Act of 1968 to give grants to states once certain requirements, none of which were environmental, were met. Since its adherence to the Safe Streets Act mandate was required, and since adherence to NEPA was discretionary, LEAA argued, it was not required to prepare impact statements.

The District Court for the Eastern District of Virginia, believing that LEAA had acted in good faith, accepted this position. But the 4th Circuit Court of Appeals reversed the lower court decision, citing Calvert Cliffs as a precedent for interpreting NEPA broadly and for requiring strict agency compliance. It rejected LEAA's narrow interpretation of its obligations, and ordered the agency to comply with NEPA's procedural requirements.

LEAA had had the opportunity to argue before Congress that it was not bound by NEPA. Under Section 103 of NEPA, LEAA, along with all other executive agencies, was charged with the responsibility to report any statutory authority that might preclude it from complying with NEPA. Yet in the Dingell subcommittee's compilation of the Section 103 statements submitted by executive agencies, no statement by the LEAA or by the Justice Department can be found.[116]

CEQ, before the lower court decision, believed that LEAA was subject to NEPA.[117] It had written to the agency, indicating that it had received neither a Section 103 statement nor a set of NEPA implementing procedures. LEAA responded by mailing to the Council a copy of the district court decision in Ely, with a note attached indicating that the note and court opinion together constituted LEAA's Section 103 report.

CEQ did not immediately press LEAA further. However, the day the citizen-plaintiffs successfully appealed the unfavorable district court decision, CEQ said to LEAA, in effect, that it expected to be informed of the steps the Administration would take to implement NEPA's procedural requirements.[118]

Davis v. *Morton*.[119] In *Davis* v. *Morton*, the secretary of the interior's approval of an Indian pueblo's leasing of its land for development was questioned. The approval had been given without preparation of an environmental impact statement. A district court decision in November 1971 supported the Interior Department's contention that it was not subject to the NEPA requirements for lease approvals of this kind. The 10th Circuit in December 1972 reversed the district court decision, holding that Interior did have to abide by the NEPA requirements with respect to its leasing actions.

The question of whether the leasing actions fell within the domain of NEPA had been aired in CEQ's review session with Interior. At the review session, the department argued the view that was to be upheld by the district court—namely, that NEPA did not apply to the secretary's approval of Indian land leases. However, CEQ did not press Interior very strongly because, in the words of a CEQ staff member, "with a big agency like Interior, there are plenty of fish to fry and the Bureau of Indian Affairs [which had principal responsibility for overseeing the leases] wasn't even one of the biggest fish." [120] When the 10th Circuit ruled against Interior, CEQ advised both the department and the solicitor general not to appeal the decision of the Supreme Court. Interior felt that for political reasons it had to ask the solicitor general to seek Supreme Court review of the 10th Circuit decision, but the solicitor general denied the request and the 10th Circuit decision went unchallenged by the government.

Summary and Conclusions

In evaluating CEQ's behavior and impact, the outside observer is confronted with an "effectiveness dilemma." One has trouble distinguishing CEQ activity that might have represented compromise in pursuit of effectiveness from activity that might have represented cooption of the Council by the administration.[121]

CEQ often was effective behind the scenes in obtaining modification of proposed agency actions. The CEQ staff itself felt that it was an effective force for promoting attainment of environmental goals within the administration. One measure is staff turnover, which through mid–1973 was quite low. When important Council and staff members left, departure was due more to alternative career goals than to dissatisfaction with the Council.[122]

The principal concern here has been the Council's role in overseeing the impact assessment process, but its accomplishments in other areas should be mentioned. The Council played an important role in promoting international environmental cooperation. It worked to establish close, regular environmental ties with Japan, Mexico, Canada, and the Soviet Union. It represented the United States' views at the Organization for Economic Cooperation and Development, at NATO's Committee on the Challenges of a Modern Society, and at the International Whaling Commission. The Council was also active in international efforts to control ocean dumping and to protect endangered species. Chairman Train headed the U. S. delegation to the 1972 UN Conference on the Human Environment in Stockholm and was accompanied by the two other members of the Council.

Two-thirds of the Council's time was devoted to preparation of the President's environmental program and development of an annual environmental report.[123] The Council drafted and shepherded through the executive clearance process a wide range of legislative proposals, particularly in areas where little or no federal legislation existed.

The Council's widely cited annual reports discussed such matters as law and the environment; the economy and the environment; and environmental indices and forecasting. In conjunction with the preparation of the annual reports and of the environmental program, the CEQ commissioned research on numerous environmental management problems.

Certainly the Council made significant advances. But its failures cannot be ignored: failures to have legislative proposals approved, to have proposed agency actions modified, and to have agencies develop sound NEPA implementing procedures.

CEQ's emphasis on its advisory role and on broad policy questions undoubtedly caused some outside observers to question the Council's effectiveness when comparing it to federal entities whose views on particular projects must be made public. The creation of the EPA in December 1970 marked the establishment of the second major exclusively "environmental" body within the federal bureaucracy. With a large decentralized staff over whose public comments on impact statements its Washington office had little control, the EPA soon gained acclaim for its public, environmentally based criticisms of federal projects. CEQ, with its policy of low keyed internal comments on impact statements, inevitably appeared ineffectual when viewed in the light of EPA's public "activism."

CEQ viewed the courts as allies in promoting implementation of NEPA but, in the public mind, CEQ may have been eclipsed when the courts captured the spotlight as apparently the most effective instrumentality for assuring the implementation of NEPA. Federal judges, through their public pronouncements and their singular ability to enjoin projects, became clothed in a cloak of "activism," which could not be worn by the CEQ.

The public activism of EPA and of the courts adversely affected CEQ's relationship with many members of its natural constituency, the environmental community. It therefore became freer, with the passage of time, in its criticism of federal agencies. Upon request, it began to release its impact statement comments to the public. CEQ's policy of releasing its review comments appears to have represented a moderation of its initial stance concerning noncriticism of federal agencies in public. CEQ realized, it seems, that to a limited extent it could publicly criticize agencies without impairing its effectiveness as a White House advisor.[124]

4

Administrative
Response
to NEPA

NEPA's broad policy objective was clear. Environmental goals and information would have to be incorporated into existing patterns of agency action, in order to increase the environmental rationality of administrative decision making. All federal agencies, especially those engaged in public works projects, would have to make environmental protection a high priority. They would be responsible for evaluating the environmental impacts of their proposed actions and they would need to examine a wider range of alternatives to such actions than they had in the past. They would also have to assure that the adverse environmental consequences of their actions were understood and compensated for to the fullest possible extent. Agencies would also have to be forthright with the public about their actions' environmental impacts. Impacts would have to be revealed sufficiently early so that environmental protection agencies and the public would be able to respond meaningfully to agency initiatives.

This chapter explores alternative ways of measuring and explaining administrative response to NEPA. It begins with a survey of pertinent theoretical writings on agency systems and decision making. The overview of the literature provides a context within which NEPA's implementation by federal decision makers can be examined.

The next section examines five major decision-making questions that NEPA and CEQ left to federal agencies. The breadth of these questions indicates the considerable latitude available to federal administrators in deciding the manner in which NEPA would be implemented.

Alternative approaches to the measurement of NEPA's implementation are explored next. Emphasis is placed on identifying valid indicators of agency response. Measures that are not useful for interagency comparisons are nevertheless useful for providing insight into the behavior of individual agencies.

The concluding section suggests possible explanations of administrative response to NEPA. It discusses some of the factors identified in the administrative behavior literature that shaped the response to NEPA by such agencies as the Department of Housing and Urban Development (HUD), the Department of Transportation (DOT), the Federal Power Commission (FPC), the Atomic Energy Commission (AEC), and the Army Corps of Engineers.

Theories of Administrative Behavior

Early students of administrative behavior believed that there existed a clear distinction between policy making and policy administration. Legislators legislated policy and administrators blindly executed the legislative will. This early belief fell into disrepute, and public policy formation is now viewed as the product of the complex interaction between legislators, administrators, and the judiciary. This is particularly true when legislators are not ready to define policy in a highly specific manner. In such instances, they may delegate to administrators the task of policy development and "hope for the best." [1]

Congress frequently delegates responsibility for statutory implementation when the conduct to be governed is technical or requires continuous decision making that is beyond congressional capabilities. Delegation leaves Congress free to enact general policies and permits development of administrative expertise in the application of legislatively developed general rules to specific situations. [2]

NEPA is an example of a broadly worded congressional enactment that lacks precise directions for administrators. Its general intent was clear, but its brevity and lack of precision left administrators considerable discretion. It is not surprising, in view of the complexity of the federal administrative system, that there often existed a gulf between the expectations of NEPA's supporters and the decision making of federal agencies.

AGENCY SYSTEMS

A federal agency is a complex, task-oriented system. [3] Administrative norms and roles within it serve an integrating purpose. These, together with the values shared by agency personnel, function as "cognitive maps" guiding administrative behavior. [4]

The structure of the agency is comprised of many channels through which messages are communicated. The manner in which the channels are interconnected guides and restricts the distribution of information within the agency. [5] It also affects the flow of information from and to the social environment within which the agency operates. [6]

Some theorists argue that an agency's activities are principally determined by a coalition of personnel within it. [7] Agency goals are established in a bargaining process in which the general character of the dominant coalition is fixed. The coalition maintains control by manipulating the "decision premises" of agency members. It directs agency decision making towards achievement of its goals by influencing the definition of problems, the distribution of power and the structure of personal interactions.[8]

Agency decision making, however, is not totally a function of internal determinants. As an open system the agency exists within a particular social environment;[9] from it resources and information are drawn and demands are made. The resources, information, and demands are processed by the agency and converted through agency choice processes to decision outputs. These, in the form of regulations, grants, licenses, permits, and the like, are inputs to other systems in the agency's environment. As such, they affect these other systems' decision outputs, which themselves influence the future demands on and resources available to the agency in question.

The agency, always somewhat dependent upon its environment, attempts to reduce external uncertainty by elaborating a set of highly predictable interrelationships with other systems. This "negotiated environment" functions both to reduce in number and to buffer unexpected threats to the agency's well-being.[10]

The process of adaptation, a quest for self-preservation and organizational maintenance, often requires an agency to retain a favorable balance of constituencies in its environment.[11] To yield effective incentives for the constituencies it desires, an agency's dominant coalition must manipulate general organizational aims in order to emphasize scoring well on those criteria that are most visible to its most important constituencies.[12] Thus, for example, if an agency's survival is dependent more on its contributions to economic development than on its role in preserving environmental quality, it may not take the latter role very seriously.

The congressional appropriations and authorizations committees with which federal agencies must deal and the clientele groups whom they regulate or upon whom they confer benefits have traditionally been the two primary components of agency environments. It has been suggested, in fact, that to implement change within an agency, proposed innovations must *necessarily* be supported both within the agency *and* by the clientele groups or the congressional committees.[13]

DECISION MAKING WITHIN AGENCY SYSTEMS

Satisficing Decision Making. Ideally, to make a rational choice, a decision maker has to select a goal, know all alternative means towards achieving the goal, and consider all the consequences of each alternative means.[14] But an agency's structure, its restricted communications net, limits the decision maker's ability to make a rational choice. Filtering will affect all the elements figuring in his decision-making process—knowledge or assumptions about future events, knowledge of sets of alternatives available for action, and knowledge of consequences attached to alternatives.[15] Consequently the decision maker's definition of a problem and its possible solutions will represent a "simplified, screened and biased model" of the "objective" situation;[16] attention will be focused on certain areas,[17] and his problem solving approach will be narrowed to particular types of procedures. When narrow approaches to problem solving are aggregated within an agency, the agency may acquire a particular character—embodiment within its structure of selected values and development of a distinctive competence or inability to frame or execute specific policies.[18]

An agency is likely to evolve a complete, highly organized set of cognitive approaches when it has been confronting one type of problem over an extended time period.[19] When these standard operating procedures become inadequate for problem solving, search is begun for a new way of coping with a situation consistent with agency decision makers' goals. But the search process is biased itself, with perception of the social environment and processing of communications from it influenced by the training, experience, social location, and goals of decision makers. With time and other resources at a premium, they must often act on the basis of limited information. Ignoring the interrelatedness of all things, they must often make decisions with relatively simple rules of thumb that do not make impossible demands upon their capacity for thought.[20] Such decisions, based on the limited evaluation of alternatives, are known as "satisficing" decisions. Unlike optimizing or rational decisions, they are not based on the full evaluation of all the consequences of all possible means of achieving an objective.

Incremental Decision Making. The "satisficing" view of administrative decision making dovetails with the "incrementalist" view of agency choice processes. Incrementalists do not view administrative decisions as rational, as based on a comparative analysis of all possible alternative actions and their consequences. They see them rather as a series of disjointed and incremental choices. According to this schema:

1. Each choice consists only of the comparison and evaluation of incremental changes.
2. Consideration is only given to a limited number of policy alternatives.
3. Analysis is reconstructive; an impossible problem is not fruitlessly attacked, but is altered to make it manageable.
4. Analysis and evaluation are serial—the same problem is continually reattacked and the renewed attacks make less alarming the neglect of certain consequences at previous stages.
5. There exists a remedial orientation; "public problem solving . . . is dominated less by aspiration toward a well-defined future state [than] by identified social ills that seem to call for remedy."
6. Problem solving, in sum, is a series of successive approximations in defining and solving a problem.[21]

NEPA, Organizational Maintenance and Incremental Decision Making. An interweaving of the satisficing and incremental decision making constructs suggests, first, that the alternatives apparent to decision makers are the product of their biased perception of the environment. Second and more importantly, certain values may be excluded from the decision-making process if they are not shared by satisficing decision makers and those with whom they interact. The resulting neglect of the same consequences over an extended period of time may systematically create irreparable damage. In short, as it pertains to the environment, incremental decision making cannot always compensate for opportunities lost and environments destroyed.

NEPA was basically directed at a multitude of federal agencies whose past lack of concern for environmental matters had produced a series of undesirable environmental consequences and a host of environmental controversies.[22] It was intended to force agencies such as the Federal Highway Administration and the Atomic Energy Commission

> to become environment conscious, to bring pressure upon them to respond to the needs of environmental quality, . . . and to reorient them toward a consciousness of and sensitivity to the environment.[23]

The framers of NEPA felt it important to give an environmental mandate to all federal agencies and to provide an action forcing means for its fulfillment, for they saw that many environmental controversies had "been caused by the failure to consider all relevant points of view and all relevant values in the planning and conduct of Federal activities."[24] This failure was attributed to technicians' overlooking the "humanistic point of view" concerning "the relationship between man and his surroundings"; to difficulty in measuring environmental impacts; and to "subjugation of environmental management needs to budgetary and fiscal considerations."[25]

NEPA was designed to put all federal agencies on notice

that the hitherto long-term, unanticipated, environmental costs produced by their parochial, incremental decision-making schemas were no longer to be tolerated; their approach to environmental problems was to be more than a mere "crisis" reaction to identified environmental ills. NEPA could be said to insist that agencies' satisficing decision-making routines would always have to incorporate an identification and evaluation of environmental impacts. The function of the impact statement was to lay bare the values, assumptions and calculations underlying processes of agency choice, the presumption being that if particular environmental costs were neglected or undervalued, increased public participation and interagency coordination would ensure their full and fair evaluation. With many reviewers of varied background evaluating an action it was hoped that all its environmental ramifications would be made clear. Moreover, agencies anticipating external review would hopefully seek to minimize future criticism by objectively evaluating environmental impacts in detail.

The environmental impact statement procedure was designed to encourage agencies to reveal the tradeoffs implicit in their actions. In situations involving two or more alternative and incompatible uses of the same natural resource, agencies proposing an action were to develop descriptions of alternatives early enough in decision making and in sufficient detail so that subsequent reviewers would be able "to consider the alternatives along with the principal recommendation." [26] It was hoped that the examination of alternatives, as mandated in two sections of NEPA, would both reduce after-the-fact expenditures for the abatement of pollution and minimize the long term costs of environmental degradation.

NEPA was a comprehensive attack on narrow agency decision-making schemas. Its goal was to overhaul fundamentally an incremental decision-making process in which the pursuit of narrow economic goals had obscured the need to weigh environmental impact. As Senator Jackson stated in the introduction to a report to his committee on a national environmental policy:

> Throughout much of our history, the goal of managing the environment for the benefit of all citizens has often been overshadowed and obscured by the pursuit of narrower and more immediate economic goals . . . .
> This report proposes that the American people, the Congress, and the Administration break the shackles of incremental policymaking in the management of the environment.[27]

Measuring Administrative Change in Response to NEPA—Conceptual Problems

In responding to NEPA's demand for change, agencies could develop procedures that would mark a vast departure from their customary forms of operation; or they could attempt to ignore NEPA as much as possible, dampen its impact, and try to carry on "business as usual." In the face of NEPA's insistence on change, what agency response was forthcoming?

From the administrative behavior literature, several potential sources of administrative opposition to change may be inferred.[28] First, there may have been calculated opposition, stemming from a desire to retain certain benefits derived from maintaining the status quo.[29] Thus, an agency that depended for its well-being on the benevolence of a particular congressional committee might have been constrained from vigorously responding to NEPA's mandate, if such response required considerable deviation from the congressionally supported traditional agency mission. Similarly, agency personnel hoping to move to high-paying positions with regulatory clientele after concluding their government service might have felt reluctant to implement a new policy that might considerably inconvenience their prospective future employers.

Second, there may have been the mere inability to change,

deriving from systemic obstacles that included the sunken costs vested in the existing system and the limited resources available for innovation.[30] Thus, for many projects initiated prior to 1970 and planned without consideration of environmental policy goals, agencies may not have been willing to make more than a token effort to respond to NEPA's requirements. Similarly, an agency with a limited staff and budget may not have had slack resources to allocate to environmental analysis, particularly if allocation of resources for environmental ends meant sacrificing achievement of goals more closely associated with the agency's traditional mission. Alternatively, an agency may not have had a decision-making structure into which the planning requirements of NEPA fit. Thus, a resource agency that was unaccustomed to advanced planning may have lacked both the manpower and the experience to respond quickly to NEPA's requirements.

Third, there may have been the inability to change created by so-called "mental blinders"—accumulations of official and unofficial constraints on behavior.[31] Thus, for example, an "environmentally protective" agency may have been unwilling to respond to NEPA's procedural requirements, believing that it was acting in the interest of environmental protection and that the NEPA procedural requirements were therefore superfluous. Furthermore, there may have been simple indifference to the goals of environmental protection. Environmental protection, like civil rights enforcement, may have been thought to require little agency attention because it was regarded as nongermane to an agency's principal activities.

On the other hand, agencies may have changed. They may have changed involuntarily, through personnel turnover;[32] or they may have deliberately induced change. They may have sought to offset systemic obstacles to change by reorganizing, importing, and concentrating new resources, avoiding sunken costs, and lifting official constraints.[33] They may have devoted resources to environmental ends if they could do so without reducing the benefits provided existing agency clientele. To lift "mental blinders" they might have recruited unorthodoxy, retrained personnel, and reduced the incentives to oppose change.[34] They might have changed in order to seize jurisdiction from a competitor agency, or they might have changed because a new, responsive, dominant coalition assumed control.

In short, agencies may or may not have changed. The larger questions, however, remain—in precise terms, what change did NEPA require, what change occurred, and how can both those quantities be defined and measured? One theorist on the subject of "organizational change" refused to define the term, fearing he would become bogged down in a semantic quagmire.[35] For three reasons that precedent will be observed here and no attempt to define organizational change will be made.

First, while the direction of organizational change dictated by NEPA was clear, the actual magnitude of the change demanded was not clear. In attempting to reach the environmental policy goals of NEPA's Title I, agencies were to act "consistent with other essential considerations of national policy." [36] Thus, NEPA's environmental goals were not absolutes, but ought to be balanced against nonenvironmental national goals. The phrase "to the fullest extent possible" in Section 102 was to be liberally interpreted, but NEPA itself did not provide specific guidance as to the manner in which a balance between the environmental goals and other "essential considerations of national policy" was to be struck. Moreover, while Section 102(b) required that environmental impacts be given "appropriate weight in decision making along with economic and technical considerations," no attempt was made to define the meaning of the word "appropriate."

Second, the actual magnitude of change that occurred is hard to assess. It is possible, on the one hand, to determine how well the environmental impacts of a proposed action were evaluated by a government agency preparing an impact statement. On the other hand, one cannot reliably determine the number of environmentally harmful actions deferred for fear their exposure to the impact statement process would subject an agency to considerable outside criticism. Similarly, in cases where an agency prepared an environmental impact statement, clearly revealing environmental trade-offs, this may only have meant that what had always been implicit had now become explicit, but no substantive change may have been made in the balancing of environmental and nonenvironmental policy considerations. Thus NEPA's procedural goal might have been attained but not its substantive goal.

Third, while the exact magnitude of the change demanded and achieved is difficult to compute, it is even harder to specify the sources or causes of the change. Some of the court cases cited in chapter 3, notably Calvert Cliffs and Greene County, were the outgrowth of deliberate administrative refusal to abide by what might be considered to be reasonable interpretations of NEPA's requirements. A multitude of additional cases can be cited where administrators refused to issue environmental impact statements, delayed release of statements, or prepared statements that inadequately assessed environmental impacts and alternatives to proposed actions. Although there were many cases in which administrators deliberately refused to carry out either the letter or spirit of NEPA, there were also, undoubtedly, many instances where nonresponsiveness derived merely from administrative inexperience with the statute.[37] The kinds of questions administrative personnel had to address are described below.

Ambiguities in NEPA's Decision-making Message

NEPA's message to the agencies was elaborated upon somewhat by CEQ. The Council established a general framework for Section 102(2)(C)'s impact statement process and urged the agencies to use it as a basis for their own detailed procedures. Agencies had the responsibility to respond creatively to several key questions:

1. Which actions require statements?
2. What analyses should statements contain?
3. When should statements be prepared?
4. How should the public be involved?
5. How should impact statements be reviewed?

Which Actions Require Statements? The first step in implementing NEPA was identification of those legislative and administrative actions requiring impact statements. Here, presumably, some threshold setting was in order to distinguish three classes of actions. First, minor decisions not usually having a significant impact on the human environment were more or less automatically exempted from environmental review and impact statement preparation procedures. Second, there were those actions that usually had such a great environmental impact that they almost always required impact statements. Sandwiched between those two classes were actions that might require impact statements if the magnitude of their environmental impact was sufficiently large. These matters required some type of preliminary environmental assessment. Conflict over whether impact statements should be prepared for agency actions often led to agency-environmentalist confrontations in the courtroom.

What Analyses Should Statements Contain? Once a decision was made to prepare an environmental impact statement, a series of subordinate decisions followed. First, what environmental impacts had to be assessed, to what degree, and over what time frame? Second, how should one determine whether a particular environmental impact was beneficial or adverse, and how much weight was the impact to be assigned in decision making? Third, once it was determined that a particular action would have adverse environmental impacts, to what extent would offsetting economic or technological benefits have to be discussed in the statement? Fourth, once adverse impacts had been noted, what range of alternatives to the proposal had to be discussed, in what detail, and over what time period?

NEPA emphasized evaluation of a wider range of alternatives than decision makers had examined in the past, but it did not specify the number or types of alternatives to be studied. It did not indicate how energy alternatives could be coherently examined in the absence of a national energy policy, how power plant siting alternatives could be discussed in the absence of a national land use policy, or how transportation needs could be evaluated in the absence of a coherent national transportation policy. Clearly, some "rule of reason" was in order. However, agency decision makers, constrained by scarce time, limited capital, clientele relationships, and professional blinders were likely to have a different view from the environmentalists as to what was to be regarded as a "reasonable" alternative. Again, the statute and the CEQ guidelines provided little specific guidance.

Furthermore, NEPA, by its nature, may have promoted a rationalizing style of impact statement writing. Since the statute did not contain a "grandfather clause" exempting projects undertaken prior to its enactment, it could be applied to current projects, some of which were environmentally controversial. Administrators, having sunk considerable resources in past decisions, may have been constrained to justify a project's existence, even when considerable environmental degradation was a likely consequence. In such instances, moreover, where there was conflict of alternative "best" uses of a natural resource—where the determination of "best" was a matter of social choice—a decision maker with one particular view of what was socially best might have avoided making a solid case for an alternative not favored by him but perhaps preferred by an intense, sizeable minority of environmentalists. The justification of current projects may have promoted both the glossing over of environmental impacts and the development of "adversary" rather than "objective" impact statements.

When Should Statements be Prepared? For the environmental evaluation to be meaningful, the statement had to be prepared sufficiently early in decision making so that the environmental impacts it described could be considered at all stages of the decision-making process. It had to come early enough to assure that environmentally preferable alternatives were not foreclosed. In the abstract that was a fine principle because an impact statement ought not be prepared so early that it provides insufficient data. A thin line existed between preparing an impact statement early enough in the process to have a meaningful role in decision making, and waiting so long to gather environmental evidence that a statement necessarily became post hoc rationalization for a chosen course of action.

How Should the Public be Involved? Implicit in NEPA was the notion that the public was to be informed of the rationale underlying environmentally impacting administrative actions. NEPA's architects also sought public involvement in decision making, but they did not indicate when it should occur or what form it should take. For example, should it start when a determination was made to prepare an impact statement, or was it to commence only after an impact statement was written and ready for circulation? The need to involve and inform the public posed a dilemma for statement writers. For instance, at what point did the statement give "adequate" detail of environmental impact without becoming so voluminous or technical as to make access to it difficult for the average layman? Also, if some laymen were presumed to have expert knowledge, did the agency have to circulate their views of its draft statement? If so, what obligation did it have, if any, to respond to the views expressed? Some of these questions were only answered through litigation.

How Should Statements be Reviewed? NEPA mandated a wider range of interagency coordination than had hitherto occurred. While for some agencies interagency coordination had existed under earlier laws, for other agencies no such coordination had been required. Many questions could be asked about the manner in which the interagency review process was to function. First, was all coordination to take place only in regard to the impact statement, or was it both to precede and follow the statement review process? Second, were the agency review comments to be directed to the quality of impact statement writing, to the substantive impact of the project in question, or to both? Third, were review comments to contain a value judgment concerning the advisability of conducting a particular project if the reviewing agency disagreed with the policy balance struck by the originating agency? Fourth and last, if an agency received comments from other agencies, was it under any obligation to respond promptly, and if so, in what detail? Agencies had considerable latitude in responding to these and other questions. The following sections describe various ways of measuring their responses.

Indicators of Agency Response to NEPA

AGENCY PROCEDURES—TIMING OF ISSUANCE

NEPA was destined to have a greater impact on some agencies than on others. It was intended to have more influence, for example, on the Federal Power Commission (FPC) than on the Subversive Activities Control Board. Therefore, specific NEPA procedures for the one might have been more appropriate than for the other. Once it has been determined which agencies needed to develop their own procedures, by measuring the time lag between enactment of the statute and promulgation of such procedures, some indication can be obtained of administrative eagerness to comply with the law.

A CEQ list from 1971 can be used for identifying those

agencies that should have developed NEPA implementation procedures. Listed in May 1971 were sixteen nondepartmental bodies and forty-four components of eleven cabinet departments. The list was subsequently revised to indicate "all agencies and subagencies for which CEQ was able to obtain apparent agency agreement that formal procedures should be prepared." [38] The final list, produced in late 1971, contained the names of twenty-one nondepartmental bodies and thirty-nine components of ten departments. The alterations in the list suggest either that some agencies were reluctant to prepare guidelines and CEQ could not obtain their consent, or that there was some doubt whether an agency was sufficiently engaged in environmentally impacting activities to require its preparation of NEPA procedures. Evidence from CEQ memoranda and from court cases suggests that CEQ was encountering at least some difficulty in obtaining agency compliance with the law.

In 1970, 1971, and 1972, CEQ published lists of those agencies that had prepared NEPA implementation procedures. The figures in Table 4-1 summarize the CEQ lists.[39] The CEQ report

Table 4–1

NUMBER OF AGENCIES PREPARING
NEPA—IMPLEMENTING PROCEDURES

Date	Depart-ments	Components of Departments	Non-departmental Agencies
August 1970	8	1	8
December 1971	9	12	16
October 1972	9	31	22
CEQ Implementation Goal*	10	39	21

Sources: "Hearings on Organizational Plans of the Council on Environmental Quality before the Subcomm. on Fisheries and Wildlife Conservation of the House Comm. on Merchant Marine and Fisheries," 91st Cong., 2d Sess. 69–163 (1970); 36 Fed. Reg. 23666 (December 11, 1971); 37 Fed. Reg. 22668 (October 20, 1972).
* Refers to number of bodies that CEQ believed required NEPA implementing procedures.

prepared in August 1970 discussed agency procedural actions in the seven month period dating from NEPA's enactment and the three and one-half month period dating from the promulgation of the CEQ interim guidelines. CEQ reported that some procedures had been adopted or tentatively drafted by eight departments, one departmental component, and eight independent agencies.

The record of the first seven months is noteworthy in several respects. First, of the twenty-one independent entities requiring procedures, only eight prepared them. Of these eight agencies, three were energy production/regulation agencies—the AEC, FPC and TVA—and two were regional planning/oversight agencies—the National Capital Planning Commission and the Appalachian Regional Commission. The remaining regional planning agencies, the Delaware River Basin Commission and the Water Resources Council, did not file procedures until the following filing period. Second, one agency not renowned for its environmental sensitivity, the Corps of Engineers, promulgated procedures that preceded even CEQ's interim guidelines. Third, virtually no procedures were prepared by subdepartmental offices. Many of the latter may have been relying on departmental procedures. Nevertheless, the absence of subdepartmental procedures may also demonstrate a lack of concern by most of these offices for implementation of NEPA.

By December 1971 the procedural situation had improved substantially. In the December 1971 CEQ compilation of procedures, nine departments, twelve departmental components, and sixteen nondepartmental bodies were shown to have guidelines. Progress was especially slow, evidently, in obtaining procedures from subdepartmental bodies. The sixteen months between the first and second CEQ summaries saw a marked increase in agency procedural preparation, but much of the increased activity occurred only in the latter four months of this period, nineteen to twenty-three months after NEPA's enactment.[40]

By October 1972 most of the agencies listed by CEQ had filed environmental impact statement preparation procedures. Among the subdepartmental bodies, eleven on CEQ's list did not prepare procedures, while three not on the list did so. One nondepartmental agency not on CEQ's list, the Central Intelligence Agency, also prepared procedures.

The record of agency procedural promulgation reveals that there was often a considerable lag between the preparation of departmental and subdepartmental NEPA procedures. For example, in early October 1971, the Interior Department published departmental procedures, a section of which ordered subdepartmental bureau heads to prepare specific procedures.[41] Of the thirteen Interior Department Bureaus affected by the order, only three had complied by December 1971. Two more filed in January, one in February and three more in March. It was not until April 1972 that the Bureau of Land Management published its procedures. All the delays, according to a knowledgeable Interior Department official, were attributable to "bureaucratic inertia."[42] Those Interior Department bureaus most likely to be sympathetic to environmental concerns—the National Park Service, Bureau of Sport Fisheries and Wildlife, and the Bureau of Outdoor Recreation, were not noticeably faster in producing procedures than other Interior Department bureaus.

AGENCY PROCEDURES—CONTENT

The existence of procedures and the timing of their promulgation provides one perspective on agency response, but it renders an incomplete view. On the one hand, agency rules and regulations could be concrete signals to administrative subordinates that a particular congressional enactment must be adopted as agency policy. On the contrary, rules and regulations could merely be symbolic gestures of statutory implementation that could be constructed in such a way as to muffle the impact of a new law on an agency's decision-making processes. Adequate agency procedures were important in promoting implementation of NEPA because CEQ, deliberately keeping its own guidelines vague, had indicated that primary responsibility for detailing procedural requirements of NEPA rested with the agencies.

Regulations of the Corps of Engineers. The Corps of Engineers' rules stand out as being the best of all those prepared within twelve months of NEPA's enactment by federal agencies.[43] They elaborated upon the environmental statement content requirements and upon the requirement for considering alternatives, they called for the consideration of environmental impacts from the beginning of project planning, and they demanded the objective, detailed evaluation of proposed projects.

In several respects, the 1970 Corps regulations anticipated interpretations of NEPA that would not become part of the CEQ guidelines until the following year. For example, they indicated that statements should provide enough of a description of a project's environmental impacts in order to permit evaluation and independent appraisal of the favorable and unfavorable environmental effects of each proposal.[44] While that requirement was implicit in the first CEQ guidelines it was not explicit. The Corps regulations also emphasized incorporating environmental considerations into project planning at the outset.[45] While that was the intent of NEPA, the need for early consideration of environmental impacts was not explicitly expressed by CEQ until 1971.[46]

The Corps rules specifically addressed the subject of responses to outside critiques, noting that statements should include and comment on the views of those opposing a project on environmental grounds.[47] Statements were also to contain summaries of the review comments of those agencies with environmental protection responsibilities.[48]

The Corps rules also placed considerable emphasis on objective analysis of projects and their alternatives. Corps officials were warned that statements should not be construed as a means for assisting or supporting project justifications. The regulations stated:

> The statement should include a full and objective appraisal of the environmental effects, good and bad, and of available alternatives. In no case will adverse effects, either real or potential, be ignored or slighted in an attempt to justify an action previously recommended. Similarly, care must be taken to avoid overstating favorable effects.[49]

In their consideration of alternatives, Corps officials were told that the preservation alternative, the alternative of taking "no action at all," was always to be discussed along with alternatives that would provide functions "similar to those provided by the proposed project but which were specifically formulated with environmental quality objectives in mind."[50] If one were to judge administrative response to NEPA solely on the basis of an evaluation of rules and regulations, then one would have to conclude that the Corps had definitely taken NEPA to heart.

Regulations of the Department of Transportation (DOT). DOT's initial regulations,[51] like the Corps', were quite impressive when compared to those of other agencies. Among their admirable features were the following: first, they provided for the preparation of "negative declarations," documents to be developed by administrators when a decision was made not to prepare an environmental impact statement.[52] Decision makers would thus be put on record that they had decided that no impact statement was required for a particular action. At the time, virtually no other agency regulations contained such "negative declaration" provisions. Second, the regulations recognized the importance of citizen input into the decision-making process, and suggested that the final impact statements discuss, where appropriate, problems and objections raised by citizens.[53] Third, the departmental rules underscored the urgency of meeting the NEPA requirements. They demanded preparation of NEPA procedures by DOT's component agencies within two weeks.[54] Fourth and last, the DOT regulations declared that if a decision maker had any doubt as to whether an impact statement should be prepared, a decision was to be made in favor of statement preparation.[55]

Regulations of the AEC. The AEC's rules and regulations were briefly described in chapter 3 in the discussion of the Calvert Cliffs case. They delayed implementation of NEPA until fourteen months after the statute's enactment and postponed consideration of the environmental impact of partially constructed plants until a later stage of AEC action. They also precluded the consideration of environmental impacts through every stage of AEC decision making, and they shifted a considerable environmental analysis burden onto opponents of nuclear power intervening in AEC licensing proceedings.

Corps, DOT, and AEC Regulations Compared. The Corps, DOT, and AEC are quite different from one another. The Corps is concerned with the planning, design and construction of its own projects. DOT is a grant-giving agency, overseeing federally financed projects planned and constructed by state agencies. AEC, in contrast, is a regulatory agency, whose function is to license projects planned, designed, constructed and paid for by utility companies.

Despite these agencies' functional differences, comparisons among their regulations may legitimately be made. If the AEC had taken its NEPA obligations seriously, the gross variations among the regulations could have been reduced considerably. In brief, the three sets of regulations represented two competing philosophies concerning an agency's responsibilities under NEPA. On the one hand, the DOT guidelines stressed the urgency of compliance. The Corps guidelines, similarly, took a liberal view of an agency's analytical responsibilities, requiring the evaluation of a broad range of alternatives to proposed actions. They advocated the application of the NEPA requirements to the fullest extent possible. The AEC guidelines, on the other hand, sought to delay and limit NEPA's implementation. They sought to postpone consideration of environmental impacts until a late stage of plant licensing proceedings, thereby permitting the de facto foreclosure of alternative actions.

Shortcomings in Other Agencies' Regulations. The AEC was not the only agency whose implementing instructions delayed the consideration of environmental impacts. Until January 1972 the Bureau of Reclamation did not provide for impact statement preparation until a late stage of its project planning. During the initial "reconnaissance" stage of Bureau decision making, the need and justification for a development or improvement is established and provisions for alternative actions made. But under the Bureau's first set of NEPA guidelines, an impact statement was not to be prepared during this crucial period when preservation options might be given more equitable weight than in later stages. The impact statement, according to Bureau regulations, was to be prepared during the second or "feasibility" stage of Bureau action, when the specific engineering and operating plan was developed and the economic justification of a project determined.[56]

Yet another example of procedural noncompliance with NEPA derives from the rules and regulations of the Federal Power Commission (FPC). As noted in the discussion of the Greene County case, the FPC decided to rely on applicants' draft environmental statements in all contested matters. Ironically, only for those hearings that were uncontested was the FPC staff to prepare a detailed environmental statement. In other words, in those instances where environmental impacts were likely to be most controversial, the staff would have a smaller role than in those situations in which they were not.

Additional examples of procedural noncompliance with NEPA abound. The Department of Housing and Urban Development (HUD), for example, instructed its regional offices to prepare impact statements solely for controversial or precedent-setting actions.[57] The HUD guidelines thus exempted a major proportion of HUD's work from the impact statement requirement. In contrast, the Corps had determined that nearly all of its projects were major actions significantly affecting the quality of the human environment and initiated plans for preparing large numbers of impact statements.[58]

The Interior Department's initial procedures were also remarkable to the extent that they diverged from the intentions of NEPA's architects. In describing the content requirements of environmental statements, they noted that the impact statements should present a brief description and *justification* of the proposed action.[59] That contrasts markedly to the Corps' injunction to its planners that "statements should not be construed as a further means for . . . project justification.[60]

QUANTITY OF IMPACT STATEMENTS PREPARED

Executive agencies had to decide which of their projects merited impact statements, that is, which actions were major and had a significant impact on the human environment. Agency impact statement output, however, does not provide a reliable comparative indicator of administrative response to NEPA, for some agencies engaged in many more environmentally impacting activities than others and as a result produced more impact statements. Moreover, even if an agency produced many statements, they may have been of such low quality that they represented nothing more than symbolic gestures of environmental concern. The following section discusses the circumstances behind the large number of impact statements produced by the Federal Highway Administration (FHWA) and the low number produced by the Environmental Protection Agency (EPA). In the case of FHWA, the large impact statement output did not necessarily represent a serious effort to implement NEPA. In the case of EPA, the low production of statements stemmed in part from a belief that statement writing would interfere with EPA's environmental protection obligations or would be superfluous to their fulfillment.

Many Statements—The Case of FHWA. In the first half of 1971, the FHWA submitted over half of all the statements reviewed by EPA and deposited with CEQ. The large number was partially the result of the FHWA's ill-defined guidance to state highway departments writing statements and may partially have been the product of an effort by state highway officials to clog NEPA review channels.

The Department of Transportation, FHWA's parent department, in its initial issuance of NEPA regulations, enumerated some of the departmental activities to which NEPA might conceivably apply. It also identified various environmental impacts likely to be significant.[61] However, it left to its component administrations the task of defining NEPA's applicability to their projects. The FHWA's first effort to implement NEPA was a draft instructional memorandum issued November 30, 1970.[62] FHWA indicated the necessity for preparing both "negative declarations" and environmental impact statements. Many actions, such as road resurfacings and lane widenings, were indicated as likely candidates for negative declarations. FHWA also indicated that impact statements would be necessary for road projects between "logical termini." Those projects could be divided into smaller proposals for purposes of receiving design or construction approval from FHWA. Little additional guidance was provided concerning likely candidates for statements.

Following the memorandum's issuance, the federal government was deluged with impact statements for highways. Often they were short, such as those describing small road segments with a negligible environmental impact. The flow of statements became so great that it was sometimes measured in pounds of paper and linear feet of shelf space.

This outpouring may have represented an earnest effort on the part of environmentally conscious state highway officials to comply with NEPA. That explanation, however, is called into question by a public-interest group study of highway impact statements.[63] The study of seventy-six final environmental statements, for proposed urban highway projects within cities of more than 50,000 population, concluded that the impact statements contained "arguments rather than findings, opinions rather than studies, and generalities rather than facts." [64] The generalities appeared repeatedly, precluded further data seeking, and ended inquiry by "affirming the notion that a safer, more efficient highway facility has a positive effect on man's environment." [65] The researchers found a reliance on standardized phrases to dismiss potentially serious environmental degradation. One-third of the seventy-six statements asserted without qualification that *all* highways increase the health and safety of the general public, 13 percent did not mention air pollution, and 44 percent did not consider the alternative of not building the projects.[66]

The research findings would appear to bear out Congressman Dingell's fear, expressed in 1972, that

> maybe we are breeding a race of environmental impact writers whose responsibility is less an honest evaluation of the environmental impact than it is sort of a medieval exorcist approach to the environment . . . by setting forth certain facts in certain forms, regardless of what the real facts may be.[67]

A second interpretation is that state highway officials were merely cautious. Anxious to avoid lawsuits charging them with failure to write statements, and unsure of which actions required statements, state highway officials developed many unnecessary statements.

A third interpretation is that they represented an attempt by state highway officials to undermine NEPA. Not only would state officials be able to point to their own paperwork, but the large number of impact statements would clog interagency review channels, producing cries by other agencies for relief from an onerous burden. Division of the analysis of lengthy highway projects into multiple impact statements would also enable highway officials to promote projects that individually might not have much environmental impact, but which cumulatively might have considerable land use, air, and noise pollution implications. Outside reviewers, swamped by impact statements describing highway segment "x"'s impact on forty redwoods and highway segment "y"'s impact on thirty oaks, and so on, might lose the forest for the trees.

Some evidence can be found to support the hypothesis that highway planners sought to undermine the NEPA review process. Highway officials complained about the burden of paperwork before a congressional committee investigating red tape in government, and at one highway conference attended by a CEQ official, an FHWA spokesman attempted to blame the Council for NEPA's paperwork load.[68]

Whatever the explanation, considerable effort was devoted to impact statement writing, although the statistical evidence in Tables 4-2 and 4-3 suggests that in only a few states was impact statement writing a burdensome administrative task. Table 4-2 lists the number of highway impact statements submitted to CEQ by the states through January 1, 1973.[69] It shows that in this period, only a few state highway departments produced large numbers of impact statements. Moreover, as Table 4-3 indicates, the impact statements produced tended to be short. Table 4-3 shows the length of the 423 draft statements prepared between June and August 1971 for which pagination could be readily obtained. Of the 423 draft statements submitted to CEQ, 37 percent were under ten pages in length, 25 percent were eleven to fifteen pages in length, and 18 percent were sixteen to twenty-five pages in length. Only 20 percent of the draft impact statements were over twenty-five pages in length. In this three month period, Alabama, which produced more impact statements than any other state through January 1, 1973, submitted eighteen draft statements, all but one of which were less than

Table 4–2

NUMBER OF ENVIRONMENTAL IMPACT STATEMENTS
PREPARED BY STATE HIGHWAY DEPARTMENTS
THROUGH JANUARY 1, 1973*

Number of Statements Prepared	*Number of State Highway Departments Preparing Statements*
0– 9	8
10–19	10
20–29	10
30–39	5
40–49	4
50–59	5
60–69	4
70–79	4
80–89	1
90–99	1
TOTAL	52**

Source: CEQ tabulation. Copy in author's files.
* Includes final statements and draft statements for which no finals had been prepared.
** Includes District of Columbia and Puerto Rico.

ten pages long. In sum, the statistical evidence suggests that in most cases, it is unlikely that statement preparation demanded a burdensome proportion of administrative time.

The flow of unnecessary impact statements became the subject of consultations between CEQ and FHWA. On August 24, 1971, with the issuance of Policy and Procedure Memorandum (PPM) 90-1,[70] FHWA sought to reduce impact statement flow by refining its administrative regulations. PPM 90-1 stressed the importance of preparing impact statements for environmentally meaningful road segments. State highway departments were told that road sections evaluated in impact statements should be as long as practicable to permit consideration of environmental matters in a broad manner, and they were warned not to "piece-meal" proposed highway improvements into multiple impact statements. Also, the list of projects

Table 4–3

LENGTH OF DRAFT STATE HIGHWAY
DEPARTMENT IMPACT STATEMENTS
JUNE TO AUGUST 1971

Number of Pages	Number of Statements
1– 5	32
6–10	125
11–15	107
16–20	45
21–25	31
26–30	26
31–35	11
36–40	10
41–45	6
46–50	4
51–55	2
56–60	4
61–65	7
66–70	4
71–75	1
76–80	1
81–85	1
85 +	6
TOTAL	423

Source: Council on Environmental Quality *102 Monitor*, July–September 1971.

eligible for negative declarations was expanded to include highway sections that were major actions but were not likely to have a significant effect on the quality of the human environment. The issuance of PPM 90-1 considerably reduced the flow of impact statements from state highway departments. Table 4-4 shows the dramatic drop in statements following its issuance.

Few Statements—The Case of EPA. EPA did not hasten to write impact statements or guidelines for their preparation. EPA was convinced that its decisions would certainly give great weight to environmental quality concerns. A young agency with

Table 4–4

DRAFT IMPACT STATEMENTS SUBMITTED TO CEQ
BY STATE HIGHWAY DEPARTMENTS
FEBRUARY 1971 TO JANUARY 1972

Month and Year	Number of Statements Submitted
February 1971	110
March 1971	96
April 1971	192
May 1971	149
June 1971	177
July 1971	126
August 1971	123
September 1971	108
October 1971	56
November 1971	68
December 1971	50
January 1972	53

Source: Council on Environmental Quality *102 Monitor* (March 1971–February 1972).

many tasks to complete within a short time, EPA looked askance at the impact statement preparation requirement.

EPA's initial impact statement preparation guidelines were not issued until January 20, 1972.[71] In accordance with CEQ's guidelines, they asserted that statements were not required for environmentally protective regulatory activities.[72] Impact statements were, however, to be prepared for sewage treatment plants whose environmental impact exceeded specified qualitative thresholds. Few plants evidently exceeded the thresholds, for by October 1973, statements had been written for fewer than one percent of the plants granted funding by EPA.[73] By October 1973, EPA had prepared only fifty-five statements.[74]

Internally, some EPA staff conceded that more effort must be devoted to impact statement preparation. In December 1971, regional administrators received a memo that summarized by region the number of environmental impact statements prepared. The memo noted that statements were few in number when compared to projects reviewed. It added:

> more effort is needed to incorporate environmental factors into the decision-making process if, for no other reason, only to guard the programs from even greater numbers of outside litigative actions on environmental issues.[75]

A year later the situation had not improved substantially, and an internal document describing EPA programs declared that EPA had to commit more of its resources to preparing environmental assessments of its actions.[76]

Legislative History. The scarcity of statements reflected in part a legal controversy arising from NEPA's ambiguous legislative history. As noted earlier, NEPA's passage through the Senate was marked by a jurisdictional dispute between Senators Muskie and Jackson. In essence, Senator Muskie did not want the activities of the Department of Interior's Federal Water Pollution Control Administration (FWPCA) and the Department of Health, Education and Welfare's National Air Pollution Control Administration (NAPCA), over both of which Muskie's Public Works Committee had jurisdiction, determined by legislation reported from Senator Jackson's Interior Committee. Senator Jackson appears to have responded to Senator Muskie's concerns, for a document entitled "Major Changes in S. 1075 as Passed by the Senate," introduced into the *Congressional Record* during senate consideration of the conference report on NEPA, stated that the provisions of Sections 102 and 103 of NEPA were not designed to change the manner in which the FWPCA and NAPCA conducted their environmental protection responsibilities.[77] Moreover, in a colloquy with Senator Jackson on the Senate floor, Senator Muskie remarked that the two of them understood that NEPA would not alter the legislative mandates of agencies like the FWPCA and NAPCA.[78] However, this apparent exception was not made any more explicit, was not written into the conference report, and

NEPA itself continued to state that *all* agencies were subject to its provisions. Three years later, in October 1972, Jackson acknowledged that the legislative history was "ambiguous with respect to the scope of the exemption sought for EPA and the policy objectives it would serve." [79]

Resourceful lawyers in *Kalur* v. *Resor*,[80] a challenge to EPA's discharge permit program for water pollution control, capitalized on NEPA's cloudy legislative history. The December 1971 holding in Kalur that NEPA applied to EPA's permit program prompted congressional discussion of a temporary exemption for the program from NEPA. The product of the debate was Section 511(c) of the Federal Water Pollution Control Act Amendments of 1972,[81] which declared that NEPA was not applicable to most of EPA's water pollution control actions.

Policy Objectives. Compelling arguments were made in support of and in opposition to a requirement that EPA prepare environmental impact statements on all its actions, particularly those of a regulatory nature. Proponents maintained that NEPA was a law whose general goal was full disclosure, and thus it should apply to EPA as well as to all other agencies. Moreover, EPA, as an environmentally concerned agency, should set an example for line agencies heretofore less concerned with environmental quality.

Proponents also contended that EPA, like any regulatory agency, could not be trusted; it might be captured by those it regulated or be subjected to political pressure that would undermine its diligence.[82] Furthermore, EPA could not be omniscient. In attempting to abate pollution of one medium, it might not consider the adverse environmental consequences such abatement might have for another medium.[83]

Finally, impact statement preparation might be desirable because EPA's staff members might wear professional blinders, like those worn by professionals in other agencies. These blinders might preclude consideration in decision making of certain environmentally protective alternatives. For example, a controversy had raged for several years concerning the comparative desirability of land versus water disposal of sewage wastes. It was argued by some that EPA engineers, brought up in the water disposal school of waste water management, gave too little weight in their planning to land disposal of sewage. As noted earlier, EPA prepared few impact statements analyzing alternatives to the sewage treatment plants it funded.

Those defending EPA's reluctance to prepare environmental impact statements responded that, under the provisions of highly specific pollution control laws like the Clean Air Act and the Federal Water Pollution Control Act, EPA had to work on a tight time schedule, and that this schedule would be upset by the procedural requirements of NEPA. They argued further that as an environmentally protective agency EPA would naturally take environmental impacts into consideration in decision making. Furthermore, said EPA's defenders, the statutes under which the agency was operating required it to develop legally defensible records supporting its regulatory decisions. These records were the functional equivalents of impact statements. Finally, EPA supporters feared that industrial opponents of pollution abatement would use NEPA's procedural requirements to entangle EPA decision making and to delay attempts at environmental improvement.

For a time, the last of those arguments seemed especially credible. A review of NEPA litigation reveals that EPA had more NEPA-based lawsuits filed against it than any agency except the Department of Transportation.[84] Large industrial corporations, particularly electric utilities, argued in lawsuits that NEPA required preparation of impact statements for EPA's environmentally regulatory activities.[85] However, when appellate courts finally adjudicated the issue of NEPA's applicability to EPA, particularly with respect to regulatory actions taken under the Clean Air Act, they ruled in favor of exemption.[86] The courts generally argued that EPA was an environmentally protective agency and that expeditious enforcement of clean air standards was necessary, so no environmental impact statements need be prepared.

Although the courts upheld EPA's position on impact statements, the agency in early 1974 indicated its willingness to prepare them for many of its actions. EPA's changed position was due in large measure to continuing pressure from Congressman Jamie Whitten. Senator Muskie, in direct response to the pressures exerted by Congressman Whitten, had a provision analogous to Section 511(c) of the FWPCA Amendments written into the Energy Supply and Environmental Coordination Act of 1974, exempting all of EPA's actions under the Clean Air Act from the impact statement requirement.[87]

EPA'S IMPACT STATEMENT REVIEW COMMENTS—
INDICATORS OF AGENCY COMPLIANCE WITH NEPA?

The search for readily quantifiable indicators of agency response to NEPA might lead one to utilize EPA review comments on impact statements as a basis for assessing the adequacy of agency environmental impact analysis. A number of assumptions must be made in order to use EPA review comments in that manner. The validity of those assumptions and the nature of EPA impact statement review in 1971 and 1972 are examined below.

As the principal line agency concerned with environmental protection, EPA might be expected to have had the most environmental expertise of any federal agency, and thus would have been best equipped to judge the adequacy of environmental assessments conducted by sister agencies. To use EPA's review comments as indicators of other agencies' behavior, however, some important assumptions have to be made:

1. EPA employed qualified reviewers with sufficient time to assess the strengths and weaknesses of individual impact statements;
2. Equal attention was paid to the impact statements of all agencies;

3. EPA environmental expertise was consistent throughout all areas of environmental impact assessment;
4. EPA personnel utilized a set of well-defined criteria in assessing other agencies' environmental impact statements; and
5. EPA environmental assessments were objective environmental analyses untainted by political considerations.

An analysis of EPA comments on environmental impact statements, part of a study of agency response to NEPA, was prepared by William J. J. Smith for the Conference Board.[88] For his analysis of EPA comments on 598 environmental statements issued during six selected months of 1972, Smith assumed that the official EPA comments offered "some systematic evidence concerning [EPA's] expert evaluations of the proposed actions and the adequacy of the environmental analyses." [89] Smith's data are presented in Table 4-5. The figures in the columns represent the number of EPA comments within each of four EPA comment categories:

Category 1. General agreement or lack of objections. EPA had no objection to the action, it suggested only minor changes in the statement or action, or it had no comments to offer.

Category 2. Inadequate information. The draft statement did not contain sufficient information for EPA to assess fully the action's environmental impact. EPA requested more information about potential hazards that had been identified in the statement, or it asked that potential hazards not addressed in the draft statement be addressed in the final statement.

Category 3. The proposed action, as described in the statement, needed major revision or major additional safeguards to adequately protect the environment.

Category 4. EPA believed the proposed action would be unsatisfactory because of its potentially harmful effect on the environment. Furthermore, the agency believed that environmental safeguards built into the project might not adequately protect the environment. Therefore, EPA recommended that alternative actions, including no action at all, be analyzed further.[90]

Smith noted that the EPA comments reflected some apparently serious controversies concerning the need for major revisions in

Table 4–5

EPA COMMENTS ON IMPACT STATEMENTS FOR
SIX SELECTED MONTHS OF 1972
BY AGENCY AND CATEGORY OF COMMENT

Agency	Category 1	2	3	4	Totals
Atomic Energy Commission	5	17	2	0	24
Corps of Engineers	32	49	15	0	96
Agriculture Department	12	22	4	0	38
Commerce Department	6	2	0	0	8
Defense Department	7	6	1	0	14
Interior Department	16	20	3	0	39
Transportation Department	177	140	7	2	326
Federal Power Commission	14	11	0	0	25
General Services Administration	2	0	1	0	3
Health, Education, and Welfare Department	4	2	0	0	6
Housing and Urban Development Department	1	10	0	0	11
National Aeronautics and Space Administration	1	0	0	0	1
Treasury Department	1	2	1	0	4
Tennessee Valley Authority	2	0	0	0	2
Veterans Administration	0	1	0	0	1
TOTALS	280	282	34	2	598

Source: Smith, *Environmental Policy and Impact Analysis* 61 (1973).

an appreciable number of Corps and DOT actions and their related NEPA statements. He concluded, however, that since EPA made no objections to about 47 percent of the statements it reviewed, and made category "4" assignments only twice, "EPA officials . . . have found relatively few draft statements seriously deficient." [91]

The Realities of Impact Statement Review by EPA. Interviews with EPA personnel conducted in 1972 and 1973 reveal that, while EPA staff may have found relatively few draft statements deficient, the 1971 and 1972 EPA comments could scarcely be useful guides to the adequacy of agency impact assessment.[92] In brief, the realities of EPA impact statement review were these: for the first two years of its existence, EPA placed emphasis on review quantity, not review quality; more attention was paid by EPA reviewers to some agencies' impact statements than to others', and EPA's comment coding scheme was tainted by political considerations.

EPA was established eleven months after NEPA's enactment.[93] It was formed by a merger of environmental units from several federal agencies, principally the Departments of Interior and HEW. EPA's authority under NEPA to review and comment upon environmentally impacting actions of other agencies was embellished with enactment in December 1970 of the Clean Air Act.[94] Section 309 of the Act gave the EPA Administrator authority to review and publicly comment upon any federal agency action affecting environmental matters within his jurisdiction.[95] The section embodied Senator Muskie's notion that environmentally protective agencies should play a strong role in policing the activities of sister agencies, and its inclusion in the Clean Air Act was motivated in part by a controversy over release to the public of agency comments on the Department of Transportation's supersonic transport (SST) proposal.[96]

Impact statement review within EPA was first governed by EPA Order 1240.1 which established a highly centralized impact statement review process. The emphasis placed in 1240.1 on centralized control was a consequence of the timing of EPA's establishment in late 1970. During this period, major decisions were made on the trans-Alaskan pipeline, the SST, and pesticide use. EPA personnel believed that most impact statement reviews would entail passing judgment on important, highly controversial agency decisions. Centralized review was therefore felt to be desirable.

The centralized procedure failed under a flood of impact statements generated by federal agencies. By August 1971 EPA was far behind in its reviews and procedures were revised to allow decentralization of the review process.[97]

It was not until November 1971 that the Office of Federal Activities (OFA), whose job it was to coordinate impact statement review within EPA, transmitted guidance to regional offices on how reviews of particular categories of action should be conducted. Two-page memos were circulated on water resource project review, on highway project review, and on pesticide review.[98] The memos were more procedural than substantive in nature. One EPA staff member interviewed suggested that the absence of substantive review guidance was a function of EPA's desire to have other agencies devote some effort to developing substantive guidelines for preparation of impact statements. EPA felt that if it developed substantive guidelines, other agencies would merely copy them. The only substantive review guidance that EPA prepared for its regions at the time was a memo containing a checklist of subjects deserving discussion in nuclear power plant impact statements.[99] The memo stressed the high priority that was to be placed on review of AEC impact statements, presumably in light of the backlog created by the Calvert Cliffs decision.

In sum, through 1971 little formal memorandum guidance was provided to regional offices for their review activity. The first formal interregional conference on impact statement review did not take place until July 1972, when such subjects as "scope and tone of review comments" and "approaches to major categories of projects" were discussed.[100] By late 1972, OFA had begun a lengthy process of preparing substantive guidelines for impact statement review. A set of draft review guidelines for highways was circulated and OFA was expressing an intention to prepare additional guidelines for power plants, airports, stream channelization, and other actions.[101]

Patterns of Review of Agency Statements. If one assumed that EPA had the technical competence to review impact statements, and that it reviewed all agency impact statements in equal fashion, comparisons might be made of agencies' response to NEPA based on EPA's review of their impact statements.

For example, Table 4-6 provides a listing of EPA's impact

Table 4–6

EPA COMMENTS ON IMPACT STATEMENTS
NOVEMBER 1971 TO JULY 1972

Agency or Department	Type of Comment (in percent)					
	1	2	3	4	2+3+4	Total
All Agencies and Departments	48.1	44.2	7.3	.3	51.8	1051
All Agencies and Departments (Except Federal Highway Administration)	40.7	47.7	11.3	.4	59.4	558
Agriculture Department (Except Soil Conservation Service)	21.2	60.7	15.2	3.0	78.9	33
Atomic Energy Commission	15.2	75.8	9.1	0	84.9	33
Commerce Department	60.7	39.3	0	0	39.3	28
Corps of Engineers	38.8	43.3	18.0	0	61.3	178
Defense Department (Except Corps of Engineers)	38.5	53.8	7.7	0	61.5	26
Federal Aviation Administration	53.4	44.7	1.9	0	46.6	103
Federal Highway Administration	56.6	40.4	2.9	.2	43.5	493
Federal Power Commission	37.0	55.6	7.4	0	63.0	27
General Services Administration	55.6	33.3	11.1	0	44.4	9
Housing and Urban Development Department	20.0	60.0	20.0	0	80.0	20
Interior Department (Except Bureau of Reclamation)	56.8	40.5	2.7	0	43.2	37
Bureau of Reclamation (Water Projects Only)	14.3	50.0	35.8	0	85.8	14
Soil Conservation Service	43.3	46.7	6.7	3.3	56.7	30
Tennessee Valley Authority	37.5	37.5	25.0	0	62.5	8
Others	50.0	33.3	16.7	0	50.0	12

Source: Lists of EPA comments published in the *Federal Register*, November 1971–August 1972. EPA comments were also reprinted in CEQ's *102 Monitor* for this period.

statement review comments by agency, providing a more specific picture than that provided in Table 4-5.[102] The next to the last column in Table 4-6 aggregates the category 2, 3, and 4 comments for each agency, and represents the percentage of agency actions and impact statements found to be inadequate by EPA. These figures would seem to suggest that both the AEC and the Bureau of Reclamation did a poorer job of implementing NEPA than did other agencies.

An examination of EPA impact statement review procedures reveals, however, that for the period studied here, making comparisons among agencies based on EPA's rating of their impact statements would be an exercise of dubious validity. Because EPA had analytical strengths concentrated in particular areas of environmental review, agencies whose projects impacted on environmental matters in which EPA had considerable competence were subjected to greater scrutiny than those agencies whose actions' impacts fell in areas of lesser EPA competence.

For example, EPA had considerable expertise in water quality management, concentrated in the large staff it inherited from the Department of Interior's Federal Water Pollution Control Administration. As a result, projects having a marked impact on water quality, especially nuclear power plants, were subjected to intensive review.[103] The attention paid the AEC's impact statements partly explains why these documents received such unfavorable ratings from EPA while they were simultaneously being praised by CEQ for being the most technically detailed and complete of all agency impact statements.

EPA's intensive analysis of AEC statements contrasted with its cursory review of Soil Conservation Service (SCS) channelization projects. EPA did not devote much attention to these projects, although they were frequently assailed for their considerable adverse consequences by the Interior Department's Bureau of Sport Fisheries and Wildlife (BSFW).[104] EPA's

organizational origins partly explain its lack of interest. When
EPA's water quality reviewers resided in the Interior Department, they left principal responsibility for reviewing the environmental impact of SCS projects to BSFW. The prime obligation for commenting on the projects' environmental impact
remained with BSFW after EPA's establishment.

Political Pressures on EPA. EPA, until early 1975, had to
have its annual appropriations approved by Congressman Jamie
Whitten's subcommittee.[105] Whitten subjected EPA officials to
tough questioning at appropriations hearings, and his committee's reports indicated his reservations about the impact statement process. For example, in its report on EPA's FY73
appropriation, the committee was concerned with the mounting
cost of impact statement preparation, and recommended that to
hold requests for detailed impact statement information to a
minimum (which requests were likely to come from environmentalists or from environmental agencies), EPA should be made
responsible for some or all of the cost of all agencies' impact
statements.[106]

EPA was also criticized by the House Public Works Committee. In early 1971 the agency released a critique of the Corps of
Engineers' authorized Tennessee-Tombigbee Waterway, a navigation project strongly supported by a large group of politically
powerful southern congressmen, including Congressman Whitten. EPA had suggested that the project was of dubious
justification.[107] The EPA critique was discussed at a Public
Works Committee Investigations Subcommittee hearing on red
tape and delays in government public works projects. When
referring to the impact statement review process, Subcommittee Chairman Jim Wright rhetorically asked EPA Assistant
Administrator Thomas Carroll:

I assume you do not regard it to be the function of the Environmental Protection Agency, once this interagency review has been
employed and a decision has been made, then to interfere with or

obstruct a project of another agency of the Government by going to the public and alerting it; or do you? [108]

Pressures on EPA emanated as well from within the administration. One EPA staffer stated that the agency was instructed by the White House not to assign category "4" ratings to nuclear power plants.[109] It is likely, therefore, that in a situation where it might have wished to assign a category "4" comment, EPA merely provided a detailed criticism and then labeled it as a category "2" or "3" comment. A review of EPA's comments on a number of nuclear power plants suggests that upgrading of ratings might have occurred. For example, in its June 1972 review of the Maine Yankee nuclear power plant, EPA commented:

> Our evaluation indicates that under present conditions the operation of Maine Yankee will not be in compliance with Maine water quality standards unless all or most of Montsweag Bay is used as a mixing zone. We believe that this commitment of a valuable and sensitive estuarine area is unacceptable from an environmental standpoint.[110]

That comment was part of a larger EPA review that indicated the agency's desire for further information. In the *Federal Register*, ERA's comment on the Maine Yankee plant was assigned to category "2" rather than to category "3" or "4," although EPA had indicated that the plant's operation was "unacceptable from an environmental standpoint." [111]

IMPACT STATEMENT ADEQUACY

Agency impact statements might be assessed on numerous criteria of adequacy and such an assessment could provide one measure of an agency's willingness and ability to fully and objectively evaluate the environmental consequences of its actions. As the study of highway impact statements cited earlier demonstrates, an agency might have produced many impact statements but these might not necessarily have contributed to more informed decision making. Through 1973, very few analyses of impact statement adequacy had been conducted; the consensus among those interviewed was that agency impact statements had improved over time although they still tended to evaluate inadequately both alternatives and secondary environmental impacts.

The Corps of Engineers appears to have been the only agency that assessed systematically the adequacy of its own impact statements. The contract assessment conducted for the Corps of its own "first-generation" statements revealed that, the Corps' detailed procedural requirements notwithstanding, a substantial number of statements were incomplete because they failed to state all the environmental impacts likely to occur.[112] Only 15 percent of the statements quantified ecological impacts, only 25 percent made mention of the presence or absence of endangered species, and only 45 percent discussed secondary impacts induced by a project.[113] While 85 percent of the statements considered the alternative of taking "no action," often this alternative was summarily dismissed because it meant foregoing a specified level of dollar benefits that a completed project would provide.[114] The study concluded that the majority of the 234 environmental statements examined "were decidedly less than adequate." [115] The researchers noted, however, that based on casual observation of "second generation" statements, those prepared after August 1971, impact statement quality was improving.

PERSONNEL ACTIONS

Comparisons of absolute numbers of personnel changes are of limited value in measuring administrative response to NEPA, because each agency had different personnel requirements. Nevertheless, an agency's willingness to hire new personnel might reflect an openness to the changes that might follow an influx of personnel having training and values different from the agency norm; therefore, agency recruitment practices can provide some insight into agency concern with NEPA's substantive goals.

The Corps of Engineers developed many new environmental positions. While some of these positions were filled by shifting engineers within the Corps, a concerted effort was made to recruit new environmental planners to all levels of the organization. The Corps' recruiting aggressiveness, in fact, was bemoaned by one regional BSFW staffer interviewed, who complained that the Corps had managed to attract one of his best environmental planners.[116]

In contrast to the Corps were SCS, the FPC, and the AEC. SCS requested no increases whatsoever in its staff or budget to fulfill its NEPA responsibilities.[117] The responses within the AEC and FPC were similar to one another and were indicative of the courts' importance in forcing implementation of NEPA. AEC staff working on impact statements increased from "a handful" to 200 following the Calvert Cliffs decision. The FPC staff multiplied almost fourfold (from 22 to 72) following the Greene County decision, after having remained at the same level for the three fiscal years following NEPA's enactment.[118]

The importance of developing adequate staff capability was underscored in the comments of a Corps environmental planner. The planner, located in a Corps division office, compared the impact statements provided him by various Corps district offices. He noted that the environmental analysis capabilities of the district offices differed, and that the district that had a seven member interdisciplinary environmental branch constantly provided analyses superior to those provided by another district whose four person environmental branch consisted solely of engineers. He observed, in addition, that inadequacies were also a function of the personal attitudes of those involved in impact statement preparation.

AGENCY RESPONSE TO SECTION 103 OF NEPA

Section 103 of NEPA required agencies to review their policies and statutory mandates so as to identify any deficiencies that might preclude their compliance with the policies of NEPA. The results of these studies were to be reported to Congress.

With perhaps one exception, little attention was paid to agency response to Section 103. In its 1970 oversight hearing on NEPA's implementation, the Dingell subcommittee showed some concern, and published the Section 103 reviews that agencies submitted.[119] In many cases, these "103 statements" were quite brief, contained undocumented assertions, and reflected lack of agency regard for the comprehensive review requirement of Section 103.

The Dingell subcommittee questioned the quality of the reviews undertaken by the agencies, contending that if the reviews had been thorough, the assertions made by most of the agencies would have been accompanied by detailed documentation.[120] The subcommittee noted that eleven agencies had concluded that the Section 102 impact statement requirement did not apply to them, but none had provided detailed documentation supporting this claim.

While registering its complaint about agency inertia, the Dingell subcommittee cited the National Park Service response as a model that should have been emulated by other agencies. The Park Service organized a task force and prepared a twenty-two page document indicating the manner in which its statutory mandate could be revised to bring it into conformance with NEPA. The subcommittee concluded its overview by urging agency heads to designate permanent investigating committees or task forces to undertake continuing review of agency environmental protection opportunities and responsibilities.[121]

Section 103, together with Section 105, gave agencies the opportunity to enlarge their mandates to include environmental protection; however, few agencies responded to the challenge.[122] The Corps of Engineers was one of the few to do so, deciding that NEPA gave it authority to deny for ecological reasons permits to dredge and fill navigable waters. The Corps decision was of considerable importance, for it provided environmentalists a handle for challenging the destruction of ecologically valuable wetlands by developers. The Corps' right to deny a dredge and fill permit on ecological grounds was contested by a developer in a landmark case, *Zabel* v. *Tabb*.[123] Based on the mandate given the Corps by NEPA, the court affirmed the agency action.

AGENCY ATTACKS ON NEPA

One certain indicator of agencies' desire to comply with NEPA was their willingness to speak in opposition to the statute and its mandated procedures. If an agency launched an especially strong attack on the statute, it was a sure sign that it cared little for compliance.

The FPC. John Nassikas, chairman of the FPC, was one of NEPA's most persistent critics. In remarks before the National Press Club in April 1973, he commented:

> There must be a critical reappraisal of the procedural requirements of the National Environmental Policy Act. The detailed, and at times, redundant procedural steps required by that statute have proven to be a windfall for those bent on blocking any and all energy development. Opponents of nuclear power, offshore oil and gas exploration and the development of Alaskan oil and gas resources have succeeded in seriously delaying these vital energy projects by utilizing the procedural roadblocks of NEPA. Often substance yields to form to the prejudice of the public interest. . . . The procedural nightmares of current legislative requirements should be carefully reexamined and revised to avoid inordinate delays.[124]

Chairman Nassikas continued his attack on NEPA in remarks before the Administrative Law Section of the American

Bar Association in August 1973. He stated that while NEPA had served important environmental goals, it had caused a disequilibrium in the nation's energy balance. He was quoted in the *Washington Post* as stating that experience had demonstrated NEPA's potential for exalting procedure over substance and "its inherent capacity to be used for non-productive dilatory tactics." [125]

The FPC's general attitude towards the consideration of environmental matters in the regulatory process was perhaps best indicated in its congressional testimony on power plant siting proposals. These measures, discussed at greater length in chapter 6, were designed to facilitate the planning of electric power generating stations while at the same time assuring that all pertinent economic, social, and environmental considerations were incorporated into the planning process. In comments on a bill introduced by Chairman Harley Staggers of the House Interstate and Foreign Commerce Committee, the Commission recommended removal of "environmental biasing language" in order to strike a balance in decision making between environmental and power needs.[126] The "environmental biasing language" to which the Commission objected was a requirement that guidelines would have to be written to assure the full NEPA-like evaluation of the environmental impacts of power plant siting. The guidelines would include criteria for evaluating the effects of proposed sites and facilities on environmental values, the relative environmental impacts of alternative sites, and the projected needs for electric power.[127]

The ICC. The FPC attitude toward environmental matters was shared by the Interstate Commerce Commission. The ICC had been the subject of one of the rare CEQ public attacks on agency implementation of NEPA, and it had filed an amicus brief supporting the FPC's appeal of the 2d Circuit decision in Greene County. Even as late as the winter of 1973, the ICC was using the energy crisis as an excuse to complain about NEPA. In a notice entitled "Energy Crisis and the Need for Emergency

Transportation Legislation" published in the *Federal Register*, the Commission commented:

> Environmentalists as well as others interested more in economic advantage have used NEPA to delay Federal action. Strained interpretations of NEPA seem to disregard the concept of "justice delayed is justice denied." In this period of severe energy shortages, one need only examine the circumstances surrounding a number of Commission activities to note how damaging such delays may be . . . .[128]

The AEC. The FPC-ICC view of NEPA contrasted markedly with the view of the law held by AEC Chairman Dr. James Schlesinger. Dr. Schlesinger commented in hearings before Congressman Dingell's committee in March 1972:

> My remarks are in no way intended to criticize the handling of NEPA by the courts. NEPA, overall, has resulted in a healthy reorientation of governmental perspectives and priorities; and the courts have in various instances played a useful, even sobering role in the process.[129]

Dr. Schlesinger's views were not shared by many members of the nuclear energy community, for the AEC had been under sustained pressure from environmentalists since NEPA's enactment. The difference of opinion was not surprising, however, for prior to his appointment, Dr. Schlesinger was not a member of the industry-AEC-Joint Committee on Atomic Energy triumvirate that constituted the nuclear "establishment" in the United States.

Factors Influencing Agency Response to NEPA

The various indicators of agency response—procedures, impact statement adequacy, personnel actions, Section 103 reports, and so forth—provide for the most part a portrait of agency uncertainty, inertia, and outright hostility, although amidst this rather gloomy picture a few instances of agency innovation, creativity, and responsiveness can be identified. Much of this agency response can be traced directly to factors described in the administrative behavior literature summarized at the beginning of this chapter. The discussion below focuses on particular external and internal forces as influencing the responses of federal agencies, and indicates how several of these factors combined to encourage change in the AEC and the Corps of Engineers.

EXTERNAL FACTORS

Important Constituencies—OMB and Congress. The central role OMB might have in all agencies' consideration of environmental impacts was alluded to in the hearings on NEPA held by Senator Jackson's Interior Committee in April 1969. Executive order 11514, however, placed primary oversight responsibility in CEQ, with little protest from OMB.

NEPA specifically mentioned agency legislative proposals as potential subjects for impact statements, but very few impact statements were prepared on legislative proposals having significant environmental consequences. Many of those for which impact statements were prepared could be regarded as environmental protection measures.[130] In its May 1970 guidelines, CEQ made only brief mention of impact statements for legislative proposals, stating that the Bureau of the Budget, OMB's predecessor, would supplement the general CEQ guidelines with specific instructions for linking the impact statement procedures to the Bureau of the Budget legislative clearance process.[131] In its bulletin 71-3, issued August 31, 1970, OMB responded by advising agencies that they should identify those of their legislative proposals requiring impact statements; they should then submit statements with proposed legislation sent to OMB for clearance.[132]

Bulletin 71-3 also provided that summaries explaining the general environmental impact of programs should accompany agencies' annual budget estimates. Each summary would also include a list of projects subject to impact statement requirements and an accounting of the status of the required statements.

The Dingell subcommittee, in a June 1971 report based on its December 1970 oversight hearings, urged OMB when it revised the interim procedures of bulletin 71-3 to require annual summaries of actions that agencies determined did not require impact statements. Those were analogous to the "negative declarations" required by some agencies in their NEPA implementation regulations. The subcommittee also urged development of procedures for regularly announcing actions that agencies anticipated would be environmentally controversial, in order to provide for maximum public participation.[133]

OMB revised its procedures in September 1971, with issuance of bulletin 72-6.[134] It weakened its impact statement requirements by stating, in effect, that agencies should try to have impact statements available for circulation with legislative proposals but that this was by no means required.[135]

OMB's lack of enthusiasm for impact statements was noticed by GAO. According to GAO, OMB felt that impact statements would provide more information than was needed for legislative analysis. GAO replied that agencies would benefit from the information developed for the impact statement, OMB's information needs notwithstanding, and recommended that OMB refuse clearance to any legislative proposal unaccompanied by an impact statement commented upon by appropriate federal agencies.[136]

CEQ privately hoped that OMB would accede to that recommendation, but the Council was unsuccessful in obtaining such an OMB commitment.[137] CEQ was only able to receive from OMB a promise that their two staffs would cooperate in identifying types of repetitive legislation requiring annual impact statements. That would assure that draft statements would regularly be prepared prior to submission of legislative proposals, so that the proposals and statements could be circulated simultaneously through the legislative clearance process. However, this agreement, noted informally in a September 1972 letter from Chairman Russell Train to OMB Director Casper Weinberger, appears to have been tenuous.[138] When CEQ circulated a draft of its revised guidelines for agency comment in early 1973, prior to their publication in draft form in the *Federal Register*, it incorporated the language of the informal CEQ-OMB understanding. However, the provisions of the agreement were deleted in the "quality of life" review process and did not appear in the proposed guidelines that were published.[139]

Congressman Dingell's subcommittee, which held several oversight hearings on NEPA, made an effort to disseminate agency documents pertaining to NEPA implementation, and requested analyses by the GAO of agency compliance with NEPA.[140] Senator Jackson's Interior Committee left the oversight responsibility largely to Congressman Dingell, whose efforts were extensive. The Interior Committee, when it chose to hold hearings, was usually responding to important court decisions construing NEPA. Except for requesting two brief Library of Congress studies on environmental indices and on proposed legislative modifications to NEPA, the Jackson committee did little to oversee administration of the statute.

Otherwise, general congressional concern with NEPA was minimal. The Joint Committee on Atomic Energy held hearings on problems in AEC licensing allegedly caused by the Calvert Cliffs decision, and the House Public Works Committee Subcommittee on Investigations and Oversight held some "red tape" hearings that focused in part on NEPA. The Senate Public Works Committee also held two brief hearings on NEPA in 1970.[141] The impact statements for controversial projects occasionally became a focus of contention in congressional debates, but only one committee, the Senate Public Works Committee, wrote into its rules a requirement that legislative proposals be accompanied by environmental impact statements. Congressional indifference is considered by two commentators to have given "comfort to those agency officials who [were] disinclined to take NEPA seriously." [142]

INTERNAL FACTORS

Agency Goals. Agencies' responses to NEPA were conditioned in part by their perception of their primary goals; nonimplementation of NEPA was evident in the behavior of developmental and environmentally protective agencies alike. For example, in the response of the AEC before Calvert Cliffs, in the response of the FPC before Greene County, and in the response of the FHWA, one sees the Neanderthal reaction of development-oriented agencies, secure in their niches, not caring to concern themselves with the potentially troublesome environmental implications of their work. A lack of concern for NEPA was evidenced as well among those agencies seemingly committed to environmental quality. The nonresponsiveness of EPA has already been described, but it can also be found in the National Park Service (NPS), the Bureau of Sport Fisheries and Wildlife (BSFW) and the Bureau of Outdoor Recreation (BOR).

While the National Park Service responded in commendable manner to Section 103 of NEPA and did not use NEPA's legislative history in an attempt to gain exemption from the statute, it did not prepare an environmental impact statement for actions in its park wilderness designation program until December 22, 1971, although it had previously made several such designations.[143] The Park Service's first environmental impact statement to accompany a national park master plan was not submitted until August 1971, although in FY71 it completed thirty-four such plans.[144] In its FY72 appropriations hearings, NPS commented on its need to review impact statements prepared by other agencies, but made no mention of impact statements for its own actions.[145]

Much the same was the case for the Bureau of Sport Fisheries and Wildlife. An understaffed agency responsible for examining the fish and wildlife aspects of federal water resource development projects, BSFW was concerned with reviewing the environmental impact statements of other agencies, but said little about preparing impact statements for its own proposals. The first BSFW impact statement for a wilderness designation was not prepared until January 26, 1972, although over a dozen wilderness studies had been completed by BSFW in 1970 and 1971.[146]

The Bureau of Outdoor Recreation behaved similarly. A small agency concerned with recreation and open space preservation, BOR did not prepare its first environmental impact statement until June 1972.[147]

The difficulty of promoting procedural compliance with NEPA by environmentally conscious agencies was alluded to by a CEQ staff member:

> It's easier to convince a highway or Corps engineer to consider the environment than to convince a park ranger, urban planner or pollution control planner. NEPA says, in effect, you haven't been doing your job before. That's why the Park Service, HUD and EPA are our biggest headaches. With the Park Service it's the development question [i.e. should access to parklands and facilities within parks be upgraded for the masses, or should accessibility and facilities be kept at a primitive level to preserve wilderness character]. With EPA it's the ignoring of the land-use impacts of waste treatment plants, that is, these plants are causing growth by anticipating it. With HUD, they think that since 1949 [the date of enactment of the first federal housing act] they've been providing decent homes and living environments.[148]

Intra-Agency, Intergroup Rivalry. Another factor influencing administrative response to NEPA was intra-agency rivalry. It was noted earlier that the Department of Transportation made a serious attempt to implement NEPA. DOT's action was a part of Secretary John Volpe's attempt to gain some measure of control for his department over the activities of its operating administrations, particularly the FHWA.

When NEPA was enacted DOT was only four years old. It was an amalgam of administrations (FHWA, Federal Aviation Administration, Coast Guard, and others) placed within DOT because of their transportation concerns. The FHWA, in particular, had well-hewn relationships with congressional committees and influential clientele groups. DOT's first secretary, liberal Democrat Alan Boyd, had made little headway in reining in the operating administrations. Secretary John Volpe was somewhat more successful, in part because he had greater credibility; a builder, a former Federal Highway Administrator and a moderate Republican, he was seen as less of a threat by the operating administrations than had been Boyd.

When NEPA was enacted, Volpe had already demonstrated his environmental concern, having established in 1969 a departmental Office of Environment and Urban Systems headed by a tough assistant secretary. NEPA provided the office with a strong statutory reason for existence, which it had previously lacked. The office was given primary responsibility within DOT for implementing NEPA, but even then its position was somewhat tenuous. Secretary Volpe, at the office's urging, would sometimes want to sidetrack, on environmental grounds, an operating administration project, but he would rely on the courts to order a project modified or halted. He would then be able to lay on others responsibility for "meddling" with the project.

NEPA's role in DOT's internecine battles was commented upon by persons both within and without the department. One CEQ staff member stated:

Volpe grabbed NEPA as an excuse to do a lot of things people had been unable to do before him . . . particularly with respect to getting secretarial control. It used to be that the Federal Highway Administration had more friends on the Hill than DOT . . . Somehow Volpe reversed that . . . though it was pretty rough sledding getting even the most outrageous highway proposals dropped.[149]

The intra-agency struggle for influence that colored DOT's implementation of NEPA can also be identified as conditioning HUD's response to the Act. But in the latter department, interests unsympathetic to NEPA prevailed. As previously noted, HUD's procedures precluded the development of impact statements for most of its actions. Moreover, as late as August 1972 HUD adhered to a narrow interpretation of NEPA's applicability to current projects, with the result that the department produced very few impact statements and was subject to numerous citizen suits.[150] HUD's susceptibility to litigation, its circumscribed view of NEPA's applicability to current projects, and its delay in developing NEPA implementing procedures, were noted by CEQ Chairman Train in an August 1972 letter to HUD Secretary George Romney. Train stated that HUD needed to assign more personnel to NEPA matters, reallocating existing manpower if necessary.[151]

One reason HUD personnel took such a narrow view of NEPA is that, like their counterparts in EPA and the Park Service, they believed they were already promoting environmental quality; they were trying to achieve the goal established by the Housing Act of 1949 of providing "a decent home and a suitable living environment for every American family." [152]

But the explanation of HUD's noncompliance goes beyond that. According to several interviewees familiar with HUD and NEPA activities, HUD is divided between persons concerned with housing production and those concerned with housing design. The former, who comprise perhaps 80 percent of the agency and dominate it, are found in the HUD production programs, while the latter are concentrated in the policy evaluation and new community development programs. NEPA implementation responsibilities were placed with the policy evaluation and community development planning minority who, it was believed, would be more receptive to environmental concerns than the production-oriented personnel. One CEQ staffer now believes this allocation of responsibility was a mistake, because although the policy planners were sympathetic to NEPA's goals, they did not have sufficient power within the agency to assure the statute's implementation.

INTERNAL AND EXTERNAL FACTORS TOGETHER

The AEC. Change in the AEC after Calvert Cliffs was a result of alterations in agency leadership combined with the diminishing influence of the Joint Committee on Atomic Energy and rising pressure exerted by environmental groups. The AEC was often singled out in the past as the prototypical regulatory agency captured by outside interests. It was long dominated by the congressional Joint Committee on Atomic Energy (JCAE), a committee characterized by one knowledgeable observer as "an enormously powerful political institution with a strong vested interest in development and exploitation of nuclear power." [153] The Commission had the task of promoting as well as regulating nuclear power, and thus developed close ties with industry in this highly technical field. For most of its existence it was chaired by scientists and engineers who had played a significant role in nuclear power development, and as late as 1969 it was successful in arguing that it did not have to concern itself with the environmental consequences of nuclear power plant operations.[154]

The Commission came under intense pressure from organized foes of nuclear power who intervened directly in highly structured quasi-judicial AEC licensing proceedings.[155] Environmentalists also brought considerable pressure to bear through the courts.[156] Among environmentalists' targets were emergency core cooling systems, the liquid metal fast breeder reactor, and other nuclear hardware falling within the Commission's regulatory jurisdiction.

Amidst all this criticism the Commission evidenced signs of change. Beginning with its decision not to appeal Calvert Cliffs to the Supreme Court, it took several actions that would have been unlikely events several years previous. For example, the Commission's Hearing and Licensing Board granted an operating license to the Consolidated Edison Company for the Indian Point II nuclear reactor, but ordered the utility to install closed cycle cooling towers to avoid damaging the fishery resources of New York's Hudson River. According to the Natural Resources Defense Council, a public interest environmental law firm, that marked the first time the Commission had ruled on behalf of an outside intervenor in one of its proceedings.[157] In October 1973 the Commission for the first time banned nuclear power near a large city when it barred construction of a nuclear power plant on the Delaware River eleven miles from Philadelphia. Plant construction had been opposed by the Commonwealth of Pennsylvania.[158] The Commission itself claimed that in several other cases, its environmental reviews produced a variety of recommendations for plant redesigns.[159] While those decisions likely resulted in large measure from pressure brought on the Commission by environmentalists, they can also be explained by a considerable change in Commission leadership.

Shortly before Calvert Cliffs, President Nixon appointed Dr. James Schlesinger as chairman of the AEC, replacing nuclear scientist Dr. Glenn Seaborg. Schlesinger was the first AEC chairman since 1953 who was not a member of the "nuclear fraternity." [160] He believed that the Commission should open up its decision making and adopt a more understanding attitude towards its environmental opponents. That view contrasted with that of Dr. Seaborg who, according to middle level AEC officials quoted by the *New York Times*, believed that policy decisions should best be made by experts without the benefit of public debate.[161] Appointed to the Commission along with Schlesinger was William O. Doub, a member of the Maryland Public Service Commission who had earned the respect of environmentalists at his Commission's hearings on the Calvert Cliffs plant.[162]

It was Schlesinger who decided against appealing the Calvert Cliffs decision. At the October 20, 1971 meeting of the Atomic Industrial Forum and American Nuclear Society, he also put the nuclear industry on notice that the AEC would no longer be its partner in the promotion of nuclear power. Schlesinger stated that he was quite "impressed . . . by the failure of industry and [the AEC] properly to distinguish between the role and responsibilities of industry and the separate role and responsibilities of the AEC." [163] A *Christian Science Monitor* correspondent described Schlesinger as determined to make the AEC "more of a public servant and less of a nursemaid for industry than it has been." [164] The *New York Times* reported the Schlesinger speech under the headline "AEC Shifts Role to Protect Public," leaving its readers with the impression that the AEC had hitherto been somewhat negligent in its defense of the public interest.[165]

When Dr. Schlesinger was shifted to another post in the Nixon administration, he was replaced by Dr. Dixie Lee Ray, a marine biologist who also had no prior ties with the nuclear industry.[166] Shortly after her appointment, Dr. Ray moved to reorganize the safety branches of the AEC. This was an effort to deflate conflict of interest charges arising from the Commission's dual responsibilities of promoting reactor development and overseeing reactor safety research.[167] This plan was opposed by only one Commission member, James Ramey, the former Joint Committee on Atomic Energy staff director appointed to the Commission by President Kennedy in 1962 at the Committee's urging.[168] The Ray action was also opposed by Dr. Milton Shaw, reactor development program chief charged by environmentalists with shortcircuiting nuclear safety research efforts.[169] Shaw subsequently resigned, and his resignation triggered an attack on the Commission by veteran Joint Committee member Representative Chet Holifield, who accused the AEC of maneuvering Shaw into a position where he had to resign.[170] Change within the Commission continued when Commissioner Ramey was not reappointed at the expiration of his term, over the protest of some members of the JCAE.[171]

The personnel situation within the "new" AEC was very much different from that within the FPC. At the time of NEPA's enactment, Carl Bagge was a member of the FPC. Bagge resigned to become president of the National Coal Association. Sitting on the Commission as chairman when Bagge departed was John Nassikas, who had served as counsel to a natural gas company from his home state of New Hampshire prior to joining the Commission.[172] Nassikas was subsequently joined by Rush Moody, who came to the FPC from a Houston law firm that had many oil and gas companies as clients.[173] Also from that law firm came Gordon Gooch, the general counsel of the Commission, and his chief assistant, Steven Wakefield.[174] Their background tied them closely to the utilities industry that they were supposed to regulate in the public interest, and, thus, the Commission's obstinate attitude towards NEPA is not surprising.

The change in personnel at the AEC was probably part of President Nixon's desire to reorganize federal energy efforts by creating a unified energy research administration that would absorb some of the AEC's responsibilities. At the same time that the AEC was threatened with reorganization, it began to lose its congressional support as key members of the Joint Committee on Atomic Energy either retired or were defeated in their reelection efforts.[175] In a "last hurrah," Joint Committee nuclear power proponents were able, in late 1974, to push through Congress a bill limiting the liability of utility companies for nuclear accidents. The bill was subsequently vetoed by President Ford, for reasons not germane to this discussion. Shortly thereafter, the AEC was dissolved and had its research and licensing responsibilities split between an Energy Research and

Development Administration and a Nuclear Regulatory Commission.

The Corps of Engineers. The Corps of Engineers civil works construction program is synonymous with pork barrel politics. A recent statistical analysis of Corps projects confirms the pork barrel, distributive nature of Corps activity. Members of the legislative and appropriative public works committees of the House and Senate obtain more new Corps projects than nonmembers; leaders of the four committees receive more favorable treatment for their states' budget requests than nonleaders, and within the appropriations subcommittees, the budgets of states represented by Democrats fare better than those of states represented by Republicans.[176] Through 1972, the Corps had constructed 3,219 projects at a total cost of $10.1 billion. In addition, 275 other projects worth an estimated $13.5 billion were under construction and another 452 were authorized.[177]

Considering the close relationship among the Corps, Congress, and developmental interests, it is surprising that on several indicators, the Corps appears to have been more attentive to NEPA concerns than most other agencies. In addition to its actions previously described, the Corps also made a vigorous attempt to involve the public in its programs, it began to take greater cognizance of nonstructural solutions to flood control problems, and it broadened the scope of its programs to include urban waste water management.[178]

The opposite reaction might have been expected, with the Corps, feeling secure in its developmental niche, paying little heed to environmental matters. The unexpected change in direction may have been prompted by several external and internal factors. The external factors include pressures from citizen suits and some limited concern with NEPA compliance on the part of the Senate Public Works Committee. The internal factors include the military presence within the Corps and the structure of the Corps' decision-making process.

The Corps was under more pressure from environmentalists than most other agencies and in response to the pressure it began to respond innovatively to environmental planning needs. Tables 4-7 and 4-8 indicate that more suits were filed against the

Table 4–7

NEPA-BASED LAWSUITS AGAINST FEDERAL AGENCIES
THROUGH MARCH 1, 1973

Agency	Lawsuits
Department of Transportation	90
Environmental Protection Agency	58
Corps of Engineers	53
Housing and Urban Development	33
Department of Agriculture	28
Department of Interior	21
Atomic Energy Commission	21
Others (17)	59
Total	363

Source: "Court and Administrative Proceedings Arising Under the National Environmental Policy Act," Memorandum to CEQ Chairman Russell Train from CEQ General Counsel Timothy Atkeson (March 22, 1973) at 2. Copy in author's files.

Table 4–8

NEPA-BASED INJUNCTIONS AGAINST FEDERAL AGENCIES
THROUGH MARCH 1, 1973

Agency	Injunctions
Department of Transportation	21
Corps of Engineers	10
Housing and Urban Development	4
Department of Agriculture	4
Others (10)	12
Total	51

Source: "Court and Administrative Proceedings Arising Under the National Environmental Policy Act," Memorandum to CEQ Chairman Russell Train from CEQ General Counsel Timothy Atkeson (March 22, 1973) at 3–4. Copy in author's files.

Corps than against any other agencies except EPA and DOT, and that except for DOT, more injunctions were imposed upon the Corps than upon any other agency. One analyst found, in addition, that a disproportionately high number of all Corps projects whose conduct was in any way affected by NEPA fell within the jurisdiction of districts that were sued at least once.[179] Furthermore, more than twice the effort was spent on the preparation of environmental statements for controversial projects than was devoted to statements for noncontroversial ones, and a significantly greater than average effort was put into the preparation of environmental statements by those Corps districts that had been subjected to NEPA based lawsuits.[180]

While the public pressure thesis has considerable merit, it provides only a partial explanation of Corps responsiveness, for it does not satisfactorily explain the Corps' reactions to NEPA in early 1970. In April 1970 the Corps ordered its offices to prepare impact statements in conjunction with FY72 budget submissions.[181] That order was shortly followed by a circular providing some basic guidance for impact statement preparation.[182] On June 2, the chief of engineers sent a personal message to domestic Corps offices indicating his strong support of the National Environmental Policy Act and its goals, and on June 6, the Corps announced creation of an environmental advisory board, comprised of six of its environmentalist critics, to advise it on environmental policy. The following months saw the issuance of additional circulars pertaining to environmental policy, culminating with the issuance in September 1970 of detailed guidance for preparation of environmental impact statements.

The Corps seems to have been somewhat aware in this period of NEPA's litigation potential, for Corps General Counsel E. Manning Seltzer sent a July 9, 1970 memo to all division and district engineers noting that all division and district NEPA procedures should provide for legal assistance and review in connection with rapidly increasing environmental management litigation.[183] However, an examination of the litigation at the time shows that a sizeable number of decisions adverse to agencies had yet to come. During the first nine months of 1970 four suits were filed against the Corps and pressure on public works projects was mounting.[184] Only one case, however, was decided.[185] Outside the Corps, four NEPA cases were decided in the same period: two resulted in injunctions and two produced narrow interpretations of NEPA favorable to agencies.[186]

A supplementary, yet somewhat tenuous explanation for the Corps' early procedural concern with NEPA arises from the Corps' need to have impact statements ready for the fall 1970 hearings on the Omnibus River and Harbor Bill. At these hearings new authorizations for Corps projects would be considered. Both the House and Senate Public Works Committees were to hold up their approval of the bill until impact statements were filed. However, the statements were poor in quality, and were not submitted to the committees until all public witnesses, including environmentalists, had testified.[187]

The Senate Public Works Committee indicated dissatisfaction with the statements in its report on the bill, but the House committee's standards seemed to be far lower. In its report the House committee stated that the environmental statements reflected a satisfactory degree of analysis based on available information.[188]

While in 1970 the Corps may perhaps have acted in anticipation of the Public Works Committee's desire for pro forma compliance with NEPA, the committees in succeeding years do not seem to have been a significant source of pressure on the Corps to become more environmentally conscious. Interviews with committee staff members and others indicate that impact statements were not a significant aspect of committee decision making. At most hearings the committees continued to show considerable willingness to accept Corps environmental assurances and demonstrated considerable skepticism of and disdain for environmental witnesses.[189] The committees were evidently willing, however, to accede to the Corps' decisions to incorporate environmental considerations into project planning and to undertake innovative programs.[190]

The Corps' reaction to NEPA may have been influenced by the presence of military engineers. In 1972 only about 1.5 percent of the total Corps' work force were military engineers and they were routinely shifted from one position to another every few years.[191] The military officers' rapid movement may have encouraged them to attend to NEPA's implementation by the civilians under their command, to ensure a minimum of "unnecessary" conflict and delay over environmental matters within their purview. Interviews indicate that some officers were deeply involved in implementation of NEPA, although the personal involvement of commanding officers differed among the Corps districts and divisions.[192] The importance of officers' personal involvement was noted in a November 1970 Corps engineering circular, issuance of which might have indicated that the Corps was building a timely resolution of environmental controversies into its reward structure. The circular, entitled "Personal Involvement of Reporting Officers in Policy Problems and Environmental Considerations," stated that district and division engineers should become personally involved at appropriate decision-making stages in order to permit the satisfactory and timely resolution of policy problems and the integration of environmental considerations in the total planning process.[193]

It was likely that the Corps' mission as a planning organization enhanced its ability to integrate NEPA into its decision making. Unlike the Bureau of Land Management or the National Park Service or many of the regulatory agencies, the Corps engaged in considerable planning, although planning per se required only a small portion of its budget. Since NEPA was, in essence, a planning statute, the Corps may have been able to adapt more readily to its demands than other less experienced agencies.

An additional, partial explanation for the Corps' willingness to develop a comprehensive procedural base for NEPA compliance lies in its lengthy, well-defined decision-making process. The planning of a Corps project, from initial study approval to completion, can take over thirteen years, and is composed of a number of distinct steps.[194] Because the steps are so well defined, and because time lags are built into the decision-making process, it may have been relatively easy to plug an environmental assessment component into Corps planning. Because the Corps program is so large, with many projects in early stages of planning, disruption induced by implementation of NEPA might not have been as great as it may have been in agencies with smaller, less diverse, and more short-term planning programs. In organization theory parlance, the Corps may have been more adaptable to required change because it had within it greater "organizational slack"—its large, diffuse program was composed of extended, well-defined, yet manipulable planning procedures, into which new components could be inserted.

Perhaps the most satisfying explanation of the early Corps response is the one that recognizes that prior to NEPA, the Corps became more environmentally sensitive, and that the statute's enactment gave an added boost to the efforts of environmentalists within the Corps who had been trying to change the agency's policies. Environmental branches had been established in some Corps offices prior to 1970, partly in response to earlier legislation. Within the Corps, a small group of strategically placed young engineers and planners, whose training often included environmental elements beyond a traditional engineering and planning curriculum, was "trying to bring [environmental] religion to the heathens." [195] Some were situated within the Corps' Institute for Water Resources, which had been organized in mid–1969, and which conducted and oversaw research on a multitude of water resource policy problems. Environmental policy was one of the Institute's three principal concerns, and its staff prepared a Corps statement on environmental policy in late 1969. The statement was ultimately released in 1970, about six months following NEPA's enactment.

Some Closing Observations

NEPA dictated the direction, but not the magnitude of a required change in decision making, and because the guidance it provided was not very specific, agency decision makers were left with considerable latitude in deciding the manner in which it would be implemented. To the extent that incrementally oriented administrators refused to enlarge their frames of reference, did not know how to enlarge them, or otherwise would or could not meet raised decision-making expectations, they fueled the conflict over NEPA's implementation. In general, they demonstrated little imagination in interpreting the statute's key messages: identify and measure environmental impacts; evaluate various alternatives; involve and advise the public to the greatest possible extent about the bases of agency action.

One factor that certainly influenced agency behavior was the seeming lack of congressional concern for either procedural or substantive compliance with NEPA. Principal oversight responsibility was vested in those committees that reported NEPA, but it was not to those oversight committees that federal agencies owed primary allegiance. Primary allegiance was owed, rather, to the legislative and appropriations committees overseeing the agencies' performance of their principal missions. If committees holding the "first mortgage" on agency allegiance did not concern themselves with NEPA, and if implementation of NEPA endangered timely achievement of agencies' principal goals, agency administrators had much less reason for risking disruption of their negotiated environments by earnestly working at compliance.

Several general patterns of agency response to NEPA are observable. First, there were those agencies like the AEC prior to Calvert Cliffs and the FPC who felt that compliance might interfere with their achievement of their traditional missions. Second, there was a lack of procedural response on the part of environmental agencies like EPA that regarded NEPA as superfluous because their decisions were already infused with environmental considerations.

Third, there were a few agencies, like the AEC after Calvert Cliffs and the Corps, in which some concerted efforts to implement NEPA was made. In the case of both these agencies, however, change occurred largely as a result of environmentalist pressure, and there continued to be considerable environmentalist dissatisfaction with the level of agency concern for environmental matters.

Fourth, some agencies showed a lack of interest in NEPA because ecological considerations did not seem germane to their principal missions, and there was little reward to be gained by allocating scarce agency resources to environmental concerns. Moreover, these same agencies were under less litigation pressure than agencies like the Corps and DOT, because their activities were of less concern to environmentalists. This fourth category contains too many agencies for enumeration here, but typical members could be said to include the Small Business Administration, Federal Trade Commission, Civil Aeronautics Board and the Arms Control and Disarmament Agency.

Even where there may have been the will to change, some agencies were better able to change than others. The Corps, for example, conducted its own planning over an extended period. It was thus in a position to phase environmental considerations into its program in an orderly fashion. In contrast were grant giving agencies like HUD and the FHWA, which, while probably able to influence the behavior of grant seekers, were not as likely to have as much control over planning and work flow as had the Corps.

The dichotomy between procedural and substantive compliance with NEPA is also worthy of note. That divergence is reflected in the significant departure of the substance of the Corps' initial impact statements from the very high procedural objectives that had been established for them. The dichotomy can also be observed when the behavior of the FHWA and its clientele is compared to that of EPA. Reams of impact statements were produced for the FHWA by state highway departments, but there is some question as to whether most of these impact statements had any meaningful substance and whether their production marked the incorporation of environmental values into highway decision making. In contrast, EPA produced few impact statements. However, considering the value orientation of EPA staff members, there was a reasonable chance that a serious effort was made to produce environmentally sensitive decisions, even though formal impact statements were not prepared.

The gross variation among agencies has been emphasized here, but differences within agencies should not be overlooked. As briefly noted above, variations were observable in the behavior of the Corps district offices. Presumably, on close examination, such variations can be found among the regional offices of other federal agencies.

In closing, the courts' impact is worth mentioning once again. Aside from whatever impact their decisions had on discrete projects, the courts induced changed hiring and administrative practices in the FPC and the AEC and changes in the impact statement preparation behavior of selected Corps districts. Moreover, just as they boosted the NEPA implementation efforts of both CEQ and Transportation Secretary Volpe, the courts likely lent added weight to the voices of environmentalists within the Corps and other agencies. The chapter that follows describes the key actions taken by federal judges to promote implementation of NEPA.

5

Judicial
Interpretation
of NEPA

On January 1, 1970 the newly enacted NEPA was a sleeper, a law whose future implications had not been recognized either by Congress or by the President. On that day, too, the environmental law movement was still a slumbering lion. From then on, NEPA and the environmental law movement grew together.

Their growth was turbulent. NEPA was simultaneously praised and damned as were environmentalists using it. The statute's most readily observed impact was in the temporary enjoining of both sizeable public works projects and many private projects contingent upon federal action.

The first portion of this chapter discusses the resources environmentalists were able to gather so that they could engage in expensive litigation, and notes how they received a financial break from the courts. The next portion explores the reasons environmentalists sought judicial relief under NEPA from federal activities regarded as prejudicial to their interests. A number of factors underlay the movement to the courts: a

general distrust of agencies, a desire to amplify NEPA's
vaguely worded action-forcing procedures, and the quest for a
new weapon to use against actions of questionable justification
and adverse environmental impact promoted by development-
oriented congressional or agency interests.

Judicial receptiveness to environmentalist petitions was
marked by a lowering of courtroom entry barriers. Gates were
opened not only for environmentalists, but also for other broad
interests (community and minority groups) underrepresented in
the political system. The succeeding portion of this chapter
examines how traditional procedural defenses to suits were
overcome, thereby easing environmentalists' achievement of
their litigation goals. The discussion focuses principally on the
manner in which environmentalists obtained standing to sue,
and briefer treatment is accorded judicial concern for the
timeliness and venue of environmental litigation.

The next section explores a major force—judicial annoyance
with abuse of agency discretion—underlying the generally
positive courtroom reception given environmentalists and other
"public interest" representatives. That concern was often combined with high regard for the strong environmental policy
embodied in NEPA's legislative history, and was most clearly
evidenced in the D.C. Circuit Court of Appeals, from which
emanated some of the most strongly worded critiques of agency
action. Judicial efforts to structure and confine agency discretion
helped clarify some of the five ambiguous areas in NEPA's
requirements noted in the preceding chapter.

The final portion of this chapter reviews the principal issues
in water resource development project litigation under NEPA
from 1970 to 1973. These cases, which provide a microcosmic
view of all NEPA litigation, involved the Corps of Engineers,
Soil Conservation Service, Bureau of Reclamation and Tennessee Valley Authority. The chronological summary of the principal decisions describes the legal environment within which

the Corps and similar agencies worked when responding to NEPA.

The Funding of Public Interest Environmental Law Organizations

In *The Logic of Collective Action*, Mancur Olson argues that an economically rational person is not likely to protect an environmental amenity from which he along with many others derives only modest benefit; the costs to the individual will be considerable and he will continue to benefit from the amenity at no cost to himself if someone else rises to defend it.[1] At first glance, the activities of public interest environmental law organizations in the late 1960s and early 1970s run counter to that theory, for individuals arose to defend the public interest in clean air and clean water against organized interests having a considerable economic stake in the alienation of these public goods for private use. A closer examination of the operation of public interest law groups suggests, however, that Olson's theory has not been completely disproven. Some of the leading public interest environmental law organizations owed their existence more to foundation generosity than to diffuse public concern with environmental quality. Foundation support enabled individual lawyers to sustain a standard of living below that which they might achieve in private practice, but which together with the psychic rewards of public litigation satisfied their needs.

Foundation contributions together with public support totaled millions of dollars. But when weighed against the cost of environmental litigation, the sum appears quite small. The public interest firms' existence was sufficiently precarious that tremors of anxiety ran through them when, in 1973, the Ford Foundation announced that it wished to end its environmental law grants. Environmental Defense Fund (EDF) Executive

Director Roderick Cameron commented, "If Ford pulls out, there will be a crash in the environmental law market."[2]

FEE SHARING: SHIFTING THE BURDEN
OF PUBLIC INTEREST LITIGATION

Anxiety over future funding produced efforts by environmental lawyers to have their fees paid by those they sued.[3] A few statutes had been enacted in the past that explicitly permitted fee recoveries, but such transfers were generally not provided for by American law. Some courts began to use their equity powers, however, to ease the financial burden of litigation borne by public interest environmentalist plaintiffs; they shifted litigation costs to defendants who might have benefited from administrative noncompliance with the law. Fees were awarded in accordance with the private attorneys-general doctrine, one of the three exceptions to the general American rule that fees cannot be awarded except where expressly permitted by statute.[4] Private attorneys-general were individuals regarded as vindicating the public interest by bringing suit against government officials who had acted in an extra-statutory manner.[5] In such instances, fee-shifting was justified because a lawsuit had effectuated a strong congressional policy that had benefited a large class of people, such private enforcement was necessary, and litigation had been undertaken at great financial burden to a plaintiff who would not reap any economic rewards from a courtroom victory.[6] Fee-shifting provided some compensation for a voluntary law enforcement effort. It was also a highly controversial judicial practice, as illustrated by the opinions written in the trans-Alaskan pipeline case.

Wilderness Society v. *Morton.*[7] The 1974 decision of the D.C. Circuit Court of Appeals in the trans-Alaskan pipeline case, in both its majority opinion and its strongly worded dissents, placed in sharp relief two opposing viewpoints concerning both the desirability of awarding attorneys fees and the "public interest" justification of environmentalist litigation efforts.

In 1970, the D.C. District Court enjoined issuance of a federal permit that would have allowed construction of the trans-Alaskan pipeline across federal lands.[8] The Interior Department had not prepared an environmental impact statement for the action, and issuance of a permit might have violated right-of-way restrictions of the Mineral Leasing Act of 1920. The district court dissolved the injunction after ruling that the Interior Department had complied with the Mineral Leasing Act, and that the nine million dollar, six volume impact statement the department finally prepared satisfied NEPA's requirements. On appeal, the D.C. Circuit Court, sitting *en banc*, reversed the district court decision. Without ruling on the NEPA issues, the court held that permit issuance would violate the Mineral Leasing Act and therefore should be enjoined.[9]

In the midst of the energy shortages of 1973, Congress asserted its authority in the matter by amending the Mineral Leasing Act to allow issuance of the pipeline permit.[10] It declared that no further administrative action pursuant to NEPA was necessary and that no further judicial review of pipeline related administrative actions would be allowed except in the most limited circumstances.

Several months after the congressional action, environmentalist attorneys, having spent over 4500 hours on the case, sought to recoup their fees. The Circuit Court voted 4 to 3, with two judges not participating, to permit a fee award.[11] Half the fees requested were assessed against the Alyeska Pipeline Company, which had intervened in the case as a defendant. An assessment of fees against the federal government was forbidden by statute,[12] and no fees were assessed against the state of Alaska, which, according to the court, had intervened to represent the public interest of those of its citizens who wished to see the pipeline built. The majority felt it was proper to assess fees against Alyeska, because its assets were far greater than the plaintiffs' litigation costs, and because it had intervened to protect its well-defined economic interest.

Judge Skelly Wright wrote the majority opinion. He noted that where the law relies on private suits to effectuate public policy in favor of broad public interests, attorneys' fees were necessary to assure that private litigants would initiate such suits.[13] Judge Wright expressed the hope that the court's decision would encourage skilled lawyers to undertake public interest litigation "on behalf of unmonied clients with just, lawful, and important claims."[14]

Judge Wright commented that the pipeline litigation prompted drafting of an extensive impact statement that benefited the public's statutory right to information about the project. It also led to refinement of the environmentally protective stipulations placed on the rights-of-way. Furthermore, although the NEPA compliance issue was never fully addressed by the circuit court, its being raised by the plaintiffs prompted Congress to include provisions in the amended Mineral Leasing Act giving the Interior Secretary broad authority to impose environmental protection stipulations on right-of-way permits.

Judge Wright believed that the course the permit controversy followed was that of a judicial remand to the legislature—an action earlier delegated by the legislature to agency discretion was passed back to the legislature as a result of judicial review of the manner in which discretion was exercised.

The majority opinion drew scathing dissents from Circuit Judges McKinnon and Wilkey. The dissenters belittled the majority opinion and presented quite a different perspective on the legislative remand and fee-sharing issues. Judge McKinnon argued, in essence, that the majority had been wrong in its initial opinion on the pipeline, that Congress was angered by this incorrect action and, as a result, had passed a bill both approving the pipeline and removing further actions taken on it from the court's jurisdiction. Judge McKinnon argued also that the plaintiffs had lost, not won, on the merits of their NEPA compliance contentions, because Congress had ordered construction of the pipeline as it was described in the final environmental impact statement. He argued that the main effect of the plaintiffs' effort was to delay the pipeline, extending the nation's dependence on foreign supplies of energy, and perhaps compelling construction of a pipeline through Canada. Judge McKinnon stated that such an effort was definitely not in the public interest.[15]

Circuit Judge Wilkey, in a dissent joined by Judges McKinnon and Robb, continued the attack on the majority opinion. Noting Congress' endorsement of the pipeline, he argued that the environmentalists were frustrating an energy development policy that Congress considered "highly desirable and of the utmost urgency." [16] He wondered sarcastically whose "public interest" the environmentalists were serving:

> It is hard to visualize the average American in this winter of 1973–74, turning down his thermostat and with a careful eye on his auto fuel gauge, feeling that warm glow of gratitude to those public-spirited plaintiffs in the Alaska Pipeline case.[17]

Noting that the decision might unleash a flood of public interest lawsuits, Judge Wilkey commented, "We can think of no greater encouragement to ill-founded litigation." [18] In sum, Judge Wilkey argued, the plaintiffs had not prevailed on an important legal issue, had not conferred a public benefit, and therefore they were not entitled to attorneys fees.

The decision in this case was one of several circuit court rulings in this period that addressed the fee-sharing issue. The D.C. Circuit's determination here was reversed in 1975 by the Supreme Court.[19] The Court, by a 5 to 2 vote, declared in broad terms that the private attorney-general doctrine could no longer be used as a basis for fee-shifting.

EQUITY BONDS: LOWERING THE
FINANCIAL BURDEN OF LITIGATION

Courts can exercise their discretionary powers to assist environmentalist plaintiffs by declining to impose sizeable bonds that may constitute onerous financial burdens. The Federal Rules of Civil Procedure, the regulations governing the conduct of civil cases in federal courts, provide that issuance of a preliminary injunction may be contingent upon a plaintiff's providing a bond to reimburse for damages any party wrongly enjoined. The rules further provide the courts with considerable discretion in determining whether such a bond will be required.[20] To the good fortune of the environmentalist cause, federal courts usually refrained from setting high bonds, for they recognized that by requiring them they might foreclose efforts by public interest groups to raise important issues pertaining to agency compliance with NEPA.

The rationale for requiring little or no equity bond was perhaps best stated in *NRDC* v. *Morton*.[21] At issue was the Bureau of Land Management's leasing of outer continental shelf lands for oil and gas exploration. From this leasing the government expected to earn millions of dollars each year. The district court granted a preliminary injunction against the lease sales and then refused the government's request that the equity bond be set at a level of $750,000 for the first month of the injunction with a provision for increasing it to $2.5 million per month thereafter. These were the sums that the federal government expected to gain from the leasing. District Judge Richey, in denying the federal request and in setting the equity bond at $100 stated that the continental shelf and its environs constitute one of the nation's most important resources. He noted the richness of its estuaries, the productivities of its fisheries, and its recreational value to millions of people. He concluded that the public interest would be more gravely damaged by his court's failure to rigorously enforce NEPA than by any leasing delays such enforcement might cause.[22]

Table 5 shows that when preliminary injunctions were granted, although substantial sums of federal, state and private money were at stake, the courts usually required only token equity bonds. Of the cases listed in which substantial bonds were required, two involved industry plaintiffs charging agency noncompliance with NEPA and one was an early decision in which the court did not set forth the rationale supporting the high bond established.[23]

Motivations for Environmentalist Legal Actions

Environmentalists tried to mobilize judicial resources in achieving their goals because their own resources were scarce. They multiplied the resources available to them by obtaining injunctions and favorable judicial constructions of NEPA. A few organizations gaining victories in key cases could significantly magnify the impact of a law like NEPA that was ripe for judicial clarification. Discrete decisions increased in importance as they became precedents for later judicial actions.

Environmentalists sought judicial redress of grievances because they regarded court rooms as more impartial forums than administrative hearing rooms; they believed environmental quality had been given insufficient consideration by mission-oriented agencies and the developmental clienteles and congressional committees to which the agencies were primarily responsive.

Litigation promoted environmental values by placing a price on them.[24] Environmentalists tried to become important elements in agencies' political environments by convincing the agencies that environmental concerns could be arbitrarily ig-

nored only at the risk of suit. Agencies had to balance legal
sanctions obtainable by environmentalists against sanctions that
might be imposed by congressional committees.

Environmentalists, in taking to the courts, paralleled the
movement of consumer protection advocates. Both reflected
diffuse interests that tended to be under represented in the
political system. Both widened the scope of conflict over issues
to include the courts when they perceived that nominally
responsible government administrators were not acting in what
the activists viewed as the public interest.[25]

Environmentalist litigation served several tactical objectives. Litigants sometimes sought judicial action merely for its
symbolic value. Alternatively, they used a lawsuit as a catalyst
to stimulate intervention by agencies other than those challenged, or they used it as a bargaining weapon.[26] A lawsuit could
also function to call legislative attention to an issue—court
ordered moratoria and remands could attract legislative interest
to a matter that had been left to administrative discretion, but
which was of sufficient import to merit additional legislative
action.[27]

NEPA, in particular, was used as a weapon in a continuing
battle against those federal actions, initiated prior to 1970,
whose abandonment or substantial modification environmentalists were insistent upon. Perhaps the best example of this is
provided by the Storm King Mountain controversy, involving
FPC approval of construction of a power plant on scenic Storm
King Mountain overlooking New York's Hudson River. Licensing of the Storm King plant had been the focus of a landmark
judicial decision in 1965,[28] and the matter was still being
considered by the FPC on January 1, 1970. One day after NEPA
became law, a staff member of a committee that had considered
NEPA advised his environmentalist friends engaged in the
Storm King litigation that they now had new grounds on which
to challenge FPC action.[29]

Table 5

EQUITY BONDS REQUIRED IN NEPA-BASED
ENVIRONMENTAL LAWSUITS

Name of Case	Project Challenged	Equity Bond	Sum Involved*
Gibson v. Ruckelshaus 1 ELR 20337 (E.D. Tex. 1971)	Sewage treatment plant	$ 500	. . .
West Virginia Highlands Conservancy v. Island Creek Coal Company 441 F.2d 232, 1 ELR 20160 (4th Cir. 1971)	Mineral exploration on national forest land	100	. . .
NRDC v. Grant 341 F.Supp. 356, 2 ELR 20185 (E.D. N.C. 1972)	SCS stream channeliza-tion	75,000**	$ 2.5 million
Wilderness Society v. Hickel 325 F.Supp. 422, 1 ELR 20042 (D.D.C. 1970)	Trans-Alaskan pipeline	100	. . .
NRDC v. Morton 337 F.Supp. 167, 2 ELR 20089 (D.D.C. 1971)	Off-shore oil leases	100	2.5 million (per month)
National Helium Corp. v. Morton 326 F.Supp. 151, 1 ELR 20157 (D. Kans. 1971)	Government contracts for helium purchase	75,000	. . .
EDF v. T.V.A. 339 F.Supp. 806, 2 ELR 20044 (E.D. Tenn. 1972)	Tellico Dam	100	40 million
EDF v. Corps of Engineers 324 F.Supp. 878, 1 ELR 20079 (D.D.C. 1971)	Cross-Florida Barge Canal	1	130 million

Table 5 *continued*

EQUITY BONDS REQUIRED IN NEPA-BASED
ENVIRONMENTAL LAWSUITS

Name of Case	Project Challenged	Equity Bond	Sum Involved*
EDF v. Corps of Engineers 331 F.Supp. 925, 1 ELR 20466 (D.D.C. 1971)	Tennessee-Tombigbee Waterway	1	6 million
Sierra Club v. Laird 1 ELR 20085 (D. Ariz. 1970)	Gila River clearing	75,000***	159,000
Texas Committee on Natural Resources v. Resor 1 ELR 20466 (E.D. Tex. 1971)	Cooper Dam-Sulfur River	0	. . .
Keith v. Volpe 2 ELR 20425 (C.D. Cal. 1972)	Highway	0	500 million
Morningside-Lenox v. Volpe 334 F.Supp. 132, 1 ELR 20629 (N.D. Ga. 1971)	Highway	0	. . .
Boston Waterfront Residents v. Romney 343 F.Supp. 89, 2 ELR 20359 (D. Mass. 1972)	Urban renewal	0	30 million
Anaconda v. Ruckelshaus 352 F.Supp. 697, 3 ELR 20024 (D. Colo. 1972)	Challenge to state Clean Air Act implementation plan	30,000	. . .

* In some instances the sums here represent the total value of the project. In other instances, these sums represent the cost to defendants of project delay. Amounts are listed only where they were readily obtainable from the court decision.
** This figure was reduced, on appeal, to $100.
*** This figure was reduced, on appeal, to $20,000.

Obtaining Access to Judicial Review

Individuals and groups seeking judicial review of administrative action had to hurdle several procedural barriers. These threshold considerations could be characterized as how, how much, when, where, and for whom judicial review should be provided.[30] Discussed below are three of these that were of particular interest in environmental litigation.[31] The "when" and "for whom" questions, involving the procedural concerns of "laches," "ripeness," and "standing," were generally answered in a manner favorable to environmentalists. The answer to the "where" question, involving the judicial requirement of proper "venue" was often of great strategic interest to environmentalist plaintiffs and federal defendants.

WHEN

The "when" criterion required that a suit be timely. A plaintiff must have exhausted his administrative remedies before seeking judicial review, and the decision challenged could not be a preliminary administrative one subject to modification at a later point in the agency review process. If the situation was otherwise then the courts might decline review. For example, a citizen suit challenging planning of a Spokane, Washington highway was ruled to be premature by a district court.[32] Similarly rejected were two environmentalist challenges to the AEC's refusal to admit environmental evidence into licensing proceedings.[33]

A lawsuit would also not be considered timely if undue delay had occurred before its initiation. The doctrine of laches was invoked by the courts in dismissing a number of environmental cases. Two such cases concerned a citizen challenge to an Alaskan timber sale and a complaint against a partially constructed highway.[34] However, the doctrine of laches could be quite flexible. For example, *Arlington Coalition on Transporta-*

tion v. *Volpe*[35] was a challenge to construction of I-66, a highway cutting through the suburbs of Washington, D.C. The original hearings on location of the highway had been held in the late 1950s. By the time the 4th Circuit handed down its 1972 decision in the case, 85 percent of the right-of-way and 95 percent of the dwellings in the proposed right-of-way had been acquired. $29 million had been expended, although no construction had begun. The previous commitments notwithstanding, the court ruled that all work had to be halted, new location hearings held, and an environmental impact statement prepared. The court commented:

> We decline to invoke laches . . . because of the public interest status accorded ecology preservation by the Congress. We believe that . . . I-66 has not progressed to the point where the costs of altering or abandoning the proposed route would *certainly* outweigh the benefits that might accrue therefrom to the general public.[36]

The words of the 4th Circuit could be found repeatedly in court decisions preliminarily enjoining federal projects on which substantial amounts of work had already been completed.

WHERE

The "where" question concerned itself with jurisdiction— was the case brought in the appropriate federal court?[37] Selection of the appropriate federal court, the choice of venue, was an important strategic decision for both plaintiff and defense counsels. Environmentalists sought to avoid nearby federal district courts in their challenges to public works projects; they felt that federal judges more removed from a locality might acquiesce less readily to the development decisions of federal agencies than locally presiding judges; the latter might share the development ethos of federal agencies or the economic aspirations of the communities in which they sat. An analysis of the backgrounds of federal judges suggests that environmentalists had good reason to avoid local federal courtrooms if local origin or residence of judges inclined them to share a community developmental ethos. An examination of U.S. district court judges in the late 1960s found that of the 124 judges studied, 30 percent were born in the city in which they presided, 29 percent within their judicial district, 13 percent within their judicial circuit and 28 percent elsewhere.[38] Moreover, at the time of their appointment, 120 of the 124 were residing in the states in which their courtroom was located.

Perhaps the clearest example of the effort environmentalists made to avoid a local jurisdiction was the Natural Resources Defense Council's (NRDC's) suit challenging TVA procurement policies for strip mined coal.[39] This suit was brought in a New York City federal court. Similarly, some environmentalists tried, when possible, to avoid the 3d Circuit. This circuit delivered some unduly narrow opinions in highway litigation under NEPA that contrasted markedly with other circuits' more liberal applications of the Act. Environmental lawyer Anthony Roisman commented: "we have had trouble with the third circuit. . . . I don't want to say it is a bad circuit, but we try not to bring our cases there." [40]

In contrast, environmentalist attorneys sought to bring suits in the D.C. Circuit, which earned a reputation for its liberal leanings and its wary view of administrative decision making. The D.C. Circuit Court handed down a number of stinging decisions rebuking federal agencies for their noncompliance with NEPA. Most notable among these was Judge Skelly Wright's opinion in Calvert Cliffs. The nine judge D.C. Circuit Court included three conservative Nixon appointees, Judges McKinnon, Wilkey, and Robb, who often dissented sharply from the opinions of the liberal majority. The conservatives constituted a minority that could be outvoted in the three-judge appellate decisions if no two sat on the same panel. Federal agencies suffered so badly at the hands of the D.C. Circuit that some Justice Department lawyers, it was rumored, were inclined to believe that the panels were deliberately "loaded" so that the conservatives would be in the minority.[41]

Environmentalists found the D.C. District Court willing to enjoin the trans-Alaskan pipeline, the Cross-Florida Barge Canal and the Tennessee-Tombigbee Waterway. In these cases, the Justice Department attempted to have the venue changed to federal district courts in Alaska, Florida, and Mississippi respectively. Venue change was denied in the pipeline case but was granted in the latter two cases. In the Tennessee-Tombigbee Waterway case, a federal district judge in Mississippi lifted the injunction against the waterway that had been issued by the D.C. District Court.[42] In the barge canal case, a Florida federal district judge issued a decision that was so skewed to favor canal proponents that the 5th Circuit in reviewing and remanding it found it did not apply proper legal standards, considered many factors that were not relevant, and failed to support its actions with proper findings of fact and conclusions of law.[43]

FOR WHOM

The "for whom" threshold pertained to standing. Standing traditionally had been granted only to those with a "legal interest" in a case, meaning that those who suffered economic injury as a result of federal action had a right to sue the government. Expansion of the concept of "legal interest" to include noneconomic interests opened the doors of the courts to groups seeking to protect noneconomically based environmental concerns. These liberalized rules for standing benefited not only environmentalists, but also civil rights activists and others.[44]

Liberalized Standing, 1965–1970. The 1965 Scenic Hudson decision[45] was the landmark opinion in the area of liberalized standing. The Scenic Hudson Preservation Conference was granted standing to challenge FPC licensing of a proposed pumped storage power project at Storm King Mountain on the Hudson River. The 2d Circuit held that, where a group had an interest in conservation rather than economic matters, it was entitled to judicial review of FPC actions affecting this interest. Such a group would be considered a party "aggrieved" by FPC action and therefore entitled to review under the judicial review provisions of the Federal Power Act.

To challenge agency actions undertaken pursuant to statutes such as NEPA that did not have judicial review provisions, environmentalists had to obtain additional rulings on standing. Their primary vehicle was the Administrative Procedure Act (APA) that provided generally that a party aggrieved by agency action could obtain judicial review.[46] Under the APA, and in accordance with the reasoning of Scenic Hudson, if a plaintiff could demonstrate that his noneconomic, conservation interest was intended to be protected by statute, he could obtain standing in court to sue. From 1965 to 1970, environmentalist plaintiffs were able to convince federal judges that environmentally protective language could be found in highway and forestry statutes, and that they therefore were entitled to standing to challenge actions taken pursuant to these laws.[47] They could be regarded as private attorneys-general seeking to protect the public interest in environmental quality.

In two major standing cases in 1970, the Supreme Court left the judicial door open to environmental groups. In two cases decided the same day, *Association of Data Processing Service Organizations, Inc.* v. *Camp*,[48] and *Barlow* v. *Collins*,[49] the Court pronounced two criteria that a plaintiff had to satisfy to obtain standing. First, the plaintiff had to show that the challenged action had injured him in some fashion, economic or otherwise. Second, the plaintiff had to show that the interest he sought to protect was arguably within the zone of interests to be protected or regulated by the statute or constitutional guarantee in question.[50] To gain standing in accordance with these criteria, environmental groups merely needed to argue that they had suffered harm to noneconomic interests and that such noneconomic interests lay, arguably, within the realm of interests that were designed to be protected by statute.

Post–1970 Standing Rulings: The Supreme Court Mineral King Decision.[51] By December 1970 an increasingly large body of case law was developed in which environmental groups were granted standing. The general tendency to liberalize the rules of standing was not observed, however, in the 9th Circuit. In two cases, *Alameda Conservation Association* v. *California*[52] and *Sierra Club* v. *Hickel* (the Mineral King case),[53] the circuit ruled that a mere general interest in conservation and environmental protection was not sufficient grounds for permitting environmental groups standing to sue.

The Sierra Club appealed *Sierra Club* v. *Hickel* to the Supreme Court, hoping that the Court would adopt the 2d Circuit's position that conservation groups, as organizations, had standing to sue to vindicate the public interest in conservation matters. The Supreme Court in a 4 to 3 decision, refused to adopt this broad view.[54] The ruling in the case nevertheless contained elements favorable to environmentalists. The Court stated that, consonant with Data Processing, standing would be granted aggrieved individuals having interests that were aesthetic, conservational, or recreational. The Court held, furthermore, that an organization whose members' individual interests were affected might represent those members in a judicial proceeding and that once standing on this basis had been established, general public interest issues might be litigated; conservation organizations would thus be serving as private attorneys-general. Only in a few isolated instances was this toughened standing requirement used to preclude environmental groups from obtaining judicial relief.

The Supreme Court Addresses the Standing Issue Again: The SCRAP Decision.[55] The Supreme Court Mineral King ruling still left the standing issue somewhat cloudy, for the Court did not specify a minimum level of individualized, noneconomic injury that had to be suffered in order to obtain standing. In the SCRAP decision fourteen months later, in June 1973, a majority of the Court indicated that environmentalist plaintiffs would not have much difficulty satisfying the minimum injury requirements.

SCRAP was an organization of five law students who sought a preliminary injunction against an ICC ruling permitting railroads to increase freight rates for recycled goods. It alleged that each of its members used the forests, streams, mountains, and other resources in the Washington, D.C. metropolitan area for camping, hiking, fishing, and sightseeing. These latter uses, it was claimed, would be disturbed by the adverse environmental impact of the decreased demand for recyclable goods that stemmed from increased freight rates. The Supreme Court, ruling on the ICC's appeal of SCRAP's victory in the district court, was willing to support standing for the plaintiffs by entertaining this circuitous logic. It is worth noting that the dissenters to this ruling contended that "the alleged injuries [were] so remote, speculative, and insubstantial in fact that they [failed] to confer standing." [56]

Judicial Response to NEPA: The Courts and Agency Discretion

The courts tended to be very responsive to NEPA because the statute's legislative history—particularly the floor remarks of Senators Jackson and Muskie and the statement of the House managers—declared in strident language that the time had come to establish a new basis for decision making. The courts found many instances of administrative discretion operating to subvert NEPA, and responded by narrowing administrators' opportunities to buffer the Act's impact.

NEPA was an exceptionally broad law, but insofar as it conveyed a strong substantive message accompanied by scantily developed procedures, it was not unique. Kenneth Culp Davis, a respected authority on administrative law, has noted that a legislative body, seeing a problem but not knowing its solution, often delegates authority to work on it. The legislature tells an administrator that what it desires is "the true, the good and the beautiful," or "just and reasonable" results, or furtherance of "the public interest." [57] The administrator, through case-by-case consideration, then divides the larger problem up into smaller, solvable ones.[58]

The exercise of some discretion is necessary in any governmental system. Discretionary opportunities allow administrators to adapt general congressional directives to specific conflict situations in an innovative fashion. Policy develops from administrators' selections among possible courses of action or inaction, with administrative choices extending to procedures, timing, emphasis, and many other decision-making factors.[59]

The availability of discretionary decision-making opportunities provides the flexibility that can result in innovative policy. But this flexibility may not be realized; agency positions may become frozen around private interests that arise.[60] Agency discretion may be exercised primarily to maintain the ties between the regulators and the regulated.

In the case of NEPA, the exercise of discretion determined whether the involvement of the public in decision making would be timely or unduly delayed, whether the methods for implementing the statute would be ad hoc or well-developed, and whether the emphasis placed on environmental values would be slight or considerable. The exercise of this discretion involved a mixing of facts, values and influences.[61] "Facts" might only have been selectively perceived; values might have been professional ones, such as those motivating FPC Commissioners to thumb their noses at NEPA; and influences might have been congressional, prompting a harried developmental agency beholden to a single committee to give little consideration to environmental concerns.

When discretion was abused, the courts could become involved. They could provide access to decision making where it had not been provided before; they could demand inclusion of values that hitherto had been excluded and they could insist on the nonarbitrary weighing of values once such values had been deemed relevant to a decision. In essence, the courts could seek to check and structure the exercise of discretion in order to foreclose its abuse.[62] They could do this not only by a post hoc review of decisions, but by providing guidance to agencies for procedural improvement, so that future decisions would not be rejected as being arbitrary.

THE BAZELON VIEW OF AGENCY DISCRETION

The rationale for judicial review of administrative decision making was perhaps best espoused in the opinions of Judge David Bazelon, Chief Judge of the D.C. Circuit Court of Appeals. In *Environmental Defense Fund* v. *Ruckelshaus*,[63] a case involving the continued government licensing of DDT sales, Judge Bazelon discoursed on the relationship between agencies and the courts. He noted that in the past courts "regularly" upheld agency action with a "bow to the mysteries of administrative expertise." [64] But courts had increasingly been setting aside agency action on the grounds that an impermissible factor had entered the proceedings, or because a crucial factor had not been considered. Thus, courts increasingly required administrators to articulate the factors underlying their decisions. Bazelon noted that this articulation was becoming even more important, as new doctrines of standing and reviewability and new statutory causes of action were causing the courts to review agency actions touching on "fundamental personal interests in life, health and property," all of which had a "special claim to judicial protection." [65] He added that to protect these interests from "administrative arbitrariness," strict judicial scrutiny was necessary. However, such scrutiny, while necessary, was not sufficient protection, for it could function to correct only the worst abuses. Judge Bazelon saw review as helping the agencies themselves curtail abuse by requiring administrators to articulate in as much detail as possible the standards and principles governing their discretionary decisions. Rules and regulations ought to be freely formulated, and discretionary decisions supported with findings of fact and reasoned opinions. Such actions would enable agencies themselves to confine and control the exercise of discretion. The end result would be a diminution in the importance of judicial review and an enhancement of the integrity of the administrative process.

Judge Bazelon delivered the opinion in *EDF* v. *Ruckelshaus* on January 7, 1971, but two years and many NEPA-related opinions later, on February 6, 1973, he found it necessary to detail his views again. *Citizens Association of Georgetown* v. *Zoning Commission of the District of Columbia*[66] was a challenge to the refusal of the D.C. Zoning Commission to rezone an area slated for high-density commercial and residential development. In noting the absence of any stated reasons in the rezoning denial decision, and in ordering their articulation, Judge Bazelon commented that the case for requiring a statement of reasons from an administrative agency was "a persuasive one." [67] A court, to know what to review, had to know what the agency had determined and should not have to speculate about the bases of administrative conclusions. A statement of reasons from the agency would "afford a safeguard against arbitrary and careless action" and was apt to create greater consistency in agency decision making.[68]

NEPA AND AGENCY DISCRETION—1970 AND 1971 CASES

The courts tended to be responsive to NEPA, but this receptiveness was considerably limited in 1970. Environmentalists obtained injunctions against the trans-Alaskan pipeline, against a Corps of Engineers project in Arizona,[69] and against a Farmers Home Administration loan for construction of a golf course in Texas.[70] Conversely, in three other opinions, the courts held that NEPA did not create court-enforceable duties and that it could not be applied retroactively.[71] To the good fortune of environmentalists, those unfavorable opinions were not carefully reasoned and therefore had little precedential value.

It was not really until 1971, in the Gillham Dam and Calvert Cliffs cases, that two courts, in careful opinions, interpreted NEPA as imposing considerable decision-making duties. The Gillham I opinion is discussed below. In Calvert Cliffs, Judge Skelly Wright held that the courts had a duty to see that congressional policy directives were "not lost in the hallways of the bureaucracy," [72] that AEC had given a "crabbed interpretation" to an act which Congress did not intend to be a "paper tiger," [73] and that agency compliance with NEPA had to be strict and would be closely reviewed by the courts.[74] Calvert Cliffs was the most widely cited of all NEPA opinions.

A non-NEPA environmental case decided by the Supreme Court in 1971 had considerable influence on later judicial reviews of agencies' discretionary actions under NEPA. *Citizens to Preserve Overton Park* v. *Volpe*[75] was an environmentalist challenge to the secretary of transportation's approval of highway construction through a Memphis, Tennessee park. The secretarial decision to approve construction had not been made after a rule-making or quasi-judicial proceeding, so there was no well-defined record for the Court to examine for "substantial evidence" supporting the determination.[76] The Court therefore used a different evidentiary test and asked whether the decision was "arbitrary and capricious": had the secretary acted within his authority and in accordance with established procedures; had he used only relevant factors and no others in making his judgment; and had he given no undue weight to any of the relevant factors? [77]

The Court declared that in checking the administrative determination in accordance with the arbitrary and capricious test, a lower court could engage in "substantial inquiry." The inquiry could be "searching," and could involve review of the entire record before the secretary at the time of his decision.[78] Perhaps realizing that its "substantial inquiry" language provided too broad a grant of authority to lower courts, the Supreme Court added that the ultimate standard of review would be narrow and a court was not empowered to substitute its judgment for that of the agency.[79]

The Overton Park decision was an important precedent for later NEPA opinions, for the substantial inquiry language provided several courts an opportunity to undertake extensive reviews of agency NEPA actions. The decision also meant that agencies, to discourage judicial remands based on lack of a supporting record, would find it desirable to develop procedures for creating a reviewable administrative record on which environmentally impacting decisions were based.

Judicial Clarification of NEPA's Ambiguities

In the preceding chapter, five areas of ambiguity within NEPA's decision-making message were noted: which actions require statements, what analyses should statements contain, when should statements be prepared, how should the public be involved, and how should statements be reviewed? The discussion that follows describes the leading judicial efforts, most of which emerged from the prestigious D.C. and 2d Circuits, to provide guidance for agencies' discretionary decisions in those areas. In certain of the areas, the judicial guidance was not great, and was limited to district court decisions of restricted precedential impact.

WHICH ACTIONS REQUIRE STATEMENTS?

The courts clearly lowered the threshold for impact statement preparation. They reserved the right to scrutinize closely agency threshold determinations as to whether a project required an impact statement. The operative criteria were that a project had to be federal, major, and have a significant effect on the environment.

The "federal" criterion was especially problematical, because many actions that were subject to NEPA were not exclusively federal. Some were joint federal-private or federal-state actions in which considerable resources had been invested by the private or state sector prior to federal involvement. In such instances, alternatives might already have been foreclosed or environmental damage might already have occurred. In a number of these, courts were willing, when future federal action was either contemplated or inevitable, to enjoin state action foreclosing alternatives.[80] For other projects, federal action had taken place at an early stage of project development, and remaining work, which might be considerable and might be environmentally damaging, was undertaken exclusively by the state. Where states tried to "defederalize" projects by completing them with state funds while transferring federal funds earmarked for them to other state endeavors, such efforts were blocked by the courts.[81]

Once an action was deemed federal, many courts used a two-test standard of "major action" and "significant effect" in deciding whether an impact statement was necessary.[82] Many more courts implicitly used a one-test standard of "significant effect" and none held that a small or minor federal project was exempted from the impact statement requirement if its environmental effects were significant. Virtually the only exceptions the courts permitted to the impact statement requirements were national security matters and temporary or emergency actions.[83] Only two agencies were exempted from NEPA.[84]

Some courts, in keeping with Judge Bazelon's dicta, made an effort to prod agencies into structuring their threshold decision making. In *Hanly* v. *Kleindienst*,[85] the 2d Circuit reviewed a General Services Administration decision to build a detention center in downtown New York City. In its first decision in the case, the court held that the agency's threshold determination as to whether a statement must be prepared had to be supported by a reviewable record covering a specified number of factors.[86] In its second decision, it stated that before making a threshold decision, the agency must notify the public of its proposed action and request submission of relevant facts that might bear on the determination.[87] In certain circumstances, a public hearing might be desirable.

WHAT ANALYSES SHOULD STATEMENTS CONTAIN?

The courts often scrutinized agency impact statements for their adequacy. As more and more opinions were written for projects of a particular type, such as water resource development projects, additional factors requiring detailed evaluation were mentioned. Some of the most important judicial findings of more general applicability were summarized by CEQ in its May 16, 1972 memo to agency heads and general counsels making recommendations for improving the NEPA implementation process.[88] Agency analyses would have to include "all known possible environmental consequences," and all "reasonably foreseeable impacts." [89] Genuine, as opposed to perfunctory, compliance with NEPA would require an agency "to explicate fully its course of inquiry, its analyses and its reasoning." [90]

While the courts demanded rigor, they did not demand perfection. This is evident from the Tennessee-Tombigbee II opinion:

> We do not fathom the phrase "to the fullest extent possible" to be an absolute term requiring perfection. . . . the phrase clearly imposes a standard . . . requiring nothing less than comprehensive and objective treatment by the responsible agency. . . . Thus, an agency's consideration of environmental matters that is merely partial or performed in a superficial manner does not satisfy the requisite standard.[91]

And in the words of the Gillham II opinion, "It is not necessary to dot all the I's and cross all the T's in an impact statement." [92]

The courts were particularly instrumental in describing the manner in which "alternatives to proposed action" were to be treated in environmental impact statements. The leading cases in that regard were *NRDC* v. *Morton*,[93] a challenge to outer continental shelf (OCS) oil and gas leasing by the Department of Interior's Bureau of Land Management; *EDF* v. *Corps of Engineers (Gillham I)*[94], a challenge to the Gillham Dam in Arkansas; and *Committee for Nuclear Responsibility* v. *Seaborg* (Amchitka),[95] a suit against an underground nuclear detonation on Alaska's Amchitka Island. *NRDC* v. *Morton* provided, most importantly, that agencies had an obligation to discuss in their impact statements alternatives to their proposed action that lay outside their jurisdiction. Gillham I also adopted a broad view of agencies' obligations to discuss alternatives. The Amchitka opinion took a far narrower view of agencies' obligations and was cited as precedent by courts narrowly construing NEPA's alternatives requirements. A close reading of the Amchitka opinion reveals, however, that courts using it in this manner in fact misconstrued it.

NRDC v. *Morton*. The majority opinion in *NRDC* v. *Morton* focused specifically on the energy policies that the Interior Department was obliged to discuss as alternatives to OCS leasing. To the extent that it discussed alternatives generally, the majority opinion could have wider application—to all areas in which no comprehensive national policy had been formulated, but in which incremental, ad hoc decision making was the norm. These areas might include, for example, energy, minerals, transportation, and housing.

NRDC v. *Morton* arose from the government's attempt to lease offshore oil and gas reserves in the Gulf of Mexico, in accordance with the President's statement in his energy message of June 1971 that there would be an increase in such leasing activity. The Interior Department prepared an environmental impact statement for the project and consonant with its interpretation of NEPA's requirements it limited its discussion

of policy alternatives to those lying within departmental jurisdiction. The discussion filled only two and one-half double
spaced, typewritten pages. NRDC brought suit, alleging departmental noncompliance with NEPA for failure to discuss adequately alternatives to the proposed leasing program lying
outside its jurisdiction.

The Interior Department offered several arguments in support of its narrow view. It stated that the only alternatives it
was required to discuss were those that could be adopted by and
put into effect by the department itself. It distinguished
environmental impact statements accompanying administrative
actions such as offshore leasing from those developed for
legislative proposals, suggesting that only for the latter was it
necessary to discuss alternative actions outside its immediate
authority. It also contended that it was not obligated to discuss
in detail remote or speculative alternatives whose impact could
not possibly be felt within the time period the chosen course of
action was designed to serve. It conceded it might have to
mention alternatives suggested by others, but that it was not
required to discuss their environmental impacts.

A preliminary injunction against the leasing action was
entered by the D.C. District Court, but it was left to the D.C.
Circuit Court majority to develop a lengthy opinion concerning
the requirements of alternatives. The majority recognized that a
search for alternatives could not proceed indefinitely, and that
such a search was not meaningfully possible in view of an
agency's limited resources. Further, it conceded that agencies
need not examine "remote and speculative possibilities," or
indulge in "crystal ball" inquiries in assessing the effects of
alternatives. While declaring that agencies only had to examine
alternatives that might be implemented in the same time frame
as their proposed course of action, the court acknowledged that
beyond this, a more precise test for the types of alternatives
that had to be considered would be quite difficult to create, and
that "the requirement as to alternatives is subject to a construc-

tion of reasonableness." [96] While emphasizing the importance of construing the alternatives requirement with some reasonableness, the majority was not prepared to uphold entirely the Interior Department's narrow view of NEPA. The department's statement, it said, had to provide "information sufficient to permit a reasoned choice so far as environmental aspects are concerned." [97] The department had to discuss opposing views that were reasonable and responsible even if these went beyond the scope of the department's authority and even if suggested by outside intervenors. Where a suggested alternative had no impact or little impact, discussion might be brief, although a rule of reason had to prevail in making this judgment.[98] The court concluded that each impact statement and its evaluation of alternatives had to be viewed as directed at the president and at Congress, so that an evaluation of alternatives that might even require legislative action was in order.

Circuit Judge McKinnon, in dissent, was willing to acquiesce to the exercise of considerable departmental discretion in the foreclosure of alternatives suggested as practical by others. He would also have left the agency little discretion in suggesting policy to Congress. He argued that it was not necessary for an impact statement such as Interior's to discuss alternatives requiring new legislative proposals, because not every impact statement was addressed to the Congress and the president, particularly when the agency was carrying out programs established by pre-existing statutes. Judge McKinnon indicated, in addition, that he saw no reasonable necessity for an agency to discuss the environmental impact of a suggested alternative that had been rejected because it was not "practical."

The majority and dissenting opinions, viewed in tandem, illustrated the difficulty of defining alternative actions deserving of detailed evaluation. What was practical in one person's judgment might be impractical in another's, and an individual's reasoning supporting the judgment of "practicality" might be arbitrary, distorted, or biased. The D.C. Circuit was divided in its views as to which specific alternatives to leasing were sufficiently realistic and nonspeculative that they merited discussion in the OCS impact statement. Alternatives viewed by the majority as realistic and deserving of discussion were not so viewed by Judge McKinnon. The majority, he stated, extended the law "to extreme and impractical ends." [99]

EDF v. *Corps of Engineers (Gillham I).* The decision in Gillham I arose from a challenge to the Gillham Dam, a project under construction on the Cossatot River in Arkansas. An impact statement for the project was issued shortly after litigation began. By insisting that the impact statement provide a thorough discussion of alternatives, benefits and costs, the Gillham I decision set a precedent for the rigorous evaluation by the courts of statement adequacy.

Initially, the court concerned itself with discussion of alternatives to the proposed project. Since the dam would be built on the last free-flowing stream in the area, the court was particularly concerned with the lack of consideration given to leaving the Cossatot in a free-flowing state by utilizing a host of nonstructural flood protection measures.[100] The court might well have noted that the nonstructural alternatives would not require Corps activity and therefore were not in the organizational interest of the Corps to discuss.

The court was also concerned with alternative means of evaluating the proposed dam. The Environmental Defense Fund (EDF) had taken issue with the Corps' benefit-cost calculations, arguing that the benefits from the dam had been inflated. The court did not wish to involve itself in a comparative evaluation of the Corps and EDF claims, stating that "the methods of calculating cost-benefit ratios are innumerable and in many cases esoteric." [101] But after describing the EDF analysis in detail, the court stated that "a critical analysis of [the Corps'] economic claims by those opposing the project . . . should also be included in any complete impact statement." [102] The court added that contentions by ordinary lay citizens opposing the project ought to be included too, even if the agency found no merit in them.[103]

Committee for Nuclear Responsibility, Inc. v. Seaborg (Amchitka). Eight months after Gillham I, environmentalists brought suit to challenge the AEC's detonation of a nuclear device in an underground chamber on Amchitka Island in the Aleutian Islands. It was feared that the detonation might cause a tidal wave and earthquakes, and Congress declared that the AEC was to proceed with the test only if the president expressly authorized it. Litigation over the test produced several D.C. District and Circuit Court rulings, and was argued at a rare Saturday session of the Supreme Court.

The D.C. Circuit was less concerned with the AEC's discussion of alternatives than it was with the omission from the impact statement of the views of scientists who disagreed with the Commission as to the likely outcome of the detonation. The disclosure requirements were somewhat narrower, however, than those that had been set forth in the Gillham I opinion. The court declared that only "responsible" opposing views had to be included. They did not have to be set forth at length, but merely referred to in a meaningful way.[104] The D.C. Circuit was concerned with differences in opinion regarding environmental impacts, not differences over viable alternatives. When certain judges sought in later cases to narrow agency obligations to discuss alternatives, they applied the standard cited above to excuse brief discussions of alternatives to proposed action.

WHEN SHOULD STATEMENTS BE PREPARED?

The courts held that impact statements must be prepared at the earliest possible time for every distinct stage of agency decision making.[105] In Calvert Cliffs the court ruled that environmental impacts had to be considered at every stage where overall balancing of environmental and nonenvironmental factors was appropriate and where actions might be modified to minimize their environmental costs.[106] Another court stated that a statement had to be prepared at the earliest practicable moment,[107] while a third stated that a statement was required once a project had reached "a coherent stage of development." [108]

Program Statements. The fact that every action involved in the early planning of a project might not be sufficiently distinctive to require an impact statement—although such planning might be important in establishing the outer boundaries of future inquiry—led to suggestions that environmental impact statements be prepared in tiers.[109] Impact statements of only limited specificity would be prepared at the broadest levels of program formulation, in accordance with NEPA's requirement that statements be prepared for "programs," and statements would then be prepared at each succeeding level of specification down to the particular projects that were a part of the larger program. Such a pattern of statement preparation would help to identify areas of potential environmental impact that might require continuing research. It would also preclude, hopefully, commitment of millions of dollars to a technology or plan of action that would later be terminated because severe, adverse environmental impacts were recognized at a later stage. Moreover, such an approach to the impact statement preparation process would be economical—certain issues that were addressed repeatedly in impact statements prepared for individual actions within a particular class would, in the future, be addressed in "generic" or "overview" statements for that class—the issues would then no longer be argued in statement after statement. An example of such program statement preparation was provided by the Bonneville Power Administration, which prepared an "overview" statement for its entire program each fiscal year supplemented by statements providing detailed information on specific projects.

CEQ endorsed the concept of program statements in its May

16, 1972 memorandum to agencies. CEQ noted that program statements might discourage "duplicative reconsideration of basic policy questions," and would promote consideration of cumulative environmental impacts that might be ignored in statements prepared on a case-by-case basis.[110]

SIPI v. AEC. The leading decision on the impact statement timing issue was *Scientists' Institute for Public Information (SIPI) v. AEC.*[111] It resulted from a 1971 challenge by SIPI to the AEC's refusal to prepare an impact statement for its Liquid Metal Fast Breeder Reactor (LMFBR) research and development program.

Environmentalists were concerned that too great a portion of the federal energy research budget was spent on a breeder technology frought with considerable environmental risk and that too small a portion was spent on more benign energy technologies. They felt that the federal government had not engaged in a sufficiently careful evaluation of the available energy alternatives. The environmentalists initiated legal action seeking AEC preparation of an LMFBR program statement that would examine the long-range environmental implications of the operation of many commercial breeder reactors and compare them with the environmental impacts of alternative technologies.

The environmentalists were unsuccessful at the district court level. The D.C. Circuit reversed the lower court, and Judge Skelly Wright, speaking for the three judge panel, ordered preparation of an LMFBR program statement. Judge Wright contended that there were two principal NEPA questions: must the AEC issue an impact statement for the entire program, or would statements for individual LMFBR facilities suffice; and assuming that a program statement must be developed, had the time come for one to be prepared? Judge Wright observed that agencies need not engage in crystal ball inquiries, and that statements prepared too early in a research and development program might resemble the work of Jules Verne or H. G. Wells.

But he also noted that if statements were not prepared until proliferating commercial breeder reactors were our most readily accessible energy sources, many less risky but comparatively underdeveloped energy options might be precluded from serious consideration as alternatives to the breeders.

Judge Wright found considerable support in NEPA's language and legislative history both for the programmatic statement concept and for its application to the LMFBR effort. As to the timing of statement preparation, he stated that the court would have to weigh four factors: how likely is the technology to prove commercially feasible and how soon will that be; to what extent is meaningful information presently available on the effects of application of the technology and of alternatives and their effects; to what extent are irretrievable commitments being made and options precluded as the developmental program progresses; and how severe will the environmental effects be if the technology does prove commercially feasible?

HOW SHOULD THE PUBLIC BE INVOLVED?

The preceding sections indicated some of the guidance the courts provided regarding public participation. For example, the courts in the Gillham I and Amchitka decisions required agencies to present, note, or discuss public views, and the 2d Circuit in Hanly II suggested a role for the public in threshold decision making. The public could find in many other decisions additional support for its important role in the impact statement process.

HOW SHOULD STATEMENTS BE REVIEWED?

The courts paid little attention to the review of impact statements by other agencies. Only one court, in *Sierra Club* v. *Froehlke*, addressed that issue at length. The court suggested that reviewing agencies might be required to conduct on-site review visits and that comments should be directed at a project's environmental impact.[112]

NEPA Water Resource Development Project Litigation—1970 to 1973

The section that follows summarizes the course of NEPA litigation involving water resource development projects from 1970 to 1973. A considerable portion of environmentalist NEPA litigation was directed against the water resource development projects of the Corps of Engineers, with a much lesser portion directed against the projects of three other agencies: the Tennessee Valley Authority, the Soil Conservation Service and the Bureau of Reclamation.

Litigation over water resource projects provides a microcosmic view of NEPA's interpretation by the courts. Among the matters dealt with were whether and how NEPA applied to projects begun before 1970; how NEPA related to the process of congressional appropriations for and authorization and oversight of projects; and what constituted an adequate impact statement in scope, objectivity and treatment of outside comments.[113] In their decisions, the courts often conducted a lengthy review of prepared environmental impact statements, prompted by plaintiffs' allegations of statement inadequacy. Through this process, the courts developed ad hoc guidelines for impact statement content and for procedural compliance with NEPA.

The water resource litigation also demonstrates how early district court decisions had considerable precedential value because appellate court decisions were absent; how both district and appellate courts sternly dismissed overt agency efforts to avoid compliance with NEPA; how, at the same time, district and appellate courts refused environmentalists' requests for injunctions when agencies conceded in court the need for NEPA compliance; and how environmentalist courtroom success diminished as agencies produced increasingly detailed environmental statements presenting substantive judgments that judges declined to overturn.

The strong court decisions of 1971 and early 1972 created a legal environment that served, undoubtedly, both to encourage environmentalist lawsuits against water resource development projects, and to promote agency procedural compliance with NEPA designed to lessen the risk of suit. In contrast, the courts' general rejection in 1973 of environmentalists' calls for additional judicial activism demonstrated the judiciary's reluctance to reverse agencies' substantive judgments.

Most of the litigation was undertaken by the Environmental Defense Fund, with many of the remaining suits initiated by the Sierra Club, Natural Resources Defense Council, and the National Wildlife Federation. Only a few cases were brought by landowners whose motivations might have been more economic than environmental, and some of these landowners were joined in their suits by environmentally concerned individuals. Environmentalist predominance in NEPA water resources litigation was reflective of all NEPA litigation.

ENVIRONMENTALIST COMPLAINTS

Benefit-Cost Ratio. In almost all cases, litigants challenged the benefit-cost justification of water resource projects. Benefit-cost ratios were utilized by agencies to assess the economic viability of proposed projects, consonant with the statement of policy in the Flood Control Act of 1936 that the benefits of proposed projects should exceed their costs. Litigants argued that projects were justified using an unrealistically low discount rate. In many cases, projects authorized in the 1940s and 1950s at low discount rates had no construction work undertaken until the late 1960s or early 1970s.[114] By this time, even though the statutory discount rate had risen, older projects were protected against reevaluation at the higher rates by "grandfather" clauses in federal regulations. Many projects, particularly those of marginal benefit-cost justification, might not have been constructed if they were reevaluated at the elevated discount rate.[115]

A second component of the attack on benefit-cost justification pertained to estimated project life. Some projects were planned with a hundred year life and others with a fifty year life. For benefit-cost purposes, the longer the project life, the higher the benefit-cost ratio was likely to be because while most costs accrued at a project's outset, benefits were returned during the many years of project operation; the more years of operation, the greater the benefits. Environmentalists argued that projects that were planned with a hundred year lifetime should only have been planned for a fifty year lifetime, thereby lowering their benefit-cost justification.

A third component of the attack on benefit-cost ratios involved quantification of environmental benefits and costs. Environmentalists often claimed that certain environmental impacts were quantified because they could be counted as project benefits, but that other environmental impacts, such as loss of natural stream recreation opportunities, were not quantified, because they counted as costs.

Statement Content. When environmental impact statements had been prepared, environmentalists often contended that the statements inadequately described project impacts and did not mention or were not responsive to outside criticism. They also maintained that the impact statements represented post hoc rationalizations.

Plaintiffs often complained that the development agencies inadequately investigated alternatives to their proposed actions. One alternative often ignored was stream preservation. This alternative encompassed several varieties of flood protection—flood insurance, flood proofing, government acquisition of the flood plain—all of which did not involve massive construction efforts.

Plaintiffs also noted that wildlife agency suggestions for mitigating project impacts were often unheeded. In channelizing projects, mitigation might mean modifying the channelization method or acquiring land to replace the wildlife-supporting land that was drained. Sometimes these mitigation alternatives were rejected outright by development agencies. Other times they were accepted but only as possible future actions dependent upon congressional funding. Unfortunately, when land acquisition was planned to follow rather than precede or occur concurrently with channelization, the amount of mitigation land available was limited because channelization raised land values in an area.

Scope of Review. Plaintiffs also argued that agencies had to comply with both NEPA's Section 102 procedural requirements and with the Section 101 substantive policy goals. Environmentalists pressed the courts to declare that the substantive obligations were as judicially reviewable as the procedural obligations. Compliance with NEPA would be meaningless, it was maintained, if agencies merely prepared impact statements without incorporating the gathered data into their substantive decision making.

NEPA WATER RESOURCE DEVELOPMENT PROJECT LITIGATION—1970 TO 1971

Litigation in 1970 and 1971 was concerned mostly with projects for which only a short, token statement had been filed, which an agency contended was adequate, and projects for which no statement had been prepared. The enjoining of work on the Gila River in June 1970 marked the first NEPA-based injunction granted against a water resource development project.[116] The opinion here, like many others in this two-year period, was brief. In the following year plaintiffs obtained preliminary injunctions in most of their litigation efforts—the Cross-Florida Barge Canal,[117] Gillham Dam,[118] Cooper Dam,[119] East Fork of the Little Miami River,[120] and the Tennessee-

Tombigbee Waterway.[121] A preliminary injunction was denied in the Kickapoo River-La Farge Dam case.[122]

In those decisions, the courts tended to reject efforts to obtain judicial review of agency benefit-cost calculations. Citing precedents dating to 1941, judges declared that benefit-cost ratios were solely the concern of Congress and the courts were not to interfere.

The Gillham I opinion of Judge Eisele of the Eastern District of Arkansas was the lengthiest of the opinions produced in this period. As previously noted, it marked the first judicial effort to undertake in-depth review of an agency impact statement for a water resource development project. In the course of his review, Judge Eisele established that certain matters would have to be discussed if an impact statement was to be regarded as adequately complying with NEPA.

The courts also uniformly rejected environmentalists' contentions that agencies' actions would have to be adjudged for their compliance with the substantive requirements of Section 101 as well as with the procedural requirements of Section 102.

Two of the decisions, Gillham I and Cross-Florida Barge Canal, enjoined projects in which the Corps of Engineers had already invested considerable money. The rationale underlying both injunctions was that before additional public funds were invested, an evaluation was required to determine whether future investments would be worthwhile. In both cases, an injunction was not regarded as delaying construction and raising costs, but as providing an opportunity for a reevaluation of project justification. One might surmise that the operative logic was similar to that evidenced in the later I-66 highway decision—because environmental protection was of such high priority, a project could be enjoined unless it was evident that the benefits that the public would derive from it would clearly outweigh the costs to the public of its continued progress.

NEPA WATER RESOURCE DEVELOPMENT PROJECT
LITIGATION—1972

The year 1971 was one of considerable environmentalist success in the courts, as indicated by the many preliminary injunctions obtained and the few denied. The following year was less successful. Several injunctions were granted from January to December, but alongside these stood several opinions in which injunctions were denied and narrow interpretations of NEPA were developed.

Environmentalists obtained injunctions against the TVA's Tellico Dam in January,[123] SCS' channelization of Chicod Creek[124] and the Corps' channelization of the Obion-Forked Deer Rivers[125] in March, and the Corps' channelization of the Cache River Watershed in December.[126] The common denominators of most of these cases were agencies' recalcitrance in applying NEPA and their raising litigation arguments contrary to the thrust of NEPA. In the Tellico Dam case, although a draft impact statement had been completed, TVA argued that NEPA did not apply to the project. For the Chicod Creek channelization, SCS had not prepared an impact statement even upon request. In the Obion-Forked Deer River and Cache River Watersheds, for which mitigation plans still had not been completed, the Corps was proceeding with channelization over the objections of state wildlife agencies.

In the larger number of cases, involving the Corps' Truman,[127] Laneport,[128] New Melones,[129] La Farge[130] and New Hope Dams,[131] environmentalists were denied preliminary injunctions. For some of those the Corps prepared voluminous final environmental impact statements. For others, no impact statements at all were prepared but the Corps conceded their necessity, or draft impact statements had been prepared and final statements were promised by a stipulated date. By middle and late 1972, many courts seemed to be operating on different assumptions from those held by injunction-granting courts in 1971. The status of compliance was somewhat different, certainly, but it also seemed that courts were assuming that construction would ultimately occur, even after environmental impact analyses were undertaken. The judicial reasoning seemed to be that if alternatives were not foreclosed by, and environmental damage did not result from continuing work while a final impact statement was prepared, resources were not wasted because construction would ultimately occur. Delay meant cost inflation, and that outweighed the cost to the environment of continued construction.

In 1972 also, a second round of litigation occurred involving projects that had been halted in 1971: Gillham Dam[132] and the Tennessee-Tombigbee Waterway.[133] In both instances, the courts were willing to provide a searching review of voluminous final environmental statements, but they indicated that perfection in environmental analysis could not be expected and would not be demanded. As long as analyses were comprehensive, objective, and provided a record on which future decision makers could base a judgment, the courts would declare agencies to be in compliance with NEPA.

There were also examples in 1972 of questionable judicial judgment. For example, in the New Hope Dam case, the judge found the impact statement discussion of alternatives adequate. He stated that the Corps did not have to describe alternatives in detail, because consonant with the Amchitka decision, an agency merely had to make meaningful reference to responsible opposing points of view. The court clearly misapplied the Amchitka standard, which was designed to be applied to disputes over environmental impacts rather to disputes over alternatives. That standard was inappropriate for the evaluation of alternatives; if alternatives were merely referenced without detailed discussion, subsequent decision makers would not be presented with sufficient information to assure them that an agency had made a serious attempt to study proposed alternatives and had made the best choice among them. NEPA litigation contains sufficient examples of agency bad faith that the discussion of alternatives in the New Hope Dam opinion has to be regarded as somewhat misguided.

Environmentalists continued to press their claims in 1972 for substantive court review of agency NEPA decisions. For most of the year the courts refused to review substantively, although the district court in the Tennessee-Tombigbee case engaged in substantive review under the guise of checking the final environmental statement for its procedural compliance with NEPA. Environmentalists finally succeeded on the substantive review issue when the 8th Circuit, in its review of the district court's Gillham II decision, declared that it had the right to review agencies' decisions for their compliance with the substantive policies of NEPA's Section 101.[134] The review would be based on "substantial inquiry" to see whether agencies' decisions were arbitrary and capricious, though the court could not substitute its judgment for the agencies'. The court recognized it was breaking new ground, so it devoted a considerable portion of its opinion to this question, seeking to find "precedent" in earlier decisions. The 8th Circuit reached this conclusion in November, but when the 6th Circuit reviewed the preliminary injunction against the Tellico Dam three weeks later, it was not prepared to rule on whether substantive review was appropriate.[135]

Throughout 1972, also, environmentalists pressed their benefit-cost review arguments. Their views were universally rejected. However, some seeds of a breakthrough were planted by the 8th Circuit when, in December, in its Cache River opinion,[136] it again considered the substantive review question. It indicated that a court could not review the balance of costs and benefits struck by the Corps for its compliance with the congressional declaration of intent, found in the Flood Control Act of 1936, that project benefits exceed costs. The 8th Circuit declared, however, that the benefit-cost balance was reviewable through the vehicle of NEPA. The agency would have to reevaluate the balance of benefits and costs struck in light of NEPA's policies. The court could then examine the agency decision to see whether the balance of costs and benefits had been arbitrarily struck.[137]

Moreover in 1972 courts began to advise environmentalists that the judiciary had limited ability to influence agency policy and that plaintiffs should look elsewhere if they wished to substantively alter federal water resource development policy. Judge Eisele in his Gillham II opinion urged environmentalist reliance on the executive and legislative decision-making process, and Judge Oliver in his Truman Dam opinion made explicit reference to congressional restiveness over environmentalists' judicial victories.[138]

NEPA WATER RESOURCE DEVELOPMENT PROJECT
LITIGATION—1973

The 8th Circuit, in its Cache River and Gillham Dam opinions, laid the groundwork for NEPA-justified substantive judicial review of agency action. Water resource development project decisions in 1973 demonstrated how substantial this judicial review could be in some instances and how restrained it could be in others.

The year 1973, like 1972, was one of mixed successes and failures for environmentalists. As in 1972, they won a few additional arguments in terms of extending the scope of review, but they also lost major cases and found themselves subjected to judicial criticism.

In 1973, environmentalists obtained injunctions against the Corps' New Hope[139] and Wallisville Dams,[140] and SCS' channelization of Blue Eye Creek in Alabama,[141] and gained a continued delay in channelization of Chicod Creek.[142] However, they lost in further attempts to enjoin construction of the New Melones[143] and Truman Dams,[144] they failed to block construction of the Corps' Gathright Dam,[145] and they found the injunction against the Tellico Dam dissolved when the TVA presented the courts with a massive final environmental statement for the project.[146]

Two strands of judicial decision making flowed from the 8th Circuit's Cache River decision. Expansive readings of it are found in the environmentalist victories in the Wallisville Dam-Trinity River Project, and the Blue Eye Creek cases. Narrow interpretations are identifiable in the environmentalist losses in the Gathright Dam and Tellico Dam cases.

In the Wallisville case,[147] District Judge Bue wrote an opinion about ten times the length of other courts' NEPA opinions, subjecting to close judicial scrutiny the entire Corps administrative record pertaining to the Wallisville Dam and Trinity River Project. He presented a detailed critique of Corps benefit-cost analysis procedures, while taking issue with Judge Eisele's contention in Gillham I that these procedures were highly esoteric matters not to be interfered with by the courts.[148] Judge Bue's criticism of the Corps' analytical procedures was similar to complaints about the techniques made by most plaintiffs in Corps-NEPA cases.

In the Wallisville opinion, Judge Bue questioned the project life and discount rate used in the benefit-cost calculations, but did not make a final determination as to whether those for the project were arbitrary. In *Montgomery* v. *Ellis*,[149] the challenge to Blue Eye Creek channelization, Judge Guin took the next step, ruling that in its project planning, SCS had used unrealistic discount rates and project lives. Because they were unrealistic, SCS decisions based on them constituted an arbitrary balancing of economic benefits and environmental costs.

A more restrained approach to judicial review was adopted by the Gathright court. Gathright Dam had a marginal 1.1:1 benefit-cost ratio, one of the lowest of all active Corps projects. Forty percent of the project benefits were attributed to water quality improvement, and the EPA administrator declared that most of the water quality benefits were unjustly claimed. In this case, however, Judge Dalton sought to avoid the difficult benefit-cost issues addressed by Judges Bue and Guin; he stated that certain aspects of the benefit-cost ratio were not reviewable. These nonreviewable matters, coincidentally, were those which were most substantively questionable.[150]

Court opinions in 1973 continued to reflect differing judicial standards for judging agency compliance with NEPA. For example, the Wallisville court stressed the articulation of agency reasoning in impact statements, and laid down guidelines for agency response to opposing views.[151] That was in considerable contrast to the Gillham II decision the preceding year, where a compilation of opposing points of view in an unindexed appendix satisfied the disclosure requirements of NEPA.[152]

The view that the courts had to act to protect environmental quality because it was such a high congressional priority was restated in the Wallisville Dam decision.[153] But in some other decisions, environmentalists found themselves subjected to significant judicial criticism. The same 6th Circuit that spoke in its 1972 Tellico decision of the importance of environmental protection criticized EDF in its 1973 opinion for raising overly technical and hypercritical objections.[154] Further, Judge Oliver, in a second Truman Dam decision, restated his concern for congressional resentment of the judiciary, and he chastized environmentalists for their attempts to block projects through the courts.[155]

Some Concluding Observations

The early 1970s saw environmentalists carving for themselves an important niche in agency politics by manipulating the resources of the judiciary to their advantage. The importance of the environmental interests and the seeming lack of agency response to NEPA produced in many instances judicial decisions requiring strict agency compliance with the statute. Some courts were not as demanding as others, but there were enough tough decisions delivered requiring agency response that agencies could no longer afford to ignore NEPA blithely. The water resource development cases show a definite trend in judicial decision making, with decisions hardest on the agencies coming in 1971 and 1972 and the courts showing considerable moderation, for the most part, by the end of 1973.

The specific impact of particular decisions can be clearly identified. For example, the Calvert Cliffs and Greene County decisions produced changes in the administrative practices of the AEC and the FPC. The court decisions in the Obion-Forked Deer River and Cache River Watershed cases led to congressional actions the following year requiring the Corps of Engineers to devote a specific and sizeable portion of its yearly project appropriations for acquisition of mitigation lands. Even where the ultimate decision to proceed with a project was unaffected by judicial decision, as in the case of Gillham Dam, the legal interpretations developed in the course of the litigation significantly influenced later judicial decisions.

The role of the courts is best appreciated in the context of the administrative behavior theory reviewed in the preceding chapter. When NEPA was enacted, agencies were presented a new law whose import for their daily activities was largely undefined. NEPA's meaning was clarified as courts showed considerable willingness to overrule deliberate agency efforts to undermine the statute. The Act's requirements were further elaborated as courts ruled on environmentalists' lawsuits alleging that agencies' procedural efforts insufficiently carried out the congressional mandate. The willingness of courts generally to define NEPA's procedural requirements, to require impact statements for a broad range of actions, and to set criteria for impact statement adequacy, meant that agencies had to adapt their behavior to a new legal environment. Agencies could no longer be insulated from considering environmental impacts merely because they or their principal clientele had little concern for such matters; environmentalists could force such considerations onto agencies' agendas. As more and more NEPA-based court decisions favorable to environmentalists were reported, concerned citizens were provided with an even larger legal reservoir from whose resources they could draw.

CEQ endeavored to alert agencies to the changing judicial requirements by circulating the leading opinions to agency offices and by incorporating the leading judicial interpretations into its guidelines. Agencies seeking to adapt to the changing legal environment, who sought to buffer potential thrusts from it, could attempt to anticipate citizen intervention and adverse judicial reaction by making an effort to comply procedurally with the statute. This effort to comply procedurally did not always augur a change in substantive agency policy, but as much of the later water resources development litigation shows, it often provided a successful first line of defense against environmentalist lawsuits alleging procedural noncompliance with NEPA.

6

Congressional
Reconsideration
of NEPA

The unanticipated consequences of NEPA's enactment, brought about by environmentalists' success in mounting legal challenges to administrative actions, prompted a congressional reaction directed against NEPA and citizen suits. This negative sentiment, most evident in 1972, was concentrated among small segments of Congress, principally in the Public Works, Agriculture, and Atomic Energy Committees, who saw their favorite programs threatened by environmentalists' courtroom victories.

Major efforts to amend NEPA emanated as well from the executive branch. CEQ and EPA proposed amendments to exempt selected EPA activities from NEPA's reach, and CEQ supported congressional efforts to modify the statute's impact on the AEC.

The resentment directed at NEPA apparently developed during the latter half of 1971. The AEC's regulations were overturned by the D.C. Circuit in July, the Corps of Engineers' Tennessee-Tombigbee Waterway was enjoined in September, and the Bureau of Land Management's off-shore lease sales were delayed in December. Together with the halting of the Cross-Florida Barge Canal and continuation of an injunction against the trans-Alaskan pipeline, those events produced considerable restlessness in the Public Works Committees. Those committees were subsequently joined by EPA and CEQ in their discontent with NEPA-based court decisions, when in the Kalur case in December, the D.C. District Court appeared to threaten the entire future of the administration's Refuse Act Permit Program. The Kalur decision, elements of the Calvert Cliffs decision, and a second questioning of AEC licensing procedures in the December Quad Cities decision prompted both CEQ and EPA to support legislation to moderate NEPA's impact.[1]

Efforts to limit NEPA's scope and the role of citizen litigation assumed three principal forms. First, attempts were made to terminate existing injunctions or preclude future ones by removing enjoined or threatened projects from federal court jurisdiction. Second, for specific programs, efforts were made to establish environmental evaluation procedures independent of NEPA's and projects formulated under the procedures would be exempted from NEPA's environmental impact statement requirements. Third, Congress considered placing restrictions on citizens' rights to sue for environmental ends.

Environmental interests were active in the fight over NEPA and citizen suits. Environmental lawyer Anthony Roisman and others concerned with the threat to NEPA established a SAVE NEPA coalition on April 11, 1972, that coordinated efforts to protect the law. Environmental lobbyists appeared at numerous congressional hearings and played a key role in defusing administrative attempts to avoid court-established obligations under the Act. They contended that administrative rule changes, rather than statutory changes, would suffice to overcome the administrative backlogs blamed on NEPA.

Congressman Dingell was NEPA's principal congressional defender. His strategy was to introduce bills providing relief from court-imposed NEPA requirements but which granted it in the narrowest of forms. He hoped these bills would reduce anti–NEPA congressional sentiment and would preclude passage of wide-ranging NEPA exemptions. They would also provide a precedent for having all bills amending NEPA pass through his subcommittee. Congressman Dingell's efforts were criticized by environmentalists, who regarded even the most narrow of NEPA amendments as precedent for future exemptions.

Exemption of Projects from Federal Court Jurisdiction

Efforts to provide project-specific exemptions from NEPA were presaged in a transcript of a spring 1972 House Public Works Committee executive session.[2] Public Works Committee members, not aware their remarks would be made public, spoke disparagingly of federal judges while discussing exemption of projects from NEPA. Acting Chairman Bob Jones, for example, annoyed by the injunction against the Tennessee-Tombigbee Waterway, stated that "you . . . have a bunch of ignoramuses who are judges who are not respecting what has been done here [in committee] . . . ." He added that lawsuits "are being maliciously used to halt the projects that Congress has worked for years and years to accomplish."

While venting their anger, committee members sought methods for circumventing NEPA. Congressman Jim Wright, a senior committee member, spoke of finding "something that will shortstop all of these little pestiferous suits that are hamstringing the programs." Committee members realized they could not directly amend NEPA because it lay outside their jurisdiction, so they discussed the possibility of exempting from it individual projects or projects authorized under broad highway and river and harbor legislation. They also considered demanding environmental statements from agencies commenting on proposed legislation. Their insistence on this procedure, they believed, would impose a heavy burden on the federal bureaucracy and would prompt administrative efforts to seek NEPA's amendment.

THE SAN ANTONIO NORTH EXPRESSWAY

The Federal Aid Highway Act considered by both Public Works Committees provided a vehicle for one of the first attempts to provide a project-specific exemption from NEPA. Provisions of both the House and Senate bills terminated the contract under which the federal government provided Highway Trust Fund revenues for the completion of the San Antonio North Expressway.[3] Road construction had been blocked by the 5th Circuit Court of Appeals on the grounds of administrative noncompliance with NEPA and other statutes.[4] Deletion of the road from the federal interstate system and its construction with state funds would remove it from federal court jurisdiction, thereby mooting the environmentalist-initiated court case.

Congressman Dingell endeavored to eliminate the San Antonio North Expressway provision from the highway bill on the House floor.[5] He believed that the provision's enactment would establish a precedent for exempting future projects from NEPA. He was supported by EPA and CEQ, which were also concerned about the precedent-setting effect of the proposed provision.[6] Although he had administration support, Congressman Dingell failed.[7]

In the Senate, the struggle to delete the provision was led by Senator James Buckley, a member of Senator Jackson's committee and an ardent NEPA supporter. Senator Buckley, too, was concerned with the provision's precedent-setting impact, and he conveyed his reservations in a lengthy floor statement. He stated that it would have a nationwide impact and would threaten the effectiveness of environmental statutes. He added that its passage would encourage other exemption efforts and would signal the agencies and courts that Congress had begun to turn its back on environmental protection. He concluded that its enactment would "hold out hope" to those wishing to avoid compliance, that if they resisted long enough they might be rescued by special legislation.[8]

Senator Buckley, like Representative Dingell, was unsuccessful in his efforts to have the provision deleted.[9] However, the conference approved highway bill containing the provision died when the House concluded its legislative session without voting on it.[10] The provision was resurrected in the 93rd Congress and was enacted as Section 154(a) of the Federal Aid Highway Act of 1973.[11]

HARRY TRUMAN DAM PROJECT

Congressman Randall's H.R.17156 provided that no court could issue a ruling impeding work on any Corps of Engineers project authorized prior to NEPA's enactment if 10 percent of the total authorized cost, or $15 million, whichever was greater, had already been spent on the project. The Randall bill was a direct response to EDF's lawsuit challenging the Corps' construction in Randall's district of the Harry Truman Dam Project. Its provisions would have exempted the Truman Dam and ninety-three other Corps projects from the reach of the federal courts.[12] It was introduced only a few days prior to adjournment of the 92d Congress and was never acted upon by the Judiciary Committee. It was reintroduced into the 93d Congress,[13] but again was never acted upon, presumably because the failure of EDF's challenge eliminated the need for it.

Project and Program Exemption by Establishment of Environmental Evaluation Procedures

Four series of bills sought to limit NEPA's impact by establishing alternative, substitute environmental evaluation procedures. Projects approved under these procedures would be exempted from NEPA's environmental impact statement requirement. One such series of bills, the Public Works and Regional Development Acts of 1972, provided for establishment of regional development commissions. The commissions would be authorized to provide in excess of $7.5 billion for public works projects.[14] After consultation with EPA and other agencies, they would promulgate guidelines designed to assure that possible adverse economic, social, and environmental effects of a proposed project had been fully considered in project development.[15] Any project determined by a commission as having been developed in compliance with these guidelines would be deemed to have satisfied the requirements of Section 102(2)(C) of NEPA.[16] These public works bills were never enacted and were reintroduced into the 93d Congress.[17]

POWER PLANT SITING

A second series of bills that seemed to provide exemption from the impact statement process were those regulating power plant siting. Increasing controversy over the location of generating stations prompted several competing proposals to simplify the siting process.[18] The administration proposed that a federal site certifying agency, a Department of Natural Resources, would establish guidelines governing the conduct of state or regional site certifying agencies to whom primary responsibility would be given for control of siting.[19] The Department of Natural Resources would be relieved from the impact statement preparation obligation when state agencies had observed a "substantially comparable procedure." [20] This NEPA exemption provision did not attract attention when it was first proposed in February 1971, prior to the major developments in NEPA litigation noted earlier. However, when Senate hearings on power plant siting were held in 1972, several environmental witnesses expressed opposition to the NEPA exemption.[21] That proposal appeared to weaken NEPA because it provided for an exemption from the Act. However, a CEQ staff member contended in an interview that this provision actually extended NEPA's scope, because it had the effect of requiring state certifying agencies to prepare documents analogous to NEPA-required environmental impact statements. The CEQ staff member conceded, however, that the proposal was poorly drafted and thus could be read as providing solely for an exemption from NEPA without establishing an equally strong alternative mechanism.[22]

No power plant siting measures were reported from committee in the 92d Congress, for reasons not germane to this discussion. A new administration siting bill, in which the language of the NEPA-related provision was clarified, was introduced into the 93d Congress.[23]

PROGRAM EXEMPTION FOR THE AEC AND EPA

Two series of bills exempting entire programs from selected NEPA requirements were rooted in court challenges to the AEC and EPA. The Calvert Cliffs court had held that for nuclear power plant licensing determinations, NEPA required the AEC, among other things, to evaluate critically the water quality certifications of state and federal water pollution control agencies—the AEC could impose stricter effluent standards than those required by these agencies. The Quad Cities court, five months later, threatened the AEC's efforts to overcome the licensing backlog created by the Calvert Cliffs decision.[24] The AEC had sought to expedite licensing by issuing interim operating licenses without public hearings or impact statements. The CEQ agreed with the new rules. In response to an environmentalist lawsuit, the D.C. District Court forbade the issuance of interim operating licenses for two nuclear power plants, holding that environmental impact statements for them had to be prepared. Finally, in the Kalur case,[25] EPA was in effect enjoined from issuing permits for major discharges of pollutants into navigable waters until impact statements for the permits were written.

Legislative Relief for the AEC. Senator Baker of Tennessee, with Senator Jackson's support, initiated efforts to override that portion of the Calvert Cliffs decision pertaining to AEC evaluation of water quality impacts. On November 2, 1971, he submitted an amendment to S.2770, the Federal Water Pollution Control Act Amendments of 1972 (the FWPCA).[26] The amendment provided that the AEC would not have to set effluent standards independent of those established in discharge permits issued by state or federal water pollution control agencies. A provision similar to Baker's was included in the FWPCA reported to the House floor, where attempts to delete it were defeated.[27]

Senators Baker and Jackson contended that the AEC would still have to add water quality impacts to its benefit-cost calculations for power plants.[28] AEC supporters on the Joint Committee on Atomic Energy, in contrast, saw the Baker amendment as removing water quality considerations entirely from the AEC decision-making calculus once a license applicant received certification from a water pollution control agency.[29] The amendment was included in both the House and Senate bills, but the dispute over its exact meaning left it with a muddled legislative history.[30]

Legislative Relief for EPA. Initial efforts to overcome the impact of the Kalur decision originated within the executive branch. In early February, CEQ appealed to the House Public Works Committee to include in the FWPCA an exemption for EPA discharge permit decisions from NEPA's impact statement provision. The Council also requested that it be given the power to exempt "environmentally protective regulatory actions" from the Section 102(2)(C) requirements.[31] CEQ's request was denied by the House Public Works Committee staff, which wished to avoid reopening hearings on the FWPCA, and which reportedly felt that any exemption from NEPA should, for jurisdictional reasons, be considered by the Dingell and Jackson committees.

CEQ next sought action from the Dingell subcommittee. For discussion purposes only, Congressman Dingell introduced H.R.14103, a narrowly worded resolution that would have provided EPA with partial, temporary relief from the Section 102(2)(C) requirements.[32] At hearings on the measure, EPA argued that the temporary exemption was necessary to prevent its discharge permit program from becoming mired in procedural requirements. John Quarles, EPA's assistant administrator for enforcement, attempted to distinguish EPA's fears of procedural delay from similar concerns voiced by the AEC prior to the Calvert Cliffs decision. He contended that with regard to the permit program, achievement of NEPA's environmental protection goals was frustrated by NEPA's procedural requirements.[33] He noted that administrative rule changes, suggested by environmentalists as alternative, nonstatutory means for circumventing the Kalur decision, probably could not withstand a legal challenge.[34] Quarles added that every day of delay in issuing permits, caused by impact statement preparation needs, meant an added day of delay in initiating pollution abatement.[35]

That logic did not appeal to environmentalists, who vigorously opposed even a temporary exemption. The SAVE NEPA coalition actively opposed H.R.14103 and other NEPA exemption bills, and its activities were reported in detail in the environmentalist press.[36] The environmentalists testified before congressional committees and met with senators, congressmen, and their staffs. They also wrote floor statements for environmentalist congressmen to use in developing court-interpretable legislative histories on NEPA-exemption legislation.[37]

The environmentalists viewed all exemption requests with suspicion, for they saw NEPA as a statute that promoted sound, open government decision making.[38] They believed that enactment of the EPA exemption would add momentum to the movement to gut NEPA and that the exemption would not even serve the purposes EPA attributed to it.[39] EPA's request for legislative relief was seen as directly comparable to other agency exemption requests that the environmentalists had seen or expected to see.[40] They did not like it. In the view of SAVE NEPA's Anthony Roisman, EPA was more recalcitrant in its implementation of NEPA than even the AEC; whereas the AEC had not appealed the Calvert Cliffs decision and promptly developed new NEPA implementing guidelines, EPA chose to appeal Kalur, and waited two months to file its notice of appeal with the circuit court. Roisman commented that EPA was not entitled to special congressional relief, because it had created an emergency situation from which it was now trying to derive legislative benefits.[41]

The environmentalists' ire was not directed solely at EPA; they were angry at CEQ. In a letter to Congressman Dingell, Roisman, who had argued the Calvert Cliffs case, accused CEQ of "dereliction of duty." He stated that the Council had become "a chief spokesman for amending NEPA and [had] been notably devoid of any constructive suggestions for administrative solutions to the problems of federal agencies." [42]

Congressman Dingell, for his part, was confronted with a dilemma. He was evidently not anxious to amend NEPA, but he recognized that for strategic purposes, he should establish a precedent of having all NEPA amendments pass through his subcommittee.[43] That was especially important, he realized, because of rising anti-NEPA sentiment in the House. In a colloquy with an environmentalist witness at the H.R.14103 hearing, he explicitly stated his strategic goals:

> I think you observe that I have been faced now twice with substantive amendments to NEPA. I think you ought to be keenly aware of that. I think you ought to be aware that we face similar threats in the future . . . .
>
> I want to ask you: Do you want statutory amendment of NEPA or do you want temporary exemption . . . ?
>
> . . . Where do you want these questions involving the future of

NEPA to be considered, in this committee or in another committee? . . .

You have observed me, and I consider myself not only a subcommittee environmentalist but a jackleg politician, and I recognize the hard facts of life as to how these things should be done—and that my primary concern is a viable intact National Environmental Policy Act.[44]

The environmentalists succeeded in convincing Congressman Dingell to stay further consideration of H.R.14103 pending receipt of the conference report on the FWPCA. The FWPCA was expected to restructure dramatically EPA's entire water quality permit program, and the NEPA exemption issue might conceivably be addressed in this broader legislation. Congressman Dingell would ultimately regret delaying action on his own bill.[45]

The conference committee reached agreement on the FWPCA towards the close of the 92d Congress. Added to a modified version of the Baker amendment was a broadly worded, ambiguous provision exempting a wide range of EPA's activities under the FWPCA from the reach of NEPA.[46] Inserted into the bill late in the conference committee deliberations, the provision was never considered at public hearings. Senator Muskie and his supporters asserted that the provision was designed to exempt most EPA action under the FWPCA from all of NEPA's requirements.[47] This added provision, argued Muskie, merely placed in statutory form his 1969 agreement with Senator Jackson that NEPA did not apply to environmentally protective activities.[48] Senator Jackson and Congressman Dingell, caught by surprise, tried to minimize the scope of the exemption provided. They argued that the conference-inserted provision exempted EPA's actions under the FWPCA only from NEPA's impact statement requirement, and not from other NEPA obligations.[49]

With the enactment of the FWPCA into law, the Environmental Protection Agency became the first agency to win an exemption from NEPA. Congressman Dingell, who had been at odds with environmentalists over the narrow exemption provided EPA by H.R.14103, suggested when the debate was concluded that perhaps the environmentalists would have been wiser to support, rather than oppose, enactment of his narrowly drawn legislation.[50]

More Legislative Relief for the AEC. The dispute over relief for the AEC from the requirements of the Quad Cities decision was similar to the controversy concerning EPA's exemption from the requirements of Kalur.

The AEC had introduced an interim licensing procedure, which it hoped would permit it to process in timely fashion the backlog of license applications resulting from the Calvert Cliffs decision. The Commission instituted the interim licensing procedure when it was advised by the Federal Power Commission that thirteen nuclear plants in the process of being licensed would have to be ready for operation to provide "necessary" power reserves for the peak energy demand periods of summer 1972 and winter 1972–1973.[51] The December 1971 Quad Cities decision, in which it was held that the AEC must prepare impact statements in conjunction with interim licensing, dashed the Commission's hopes of placing two or three of the requisite plants on line by the time they were needed.

The Commission suspected by late January 1972 that the Quad Cities decision might have an adverse impact on energy supplies.[52] However, it was not until six weeks later, in early March, that it submitted interim licensing legislation designed to surmount the identified energy supply problem.[53] The AEC's effort to obtain statutory relief was supported by the CEQ, for the Council had viewed the Commission's post–Calvert Cliffs, pre-Quad Cities licensing regulation as "a reasonable transitional arrangement, compatible with . . . NEPA."[54]

The legislation proposed by the AEC was designed to give it statutory authority to issue interim licenses, authority that had been called into question by the Quad Cities litigation. A companion measure introduced by Congressman Craig Hosmer, an influential member of the Joint Committee on Atomic Energy and an avid proponent of nuclear energy, sought to truncate the licensing procedure by reducing public participation.[55]

Environmentalists' testimony on the interim licensing legislation echoed their remarks on Congressman Dingell's legislation exempting EPA from NEPA. First, they asserted that the legislation was not necessary, for administrative means were available to the AEC for circumventing the Quad Cities decision.[56] Second, they added that the interim licensing law would not significantly contribute to resolving the key problem at issue, for it would assist in placing on line very few of the power plants the FPC and AEC had said were necessary to provide adequate reserve margins.[57] Third, they argued that the AEC proposal, if enacted, would tempt many other agencies to propose NEPA-modifying legislation.[58] Joseph Karaganis, the attorney for the Izaak Walton League in Quad Cities, stated that the proposal would mark the "opening of the floodgates of . . . environmental regression." [59] Fourth, they contended that the proposed legislation would unduly restrict citizen access to the administrative decision-making process.[60]

The Joint Committee on Atomic Energy reported the interim licensing legislation, but it was replete with concessions to the environmentalists insisted upon by committee member Senator Baker.[61] The concessions, most of which loosened the restrictions on citizen participation, rendered ambiguous the procedural changes proposed in the bill.[62] On the House floor, environmentalist congressmen sought to develop a legislative history of the ambiguous bill favorable to public participation, and some of them delivered speeches written by environmental lawyers Anthony Roisman and Myron Cherry.[63] In response, Congressman Hosmer spoke in support of a highly restrictive view of public participation.[64] The bill was passed by both houses of

Congress and signed into law, but its implications were unclear.[65]

The interim licensing measure did not directly amend NEPA and did not explicitly relieve the AEC of responsibility for preparing impact statements for interim licenses. A direct amendment to NEPA permitting interim licensing without completion of the impact statement process was, however, introduced by Congressman Dingell, and it provided for a narrow exemption. The motivation behind the Dingell bill, H.R.13752, was similar to that behind H.R.14103—to stave off stronger attacks on NEPA.[66] H.R.13752 would have permitted the AEC to grant interim operating licenses for nuclear power plants even though final environmental statements for the plants had not been filed. For each plant, the Commission would determine whether plant operation was necessary to meet an energy emergency, and whether licensing would cause a significant, adverse environmental impact.[67]

At the H.R.13752 hearings, Dr. James Schlesinger, chairman of the AEC, conceded that delays in power plant licensing could not be blamed principally on environmentalists.[68] FPC figures cited by Schlesinger revealed that unduly short utility company schedules contributed to delays in ten of the thirteen critically needed plants. Six of the thirteen had suffered from late delivery of equipment. While intervention by private or public organizations was listed as causing delay in eight of the thirteen licensing cases, in no instance was delay due solely to citizen intervention. It was demonstrated that the Quad Cities units that would benefit from interim licensing legislation were delayed because of scheduling, labor, equipment, and regulatory reasons.[69]

The environmentalists' testimony on H.R.13752 was, substantively, a repeat of their remarks on the earlier interim licensing legislation. Over their objections, H.R.13752 was reported to the full House and passed.[70] The bill, however, was defeated in the Senate. The SAVE NEPA coalition produced a

hundred telegrams from environmental organizations supporting its position at a Senate Interior Committee meeting, and
convinced the Committee that the bill would be useless in
enabling AEC and FPC to meet short-term energy demands.
The bill died in the Interior Committee.

Restriction of Citizen Litigation

The extended impact of the citizen lawsuit, particularly in
the arena of environmental protection, prompted some congressional caution in the enactment of new legislation containing
citizen suit provisions. For example, considerable controversy
was generated by efforts to incorporate citizen suit provisions in
proposals for reform of federal pesticide registration and water
pollution control procedures. In both instances, there were
attempts to introduce citizen suit provisions similar to those
included in the 1970 Clean Air Act.[71] The Clean Air Act permits
individuals to sue those who violate it, as well as the EPA
administrator when he has allegedly failed to perform a duty
mandated by the Act. A court is also permitted to award
attorneys fees to the plaintiffs in such suits. Attempts to
introduce provisions such as those into the pesticide and water
pollution control bills were opposed by committees protective of
agricultural and developmental interests.

CITIZEN SUITS AND THE PESTICIDE BILL

The Nixon administration's tough pesticide control proposal
contained citizen suit provisions when it was referred to the
House Agriculture Committee. The administration bill would
have permitted challenges to EPA pesticide rulings by those
"adversely affected" by such determinations.[72] That portion of
the administration bill was not formally labeled a "citizen suit
provision," but under existing doctrines governing standing to
sue, it provided a means for environmentally concerned individ-

uals and groups to challenge EPA pesticide registration orders in court.

The bill ultimately reported by the House Agriculture Committee was quite different from the administration proposal. The committee bill declared that only persons "at interest" to a proceeding, that is, manufacturers, would be granted standing to challenge an EPA order.[73] Environmentalist congressmen, dismayed at that and other committee actions, sought to amend the committee bill on the House floor, but their efforts were rebuffed.[74]

The bill was then referred to the Senate Agriculture Committee. The committee restored the "adversely affected" test for standing and permitted judicial review of all EPA actions taken under the law. However, it rejected a proposal to include even broader citizen suit provisions similar to those in the Clean Air Act. In accordance with an intercommittee agreement, the bill then passed to the Senate Commerce Committee Subcommittee on the Environment, chaired by environmentalist Senator Philip Hart. The Hart subcommittee promptly enlarged the citizen suit provisions by adopting the proposals rejected by the Senate Agriculture Committee.[75] In a printed rebuttal to the Hart subcommittee, the Agriculture Committee opposed the liberalized citizen suit provisions, stating that they "may encourage suits by professional litigants and interfere with the orderly administration of the law." [76] The Agriculture Committee added:

> The courts are already overburdened with judicial responsibilities, so that criminals go untried and unpunished for long periods.
> The courts should not be further burdened with suits by citizens who disagree with the manner in which the President [through EPA] is executing the laws.[77]

After lengthy negotiations between the Senate committees, a compromise on the citizen suit provisions was announced. The substitute bill provided for citizen suits against the EPA administrator for failure to perform mandatory duties, but did not include the Hart subcommittee provisions, which would have permitted citizen suits against manufacturers, distributors, and others, and which would have permitted payment of plaintiffs' attorneys' fees.[78] The compromise Senate view of citizen suits ultimately prevailed in conference over the very restrictive House view.[79]

CITIZEN SUITS AND THE FWPCA

The backlash against citizen lawsuits was evident as well in the House Public Works Committee's treatment of the FWPCA. The Senate version of the FWPCA contained the liberal citizen suit provisions of the Clean Air Act, but the House Public Works Committee incorporated them in a substantially modified form. The House committee's version sought to deliberately restrict environmentalist litigation. It did so by limiting standing to sue to those individuals residing in the geographic area in question who had a direct interest that might be affected by the private or public action being challenged. For groups, it limited standing to those that had been "actively engaged in the administrative process" and had thereby shown a "special interest in the geographic area in controversy." [80] That latter provision was apparently aimed at such successful litigants as the Natural Resources Defense Council and the Environmental Defense Fund, both of which had instituted suit throughout the country but neither of which had been well organized on a regional membership basis.

The weak citizen suit provisions supported by the Public Works Committee majority were attacked in a minority report submitted by committee members Bella Abzug and Charles Rangel.[81] The Abzug-Rangel report criticized the general vagueness of such terms as "geographic area in controversy," "actively engaged," and "special interest." Abzug and Rangel also argued against requiring potential plaintiffs to have actively engaged in the administrative process. They observed that the doctrine of laches provides ample judicial authority for dismissing suits by organizations who have not participated in administrative proceedings. They added that all too often, the administrative process is "clothed in secrecy," or citizen groups do not have time to prepare adequately for participation in a "hurried" administrative procedure. In such instances, having been "edged out" of the administrative proceedings, the groups would also, under the committee bill, be foreclosed from gaining standing to obtain judicial relief.[82] Abzug and Rangel also contended that the question of standing should be left to the courts to determine. They argued that the restricted standing provisions were a "drastic departure from the pattern and policy which the Congress has already adopted to enable citizens to go to court to protect the environment." [83]

The House committee bill also provided for reimbursement of legal fees, but this was not meant to encourage citizen use of the courts, as had similar provisions in the Hart subcommittee's pesticide bill amendments. Rather, those provisions were designed to prevent "frivolous" use of the citizen suit provisions and "needless harassment" of prospective defendants.[84]

Environmentalist congressmen sought to strengthen the weak Public Works Committee version of the FWPCA, but the committee defeated their attempts.[85] Congressman Hosmer of the Joint Committee on Atomic Energy undoubtedly summarized the views of many congressmen who opposed liberalizing the citizen suit provisions when he stated:

We already have itinerant intervenors who go around the country and persons meddling in problems that have significance locally and not nationally . . . if this amendment were adopted, they could take over an installation and hold it for ransom, because of the delay in time involved in the litigation, and cause the expenditure of millions of dollars . . . .[86]

In conference, the broad Senate view of citizen suits prevailed, and the restrictive House provision concerning standing was dropped. For the purposes of determining standing, "citizen" was defined by the conference to mean any person or group with an interest "adversely affected" by agency action.[87] The conference report observed that this definition of "citizen" was designed to reflect the decision of the U.S. Supreme Court in the Mineral King litigation.[88]

In the cases of both the FWPCA and the pesticides bills, the more liberal Senate view of citizen suits prevailed. Nevertheless, the repeated attempts by the Agriculture Committees and the House Public Works Committee to restrict citizen suits represented recognition that programs under their jurisdiction would be subject to increased pressure from environmentalists if strong citizen suit provisions were enacted. The marked success of the environmentalists in bringing litigation under NEPA and other laws was certainly instrumental in prompting these insular committee efforts.

Summary and Conclusions

The reaction against NEPA and citizen intervention in the administrative process stemmed from NEPA's unanticipated impact on both environmental protection and public works programs. One part of the NEPA amendment/exemption effort was directed at correcting what Senator Muskie and his colleagues viewed as judicial misinterpretation of the legislative history of NEPA, particularly the applicability of NEPA to environmentally protective agencies. But the major portion of the effort evolved from certain congressional committees' discontent with NEPA's impact on programs that hitherto had been immune to challenge owing to the fraternal relationship of the committees to the administrative agencies.

The lack of congressional tolerance for citizen action forcing implementation of NEPA suggests that the statute's impact would have been diminished had Congressman Aspinall's narrow view of it prevailed. Agencies would have been under scant pressure from their oversight committees to implement the law, and would have been left with considerable discretion in responding to its requirements.

Environmental groups played a different role in the 1972 struggle over NEPA from the one they played during NEPA's enactment. To some extent, the increased effort was merely a function of the evolution of environmental lobbying into a larger, more sophisticated operation. But the active role environmentalists played—in public hearings, in developing legislative histories, and in promoting widespread awareness of the significance of the attacks on NEPA—was a result also of their recognition of NEPA's importance; a recognition not manifested at the time the statute was enacted.

Although initial efforts to undermine NEPA met with mixed success, the stand-off in the 92d Congress represented only the first skirmish in a lengthy battle. In the 93d Congress, many of the bills were reintroduced, and exemptions were voted for the San Antonio North Expressway and the trans-Alaskan pipeline. In early 1974, some influential presidential advisors advocated major exemptions to or repeal of NEPA. Those suggestions prompted threats of resignation from Russell Train, who by then had become EPA administrator, and from Russell Peterson, Train's successor as CEQ chairman. Increasing concern over energy shortages and domestic economic tranquility will undoubtedly spur further attempts to modify NEPA.

7

Some
Closing
Observations

NEPA "clearly established itself as one of the most controversial environmental measures of all time."[1] It is likely that "no federal statute of modern times [was] read by a greater proportion of federal officials."[2] One writer described NEPA as penetrating the bureaucratic structure "like a whiplash," noting that "not since women received the vote had the discretion of government been so thoroughly bruised."[3] In reference to the emotions generated by the law, environmental lawyer David Sive jokingly suggested that those familiar with NEPA could be divided into two categories—those who regarded Section 102 almost like the 23d Psalm, with the words "major federal action" the equivalent of "The Lord is my shepherd," and those on the other side, the federal bureaucrats who, it was rumored, were threatening en masse to jump off Calvert Cliffs.[4]

NEPA's ambiguities would appear to have been at the root of much of the conflict over the Act. The American Petroleum Institute argued that "none of the problems that [arose] under

NEPA [were] the result of unwillingness to comply with either the letter or spirit of the statute," but came about "because of its ambiguities." [5] Sierra Club attorney James Moorman, in contrast, argued with respect to NEPA and other environmental laws that federal agencies used administrative interpretation—opinions of counsel, rule making, and so forth—to avoid statutory mandates.[6] Whether administrative agencies failed to comply with NEPA out of ignorance or out of deceit, the question of their compliance with the Act was the subject of numerous judicial opinions. As one commentator noted, "the courts . . . shaped NEPA, and the federal process under it, in a manner unprecedented in the history of the development of federal programs." [7]

The lesson to be learned from reviewing the history of NEPA's implementation is that Congress did not create a national environmental policy when it enacted NEPA. Rather, NEPA laid the groundwork for establishing a series of procedures whereby environmental considerations could be fed into agency decision-making routines. The national environmental policy in the early 1970s was not so much the congressional statement in Title I of NEPA, but rather, it was the sum of all administrative decisions that were environmentally impacting.

Although NEPA was at the center of considerable controversy for its first few years of existence, its potential for promoting administrative change and intelligent, environmentally conscious planning prompted many states to enact similar laws.[8] Also spurred by NEPA was a 1972 Senate Commerce Committee proposal that would have required energy impact statements for certain federal actions.[9] In that case, however, the Committee insured that the energy statement requirements would be enforceable only by an Energy Policy Council, and not by outside parties engaging in litigation.[10]

The impact statement notion was also suggested for other areas: "public impact statements" describing the effect on competition of consent decrees proposed in antitrust case settlements; "judicial impact statements" describing the impact of federal legislative proposals on the courts; and "inflation impact statements" describing the economic impact of new federal regulatory actions.

It is ironic that, amidst the calls for new kinds of statements, agencies remained lethargic in meeting demands for environmental statements. Administrative neglect of NEPA paralleled agency disdain for broad "social policy" statutes of another type—civil rights laws. In October 1970 the United States Civil Rights Commission stated that "executive branch enforcement of civil rights mandates was so inadequate as to render the law practically meaningless," and added that "this deplorable situation did not develop accidentally." [11] In its February 1973 report, the Commission observed that "the inertia of agencies in the area of civil rights has persisted." The Commission noted the FPC's refusal to enforce fair hiring standards in the utility industry despite a Justice Department opinion that it had authority to do so, the ICC's eighteen month delay in reaching a decision on that same point, the IRS's viewing "in an unjustifiably narrow manner" its job of keeping segregated private schools from receiving tax exemptions, and the failure of the IRS and HEW to cooperate on that tax matter.

Because congressional enactments tended, in the words of the Calvert Cliffs decision, to be lost in the hallways of the bureaucracy, the courts played a significant role in promoting compliance with civil rights laws by agencies and their clientele, just as federal judges promoted agency and agency clientele implementation of NEPA. The courts' importance in prodding agencies to enforce civil rights laws is most noteworthy in the fields of broadcasting and education.[12]

By 1975, as this final chapter is written, substantive changes in agency decision making are appearing. For example, the Corps of Engineers maintains that NEPA has been responsible for modifications, delays, or halts in 350 of its projects.[13] One of every four projects under study or construction has been changed and the operating procedures of one of every two completed ones have been modified to improve their social and ecological impact. Those Corps assertions of change must be examined critically in order to determine whether NEPA is indeed the predominant element in altering the agency's decisions. There is little doubt, however, that the Corps' activities are now conducted with somewhat greater environmental sensitivity, even though the agency still builds environmentally impacting projects of dubious economic value.

A second example of substantive change in agency decision making is found in the Forest Service. Academic monitors of the NEPA process have noted that impact statements have helped this agency in its efforts to impose more stringent controls on development in national forests. The service is able to stimulate "environmentalist pressures" on itself by highlighting project deficiencies in draft impact statements, or by prompting prospective commentators by telephone.[14] The experience in the Forest Service suggests that the strengthening of NEPA's procedural requirements by judicial action has opened a more direct access route to agency decision makers for environmentalists than had been available. When impact statements are prepared late in the decision-making process, the effects of the environmentalists' input by that route may be minimal. But where impact statements are prepared early, or where environmentalist participation is invited in the pre-impact statement stage (in order to discourage later criticism) one would imagine that the ability to influence policy is increased.

The recognition that impact statements are often produced too late has spurred efforts to move their preparation to earlier points in the decision-making process. Emphasis is now placed on programmatic impact statements and on tiers of statements, as discussed in chapter 5. Efforts are also being made to tie environmental analysis closer to the budgeting process. Since it is in budgeting that environmentally impacting policy choices are so often made, it is important to produce some form of environmental assessment document for budget purposes, the lack of OMB interest notwithstanding. In 1975, the Sierra Club obtained from the D.C. District Court a ruling that OMB and the Interior Department must prepare impact statements to accompany funding proposals for national wildlife refuges.[15]

The effort to obtain early input has also led agencies to publish periodically lists of actions for which impact statements are planned. Those lists, published in the *Federal Register* and *102 Monitor*, are required by CEQ's 1973 guidelines. Their appearance might prompt an interested individual to alert agencies to important environmental impacts that should be assessed early in project planning.

An increasingly crucial question in the future will be the extent to which agencies will use Sections 103 and 105 of NEPA to add environmental protection to their existing substantive mandates. As noted in chapter 4, agency efforts to utilize those sections to expand their mandates have not been ambitious. In early 1975, the question of how much NEPA enlarged mandates was brought into focus by a Food and Drug Administration determination that it lacked authority to deny on environmental grounds approval for plastic bottles proposed for use by beverage manufacturers.[16] Whether or not bottles might cause a solid waste problem could not influence its decision, the agency claimed, because it could only refuse to approve the bottles if they were a hazard to public health and safety. FDA contended that it had to disclose the bottles' adverse environmental impacts in an environmental impact statement, but that it could not, by statute, deny them approval on environmental grounds. FDA openly invited a lawsuit on this matter, and the Environmental Defense Fund rose to the occasion.[17]

Agency decisions have been altered by and have benefited from the NEPA procedures, but it is not difficult to uncover a sizeable quantity of NEPA "horror stories." One is reminded, for example, of the Bureau of Reclamation including in one final impact statement many pages of brief, general comments from a junior high school English class—replete with misspelled words.[18]

While such action by a federal agency might be laughable, other horror stories are not so funny. They relate gross analytical mistakes that might be embarrassing to an agency even if made in a nonenvironmental context. For example, two academic observers noted that the Corps of Engineers predicts recreation benefits for proposed projects by using assumptions based on "most similar other projects," but often the assumptions underlying the comparison are invalid because the projects compared are fundamentally different.[19] The same observers noted a gross error in the impact statement prepared by the Forest Service for the Mineral King ski development. The subject of litigation dating at least to 1969, the Mineral King development was still being contested in 1975. In its environmental impact statement for the project, the Forest Service, in projecting skier use of the facility, made a simple arithmetic error, which had the effect of overstating demand by 600 percent.[20]

While the courts opened up the decision-making process to activists, their decisions probably had the unfortunate side effect of encouraging the production of bulky but misguided statements. By demanding full disclosure of information, the courts spurred agencies, seemingly, to reproduce drawers full of material for inclusion in impact statements, even if the information had little analytical value. For example, statements often contain inventories of wildlife or lists of species found in a locale where an action is planned. The inventories may be useful if they reveal the presence of endangered species, but they do not describe the dynamics of the ecological system that will be impacted by the particular action.

NEPA is still with us. By now there is considerable agency and judicial experience with NEPA. A large body of case law exists providing precedent for the application of NEPA procedures to a wide array of agency actions. Great sums are allocated for NEPA-induced environmental impact analysis, though in many instances the exact magnitude of these sums is difficult to determine. Agencies and private parties alike are devising methodologies for environmental impact assessment to fill the analytical void that has existed in the early 1970s.

Of all the projects now affected by NEPA a greater proportion than ever before were likely initiated after January 1, 1970. It seems that the pattern of conflict over environmental impacts and the nature of impact assessment may be changing. With a large number of impact statements now resting in repositories across the country, the opportunity exists for measuring in some rigorous way the pattern of conflict and compromise over impact statements, as reflected in their contents, comments on them, and responses to comments. Similarly, insight can be obtained into NEPA's impact on agency decision making by examining the roles of those individuals hired by agencies to conduct environmental analyses. Interviewing might indicate whether NEPA's enactment has influenced decision making not only by changing the information underlying decisions, but by changing the intra-agency configuration of participants in the decisions.

It is difficult to obtain a complete picture of the changes in agency decision making that are attributable to NEPA. In anticipation of possible adverse public reaction, agencies may be foregoing some actions, or may be modifying others in a manner that would not have occurred prior to NEPA's enactment. Because of their own raised ecological consciences, and because of aggressive environmentalist oversight, agencies are probably compiling more complete records of their projects' environmental implications. In those instances where ecological consequences have been exhaustively researched, and are expected to be grave and extensive, perhaps agencies are reconsidering committing themselves to projected courses of action. But if environmental ends are continually and substantially subordinated to other ends, then the next generation may have, if nothing else, a highly detailed record of how this generation systematically abused the natural environment.

Appendix

National Environmental Policy Act of 1969

42 U.S.C. § 4321 *et seq.* (originally enacted as Act of Jan. 1, 1970, Pub. L. No. 91-190, 83 Stat. 852)

Be it enacted by the Senate and House of Representatives of the United States of America in Congress assembled, That this Act may be cited as the "National Environmental Policy Act of 1969".

PURPOSE

SEC. 2. The purposes of this Act are: To declare a national policy which will encourage productive and enjoyable harmony between man and his environment; to promote efforts which will prevent or eliminate damage to the environment and biosphere and stimulate the health and welfare of man; to enrich the understanding of the ecological systems and natural resources important to the Nation; and to establish a Council on Environmental Quality.

TITLE I

DECLARATION OF NATIONAL ENVIRONMENTAL POLICY

SEC. 101. (a) The Congress, recognizing the profound impact of man's activity on the interrelations of all components of the natural environment, particularly the profound influences of population growth, high-density urbanization, industrial expansion, resource exploitation, and new and expanding technological advances and recognizing further the critical importance of restoring and maintaining environmental quality to the overall welfare and development of man, declares that it is the continuing policy of the Federal Government, in cooperation with State and local governments, and other concerned public and private organizations, to use all practicable means and measures, including financial and technical assistance, in a manner calculated to foster and promote the general welfare, to create and maintain conditions under which man and nature can exist in productive harmony, and fulfill the social, economic, and other requirements of present and future generations of Americans.

(b) In order to carry out the policy set forth in this Act, it is the continuing responsibility of the Federal Government to use all practicable means, consistent with other essential considerations of national policy, to improve and coordinate Federal plans, functions, programs, and resources to the end that the Nation may—

    (1) fulfill the responsibilities of each generation as trustee of the environment for succeeding generations;

    (2) assure for all Americans safe, healthful, productive, and esthetically and culturally pleasing surroundings;

    (3) attain the widest range of beneficial uses of the environment without degradation, risk to health or safety, or other undesirable and unintended consequences;

    (4) preserve important historic, cultural, and natural aspects of our national heritage, and maintain, wherever possible, an environment which supports diversity, and variety of individual choice;

    (5) achieve a balance between population and resource use which will permit high standards of living and a wide sharing of life's amenities; and

    (6) enhance the quality of renewable resources and approach the maximum attainable recycling of depletable resources.

(c) The Congress recognizes that each person should enjoy a healthful environment and that each person has a responsibility to contribute to the preservation and enhancement of the environment.

SEC. 102. The Congress authorizes and directs that, to the fullest extent possible: (1) the policies, regulations, and public laws of the United States shall be interpreted and administered in accordance with the policies set forth in this Act, and (2) all agencies of the Federal Government shall—

    (A) utilize a systematic, interdisciplinary approach which will insure the integrated use of the natural and social sciences and the environmental design arts in planning and in decisionmaking which may have an impact on man's environment;

    (B) identify and develop methods and procedures, in consultation with the Council on Environmental Quality established by title II of this Act, which will insure that presently unquantified environmental amenities and values may be given appropriate consideration in decisionmaking along with economic and technical considerations;

(C) include in every recommendation or report on proposals for legislation and other major Federal actions significantly affecting the quality of the human environment, a detailed statement by the responsible official on—

   (i) the environmental impact of the proposed action,

   (ii) any adverse environmental effects which cannot be avoided should the proposal be implemented,

   (iii) alternatives to the proposed action,

   (iv) the relationship between local short-term uses of man's environment and the maintenance and enhancement of long-term productivity, and

   (v) any irreversible and irretrievable commitments of resources which would be involved in the proposed action should it be implemented.

Prior to making any detailed statement, the responsible Federal official shall consult with and obtain the comments of any Federal agency which has jurisdiction by law or special expertise with respect to any environmental impact involved. Copies of such statement and the comments and views of the appropriate Federal, State, and local agencies, which are authorized to develop and enforce environmental standards, shall be made available to the President, the Council on Environmental Quality and to the public as provided by section 552 of title 5, United States Code, and shall accompany the proposal through the existing agency review processes;

(D) study, develop, and describe appropriate alternatives to recommended courses of action in any proposal which involves unresolved conflicts concerning alternative uses of available resources;

(E) recognize the worldwide and long-range character of environmental problems and, where consistent with the foreign policy of the United States, lend appropriate support to initiatives, resolutions, and programs designed to maximize international cooperation in anticipating and preventing a decline in the quality of mankind's world environment;

(F) make available to States, counties, municipalities, institutions, and individuals, advice and information useful in restoring, maintaining, and enhancing the quality of the environment;

(G) initiate and utilize ecological information in the planning and development of resource-oriented projects; and

(H) assist the Council on Environmental Quality established by title II of this Act.

SEC. 103. All agencies of the Federal Government shall review their present statutory authority, administrative regulations, and current policies and procedures for the purpose of determining whether there are any deficiencies or inconsistencies therein which prohibit full compliance with the purposes and provisions of this Act and shall propose to the President not later than July 1, 1971, such measures as may be necessary to bring their authority and policies into conformity with the intent, purposes, and procedures set forth in this Act.

SEC. 104. Nothing in section 102 or 103 shall in any way affect the specific statutory obligations of any Federal agency (1) to comply with criteria or standards of environmental quality, (2) to coordinate or consult with any other Federal or State agency, or (3) to act, or refrain from acting contingent upon the recommendations or certification of any other Federal or State agency.

SEC. 105. The policies and goals set forth in this Act are supplementary to those set forth in existing authorizations of Federal agencies.

TITLE II

COUNCIL ON ENVIRONMENTAL QUALITY

SEC. 201. The President shall transmit to the Congress annually beginning July 1, 1970, an Environmental Quality Report (hereinafter referred to as the "report") which shall set forth (1) the status and condition of the major natural, manmade, or altered environmental classes of the Nation, including, but not limited to, the air, the aquatic, including marine, estuarine, and fresh water, and the terrestrial environment, including, but not limited to, the forest, dryland, wetland, range, urban, suburban, and rural environment; (2) current and foreseeable trends in the quality, management and utilization of such environments and the effects of those trends on the social, economic, and other requirements of the Nation; (3) the adequacy of available natural resources for fulfilling human and economic requirements of the Nation in the light of expected population pressures; (4) a review of the programs and activities (including regulatory activities) of the Federal Government, the State and local governments, and nongovernmental entities or individuals, with particular reference to their effect on the environment and on the conservation, development and utilization of natural resources; and (5) a program for remedying the deficiencies of existing programs and activities, together with recommendations for legislation.

SEC. 202. There is created in the Executive Office of the President a Council on Environmental Quality (hereinafter referred to as the "Council"). The Council shall be composed of three members who shall be appointed by the President to serve at his pleasure, by and with the advice and consent of the Senate. The President shall designate one of the members of the Council to serve as Chairman. Each member shall be a person who, as a result of his training, experience, and attainments, is exceptionally well qualified to analyze and interpret environmental trends and information of all kinds; to appraise programs and activities of the Federal Government in the light of the policy set forth in title I of this Act; to be conscious of and responsive to the scientific, economic, social, esthetic, and cultural needs and interests of the Nation; and to formulate and recommend national policies to promote the improvement of the quality of the environment.

SEC. 203. The Council may employ such officers and employees as may be necessary to carry out its functions under this Act. In addition, the Council may employ and fix the compensation of such experts and consultants as may be necessary for the carrying out of its functions under this Act, in accordance with section 3109 of title 5, United States Code (but without regard to the last sentence thereof).

SEC. 204. It shall be the duty and function of the Council—

(1) to assist and advise the President in the preparation of the Environmental Quality Report required by section 201;

(2) to gather timely and authoritative information concerning the conditions and trends in the quality of the environment both current and prospective, to analyze and interpret such information for the purpose of determining whether such conditions and trends are interfering, or are likely to interfere, with the achievement of the policy set forth in title I of this Act, and to compile and submit to the President studies relating to such conditions and trends;

(3) to review and appraise the various programs and activities

of the Federal Government in the light of the policy set forth in title I of this Act for the purpose of determining the extent to which such programs and activities are contributing to the achievement of such policy, and to make recommendations to the President with respect thereto;

(4) to develop and recommend to the President national policies to foster and promote the improvement of environmental quality to meet the conservation, social, economic, health, and other requirements and goals of the Nation;

(5) to conduct investigations, studies, surveys, research, and analyses relating to ecological systems and environmental quality;

(6) to document and define changes in the natural environment, including the plant and animal systems, and to accumulate necessary data and other information for a continuing analysis of these changes or trends and an interpretation of their underlying causes;

(7) to report at least once each year to the President on the state and condition of the environment; and

(8) to make and furnish such studies, reports thereon, and recommendations with respect to matters of policy and legislation as the President may request.

Sec. 205. In exercising its powers, functions, and duties under this Act, the Council shall—

(1) consult with the Citizens' Advisory Committee on Environmental Quality established by Executive Order numbered 11472, dated May 29, 1969, and with such representatives of science, industry, agriculture, labor, conservation organizations, State and local governments and other groups, as it deems advisable; and

(2) utilize, to the fullest extent possible, the services, facilities, and information (including statistical information) of public and private agencies and organizations, and individuals, in order that duplication of effort and expense may be avoided, thus assuring that the Council's activities will not unnecessarily overlap or conflict with similar activities authorized by law and performed by established agencies.

Sec. 206. Members of the Council shall serve full time and the Chairman of the Council shall be compensated at the rate provided for Level II of the Executive Schedule Pay Rates (5 U.S.C. 5313). The other members of the Council shall be compensated at the rate pro-vided for Level IV of the Executive Schedule Pay Rates (5 U.S.C. 5315).

SEC. 207. There are authorized to be appropriated to carry out the provisions of this Act not to exceed $300,000 for fiscal year 1970, $700,000 for fiscal year 1971, and $1,000,000 for each fiscal year thereafter.

Approved January 1, 1970.

_____

[This text of NEPA does not include the amendments to the law provided by Pub. L. No. 94–52 89 Stat. 258 (enacted July 3, 1975) and Pub. L. No. 94–83, 89 Stat. 424 (enacted August 9, 1975).]

Selected Bibliography

BOOKS

Anderson, Frederick R. "The National Environmental Policy Act." In *Federal Environmental Law*, pp. 238–419. ed. Erica Dolgin and Thomas Guilbert. St. Paul: West Publishers, 1974.

———. *NEPA in the Courts*. Baltimore: Johns Hopkins Press for Resources for the Future, 1973.

Cyert, Richard, and March, James. *A Behavioral Theory of the Firm*. Englewood Cliffs: Prentice-Hall, 1963.

Davis, Kenneth Culp. *Administrative Discretion*. Urbana: University of Illinois Press, 1971.

Flash, Edward S., Jr. *Economic Advice and Presidential Leadership: The Council of Economic Advisors*. New York: Columbia University Press, 1965.

Hage, Jerald, and Aiken, Michael. *Social Change in Complex Organizations*. New York: Random House, 1970.

Jaffe, Louis L. *Judicial Control of Administrative Action*. abridged student ed. Boston: Little, Brown, 1965.

Katz, Daniel, and Kahn, Robert. *The Social Psychology of Organizations*. New York: Wiley, 1967.

Kaufman, Herbert. *The Limits of Organizational Change*. University, Alabama: University of Alabama Press, 1971.

Lawrence, Paul, and Lorsch, Jay. *Organizations and Environment*. Homewood: Irwin, 1969.

Lindblom, Charles. *The Intelligence of Democracy*. New York: The Free Press, 1965.

———. *The Policy-Making Process*. Englewood Cliffs: Prentice-Hall, 1968.

March, James, and Simon, Herbert. *Organizations*. New York: Wiley, 1958.

Nadel, Mark. *The Politics of Consumer Protection*. Indianapolis: Bobbs-Merrill, 1971.

Olson, Mancur. *The Logic of Collective Action*. Cambridge: Harvard University Press, 1965.

Sax, Joseph. *Defending the Environment*. Consumers Union ed. New York: Knopf, 1971.

Simon, Herbert. *Administrative Behavior*. 2nd ed. New York: The Free Press, 1965.

Thompson, James D. *Organizations in Action*. New York: McGraw-Hill, 1967.

ARTICLES

Barfield, Claude. "Environment Report/Exemption from NEPA Requirements Sought for Nuclear Plants, Pollution Permits," *National Journal* 4 (June 17, 1972): pp. 1025–34.

———. "Environment Report/Water Pollution Act Forces Showdown in 1973 Over Best Way to Protect Environment," *National Journal* 4 (December 9, 1972): pp. 1871–82.

———. "Environment Report/Pollution Law May Produce Delays in Nuclear Power Licensing Process," *National Journal* 5 (January 27, 1973): pp. 128–34.

———, and Corrigan, Richard. "Environment Report/White House Seeks to Restrict Scope of Environmental Law," *National Journal* 4 (February 26, 1972): pp. 336–49.

Carter, Luther. "Environmental Law (I): Maturing Field for Lawyers and Scientists," *Science* 179 (March 23, 1973): pp. 1205–09.

———. "Environmental Law (II): A Strategic Weapon Against Degradation?" *Science* 179 (March 30, 1973): pp. 1310–11, p. 1350.

Corrigan, Richard, and Barfield, Claude. "Energy Report/Pipeline Lobby Uses its Political Muscle to Bypass Environmental Law," *National Journal* 5 (August 11, 1973): pp. 1172–78.

Cramton, Roger, and Berg, Richard K. "On Leading a Horse to Water: NEPA and the Federal Bureaucracy," *Michigan Law Review* 71 (January 1973): pp. 511–36.

Gillette, Robert. "National Environmental Policy Act: Signs of Backlash are Evident," *Science* 176 (April 7, 1972): pp. 30–33.

———. "National Environmental Policy Act: How Well is it Working?" *Science* 176 (April 14, 1972): pp. 146–50.

———. "Nuclear Safety (I): The Roots of Dissent," *Science* 177 (September 1, 1972): pp. 771–76.

———. "Nuclear Safety (III): Critics Charge Conflicts of Interest," *Science* 177 (September 15, 1972): pp. 970–75.

Holden, Matthew. "Imperialism in Bureaucracy," *American Political Science Review* 60 (December 1966): pp. 943–51.

Lindblom, Charles. "The Science of 'Muddling Through'," *Public Administration Review* 19 (Spring 1959): pp. 79–88.

Yarrington, Hugh J. *The National Environmental Policy Act*. Washington: BNA Environment Reporter, Monograph No. 17, 1974.

GOVERNMENT DOCUMENTS

U.S. Congress. House. Committee on Merchant Marine and Fisheries. *Administration of the National Environmental Policy Act. Hearings before the Subcommittee on Fisheries and Wildlife Conservation on Federal Agency Compliances with Section 102(2)(C) and Section 103 of the National Environmental Policy Act of 1969,* 91st Cong., 2d sess., 1970 (Parts 1 and 2).

U.S. Congress. House. Committee on Merchant Marine and Fisheries. *Administration of the National Environmental Policy Act (P.L. 91-190).* H. Rept. 316, 92d Cong., 1st sess., 1971.

U.S. Congress. House. Committee on Merchant Marine and Fisheries. *Administration of the National Environmental Policy Act–1972. Hearings before the Subcommittee on Fisheries and Wildlife Conservation on NEPA Oversight,* 92d Cong., 2d sess., 1972.

U.S. Congress. Senate. Committee on Interior and Insular Affairs. *Calvert Cliffs Court Decision. Hearings on Environmental Constraints and the Generation of Nuclear Electric Power: The Aftermath of the Court Decision on Calvert Cliffs,* 92d Cong., 1st sess., 1971 (Parts 1 and 2).

U.S. Congress. Senate. Committee on the Judiciary. *Legal Fees. Hearings before the Subcommittee on Representation of Citizen Interests on the Effect of Legal Fees on the Adequacy of Representation,* 93d Cong., 1st sess., 1973 (Parts 3 and 4).

U.S. Congress. Senate. Committees on Public Works and Interior and Insular Affairs. *National Environmental Policy Act. Joint Hearings on the Operation of the National Environmental Policy Act of 1969,* 92d Cong., 2d sess., 1972.

U.S. Council on Environmental Quality. *Environmental Quality—The Annual Report of the Council on Environmental Quality.* Washington, D.C.: Government Printing Office, 1970–   (annual).

U.S. Council on Environmental Quality. *102 Monitor.* Washington, D.C.: Government Printing Office, February 1971–   (monthly).

U.S. General Accounting Office. *Improvements Needed in Federal Efforts to Implement the National Environmental Policy Act of 1969,* Report No. B-170186. Washington, D.C., 1972.

DISSERTATIONS

Andrews, Richard N. L. "Environmental Policy and Administrative Change: The National Environmental Policy Act of 1969 (1970–71)." Ph.D. Dissertation, Department of City and Regional Planning, University of North Carolina, 1972.

Ferejohn, John. "Congressional Influence on Water Politics." Ph.D.

Dissertation, Department of Political Science, Stanford University, 1972.

Finn, Terence T. "Conflict and Compromise: Congress Makes a Law, The Passage of the National Environmental Policy Act." Ph.D. Dissertation, Department of Government, Georgetown University, 1972.

REPORTING SERVICES

Environmental Law Reporter. Washington: Environmental Law Institute, 1971–   (monthly).

Notes

Chapter 1

1. Story from *Playboy*, February 1975, related in speech by Russell Peterson, Chairman, Council on Environmental Quality before the American Association for the Advancement of Science, January 30, 1975. Printed text at 1.

2. 42 U.S.C. §§4321 *et seq.*, Pub. L. No. 91-190, 83 Stat. 852. See appendix for text.

3. Harnik, "Testing the Movement. It's time to save NEPA," *Environmental Action*, April 15, 1972, at 3; "Environmental Policy and the Congress," 11 *Nat. Res. L.* 407 (1971).

4. Quoted in Gillette, "National Environmental Policy Act: Signs of Backlash are Evident," 176 *Science* 30 (1972); February 7, 1972 editorial cited in Barfield and Corrigan, "Environment Report/White House Seeks to Restrict Scope of Environmental Law," 4 *Nat'l. Jn'l.* 347 (1972); Harnik, *supra* note 3, at 4.

5. Schachter, "Standards for Evaluating a NEPA Environmental Statement," *Pub. Util. Fort.*, Aug. 31, 1972 at 29; J. Feinberg in Hanly v. Mitchell, 2 ELR 20217, 20217 (2d Cir., May 17, 1972); J. Friendly in City of New York v. U.S., 2 ELR 20275, 20276 (E.D. N.Y., January 20, 1972).

6. K. C. Davis, *Discretionary Justice* 55 (1971).

7. For the caveats attendant to this generalization, see chapter 5.

Chapter 2

1. 42 U.S.C. §§4321 *et seq.*, Pub. L. No. 91-190, 83 Stat. 852. See appendix for text.

2. See Senate Comm. on Interior and Insular Affairs, "National Environmental Policy Act of 1969," S. Rep. No. 91-296, 91st Cong., 1st Sess. *passim* (1969) [hereafter cited as S.1075 Report].

3. §§201 and 204(7). See appendix.

4. A general discussion of reorganization is presented in Bailey, "Managing the Federal Government," in *Agenda for the Nation* 301 (K. Gordon ed. 1968). It is reprinted in "Hearing on S.1075, S.237 and S.1752 before the Senate Comm. on Interior and Insular Affairs," 92d Cong., 1st Sess. 45 (April 1969) [hereafter cited as S.1075 Hearing]. It is worth noting that many of the earlier institutional proposals were focused on resources rather than on the larger issue of environmental quality.

5. *E.g.*, President's Science Advisory Committee, *Restoring the Quality of Our Environment: Report of the Environmental Pollution Panel* (1965). See also S.886, Department of Natural Resources Act, introduced into the 90th Congress by Senator Moss; S.2549, Proposed Resources and Energy Conservation Act of 1960, introduced into the 86th Congress by Senator Murray; and S.2805, introduced into the 90th Congress by Senators Kuchel and Jackson. Lynton Caldwell observed that under the Kennedy administration, the nation had moved "indecisively" toward a policy for the environment, in the course of addressing natural resource matters. He adds that concern became more focused during the Johnson administration. Congress backed into a national policy for the environment while trying to urge the executive branch, especially the Interior Department, to give greater attention and higher priority to ecological values. See *Environment: A Challenge to Modern Society* 191–212 (1970).

6. Staff of Subcomm. on Science, Research and Development, House Comm. on Science and Astronautics, 90th Cong., 2d Sess., "Managing the Environment" (Comm. Print 1968).

7. Legislative Reference Service, Library of Congress, for Senate Comm. on Interior and Insular Affairs and House Comm. on Science and Astronautics, 90th Cong., 2d Sess., "A Congressional White Paper on A National Policy for the Environment" (Comm. Print 1968).

8. Trop and Roos, "Public Opinion and the Environment," in *The Politics of Ecosuicide* 58 (L. Roos ed. 1971).

9. For the text, see S.1075 Hearing, *supra* note 4, at 1.

10. *Id.*, at 83.

11. For a list of federal agencies having environmental responsibilities, see Appendix C in L. Caldwell and W. Van Ness for Senate Comm. on Interior and Insular Affairs, 90th Cong., 2d Sess., "A National Policy for the Environment" (Comm. Print 1968).

12. See, e.g., testimony of Anthony Wayne Smith, S.1075 Hearing, *supra* note 4, at 177.

13. *Id.*, at 151.

14. *Id.*, at 112–28.

15. *Id.*, at 117.

16. Those amendments were embodied in the S.1075 reported by his committee. See S.1075 Report, *supra* note 2, at 1.

17. *Id.*, at 2.

18. Interview with the author.

19. For BOB's view, see S.1075 Report, *supra* note 2, at 27.

20. 115 Cong. Rec. 15544 (June 12, 1969).

21. 115 Cong. Rec. 29050.

22. For the relevant text see 115 Cong. Rec. 29051.

23. §102(b), in S.1075 Report, *supra* note 2 at 2.

24. §102(b), at 115 Cong. Rec. 29051.

25. The §103 of Senator Jackson's S.1075 that had extended agency authority became, with slight modifications, §104 of the Muskie-Jackson S.1075.

26. 115 Cong. Rec. 29061 (October 8, 1969).

27. The interagency committee is discussed *infra*.

28. The text of H.R.6750 is printed in "Hearings on H.R. 6750, H.R. 11886, H.R. 11942, H.R. 12077, H.R. 12190, H.R. 12207, H.R. 12209, H.R. 12228, H.R. 12264, H.R. 12409 before the Subcomm. on Fisheries and Wildlife Conservation of the House Comm. on Merchant Marine and Fisheries," 91st Cong., 1st Sess. 3 (May–June 1970) [hereafter cited as 1969 Dingell Hearings].

29. H.R.7796, introduced March 23, 1967.

30. The subcommittee's views, and its general "technology assessment" approach to environmental quality, are described in Wandesforde-Smith, "National Policy for the Environment: Politics and the Concept of Stewardship," in *Congress and the Environment* 205 (R. Cooley and G. Wandesforde-Smith eds. 1970).

31. Exec. Order No. 11472, 3 C.F.R. 122 (1969 Comp.).

32. The Jackson-White House talks are described in the *Christian Science Monitor*, June 4, 1969.

33. The administration was restrained in its actions throughout NEPA's consideration by Congress, in part because it thought it would need Jackson's support in an upcoming legislative debate on national security and the ABM. Jackson, for his part, did not undertake to disabuse the administration of that notion. Agencies within the administration did not adopt a unified stance on NEPA, as evidenced in their letters and testimony in congressional hearing records. A summary of the executive views can be found in H. Rep. No. 91-378, "Council on Environmental Quality" 91st Cong., 1st Sess. 2-3 (1969).

34. 1969 Dingell Hearings, *supra* note 28, at 355–401.

35. The Office of Science and Technology was eliminated several years later by executive order.

36. See, e.g., testimony of Robert Burnap, 1969 Dingell Hearings, *supra* note 28, at 159.

37. *Id.*, at 40–41.

38. *Id.*, at 96, 242, 451.

39. Statement of staff aide in interview with the author.

40. Statement of staff aide in interview with the author.

41. H.R.12143 is reprinted in 1969 Dingell Hearings, *supra* note 28, at 9.

42. *Id.*, at 12–14.

43. *Supra*, note 35.

44. H.R.8447, introduced March 6, 1969, by Reuss and H.R.7923, introduced February 27, 1969, by Howard.

45. Information obtained from staff aide in interview with author.

46. Statement of Aspinall before the Rules Committee. On file at the House Interior Committee.

47. 115 Cong. Rec. 26586, 26589.

48. 115 Cong. Rec. 26589.

49. See note 25, *supra*.

50. 115 Cong. Rec. 26587.

51. 115 Cong. Rec. 26588–89.

52. 115 Cong. Rec. 26590.

53. Statement of staff aide in interview with the author.

54. Statement of staff aide in interview with the author.

55. Statement of staff aide in interview with the author.

56. Interview with the author.

57. Interview with the author.

58. The "environmental rights" provision was §101(b) of the Muskie-Jackson version of S.1075.

59. See discussion in "Statement of the Managers on the Part of the House," appended to the conference report and reprinted at 115 Cong. Rec. 39702 (December 17, 1969).

60. The compromise version became §102(2)(B) of NEPA. See appendix.

61. See text at 115 Cong. Rec. 29051 (October 8, 1969).

62. Subsections (a)–(f) were, mostly, the precursors of §§102(2)(A)–(F) of NEPA.

63. See appendix for balance of text.

64. *Supra*, note 59.

65. See appendix for text of §§103 and 105.

66. *Supra*, note 59.

67. *Id.*, at 115 Cong. Rec. 39703.

68. *Id.*

69. 115 Cong. Rec. 40926 (December 22, 1969).

70. 115 Cong. Rec. 40927.

71. 115 Cong. Rec. 40927–40928.

72. 115 Cong. Rec. 40422.

73. *Supra*, note 59.

74. Statement of staff aide in interview with the author.

75. One writer commented that the change from findings to statement probably tended to enlarge the scope of judicial review. See Note, "Evolving Judicial Standards under the NEPA and the Challenge of the Alaska Pipeline," 81 *Yale L. J.* 1592, 1594 n. 13 (1972).

76. "Citizen-initiated lawsuit" means a legal action begun by individual citizens or environmental groups. The suit is designed to obtain compliance with environmental statutes and is environmentally, rather than economically motivated.

77. Fisher, "Environmental Law," 24–30.

78. *Environmental Law* (Northwestern School of Law) and *Environmental Affairs* (Boston College Environmental Law Center); *Environmental Law Reporter* (Environmental Law Institute) and *Environment Reporter* (Bureau of National Affairs).

79. The Environmental Defense Fund, founded in 1967, was the first group organized exclusively for environmental litigation. It was joined in 1969 by the Center for Law and Social Policy and by Berlin, Roisman and Kessler, the latter a *pro bono* firm that often represented environmental groups. The Natural Resources Defense Council was founded in 1970, and in January 1971 the National Wildlife Federation hired its first full-time environmental lawyer. In 1971, the Sierra Club Legal Defense Fund was organized, although the Sierra Club had been engaged in environmental litigation since the middle of the 1960s. Similarly, in 1972, The Izaak Walton League organized its legal defense fund, although its legal activity dated back to 1969.

80. Staff aide interviews with the author.

81. My treatment of the legislative history of NEPA is consistent with the two other lengthy, interview-based legislative histories. See Richard N. L. Andrews, "Environmental Policy and Administrative Change: The National Environmental Policy Act of 1969 (1970–71)," 76–109 (Ph.D. dissertation, Department of City and Regional Planning, University of North Carolina, 1972); and Terence T. Finn, "Conflict and Compromise: Congress Makes A Law, The Passage of the National Environmental Policy Act" (Ph.D. dissertation, Department of Government, Georgetown University, 1972). The interviews for the legislative history presented here were conducted soon after the interviews by Andrews and Finn.

Chapter 3

1. Most of the Council's mandate is found in Title II of NEPA, although §102(2)(B) mentions the Council as consulting with agencies to develop methods for weighing environmental values in decision making and §102(2)(C) indicates that the Council is to be furnished environmental impact statements. The responsibility to conduct ecological systems studies mandated by §204(5) was shifted to the EPA in December 1970. See 5 U.S.C. Reorg. Plan of 1970 No. 3. CEQ still retained authority, however, for conducting environmental quality studies. The Council also was given statutory authority in the Environmental Quality Improvement Act of 1970 (42 U.S.C. §§4371 *et. seq.*, Title II of Pub. L. No. 91-224, 84 Stat. 91), which established an Office of Environmental Quality in the executive office of the president. That was the office Senator Muskie had proposed in June 1969, as a counter to Senator Jackson's Council on Environmental Quality. The office never had an institutional identity of its own, and its authorizations, and coordination and evaluation responsibilities were assigned to CEQ.

2. See Senate Comm. on Interior and Insular Affairs, "National Environmental Policy Act of 1969," S. Rep. No. 91-296, 91st Cong., 1st Sess. 25 (1969) [hereafter cited as S.1075 Report].

3. 35 Fed. Reg. 4247 (March 5, 1970), ELR 45003.

4. See §3(h).

5. Interview with CEQ staff.

6. 35 Fed. Reg. 7390 (May 12, 1970), 1 ELR 46001.

7. §10(b). NEPA had made no distinction between "draft" and "final" statements, mentioning only one "detailed" statement.

8. §7(a)(iii).

9. NEPA does not have a "grandfather clause" exempting from its provisions actions taken prior to a specified date. §11 of the CEQ guidelines stated: "To the fullest extent possible the Section 102(2)(C) procedure should be applied to further major Federal actions having a significant effect on the environment even though they arise from projects or programs initiated prior to enactment of P.L. 91-190 on January 1, 1970. Where it is not practicable to reassess the basic course of action, it is still important that further incremental major actions be shaped so as to minimize adverse environmental consequences. It is also important in further action that account be taken of environmental consequences not fully evaluated at the outset of the project or program."

10. §105 of NEPA. See appendix.

11. "Hearings on Federal Agency Compliances with Section

102(2)(C) and Section 103 of the National Environmental Policy Act of 1969 before the Subcomm. on Fisheries and Wildlife Conservation of the House Comm. on Merchant Marine and Fisheries," 91st Cong., 2d Sess. (1970) [hereafter cited as Dingell 1970 Oversight Hearings].

12. 36 Fed. Reg. 7724 (April 23, 1971), ELR 46049.

13. The memo is reprinted in "Hearings on the Operation of the National Environmental Policy Act of 1969 before the Senate Comm. on Public Works and the Senate Comm. on Interior and Insular Affairs," 92d Cong., 2d Sess. 40, 41 (1972) [hereafter cited as Joint 1972 NEPA Hearings].

14. 38 Fed. Reg. 20549 (August 1, 1973).

15. See the discussion of §102 in the section-by-section analysis of NEPA inserted by Senator Jackson in 115 Cong. Rec. 40419–20 (December 20, 1969).

16. *Id.*

17. This was one element of the Muskie-Jackson compromise. Also, the S.1075 Report, *supra* note 2, at 8, commented that in past environmental decision making, "Public desires and aspirations were seldom consulted."

18. The theme of public involvement was not well-developed in the legislative history. Jackson, in comments on the Senate floor [115 Cong. Rec. 40416 (December 20, 1969)] declared that environmentally impacting decisions must be made "in the light of public scrutiny." The theme of public involvement was made quite explicit, however, in exec. order No. 11514, *supra* note 3, §2(b), which requires federal agencies to develop procedures to ensure the fullest practicable provision of timely public information and understanding of federal plans and programs with environmental impact in order to obtain the views of interested parties.

19. Calvert Cliffs' Coordinating Committee v. AEC, 449 F.2d 1109, 1 ELR 20346 (D.C. Cir. 1971), *cert. denied*, 404 U.S. 942 (1972).

20. The CEQ memo is reprinted in Joint 1972 NEPA Hearings, *supra* note 13, at 43.

21. *Id.*, at 45.

22. *Id.*, at 47. The eight points were: 1. NEPA is an environmental full disclosure law. 2. NEPA mandates a systematic balancing analysis of environmental and nonenvironmental costs and benefits. 3. Agencies cannot sit back and resolve environmental issues others may raise, but must take the initiative in probing environmental considerations. 4. Agencies must conduct research into the environmental impact of their actions. 5. Agencies must include economic data in their NEPA mandated analyses. 6. In choosing a particular course of action,

agencies must consider less environmentally damaging alternatives. 7. "The full range of responsible opinion" on environmental effects must be treated in an impact statement. 8. Courts will not act to overturn substantive administrative judgments on their merits. But if the agency's decision making is procedurally deficient, then the courts have the responsibility to enjoin administrative actions until compliance has been achieved.

23. *Id.*, at 45.

24. Reprinted at 2 ELR 46162.

25. Comptroller General of the United States, "Report to the Subcomm. on Fisheries and Wildlife Conservation, House Comm. on Merchant Marine and Fisheries, Improvements Needed in Federal Efforts to Implement the National Environmental Policy Act of 1969," (May 18, 1972) [hereafter cited as GAO Report].

26. The October 5, 1971 OMB memo establishing the quality of life review process is reprinted at ELR 46001.

27. §102(2)(C). See appendix.

28. See S.1075 Report, *supra* note 2, at 25.

29. Council on Environmental Quality, *102 Monitor*, May 1973, at 103.

30. Dingell 1970 Oversight Hearings, *supra* note 11, pt. I, at 58–59.

31. *Environmental Quality—The Second Annual Report of the Council on Environmental Quality* 26 (1971) [hereafter cited as CEQ Second Annual Report].

32. Undated staff memo at 3. Copy in author's files.

33. *Supra*, note 25.

34. *Id.*, at 47.

35. *Id.*, at 46.

36. *Id.*, at 3.

37. See Dingell's opening statement in Dingell 1970 Oversight Hearings, *supra* note 11, pt. 1 at 1–2.

38. *Id.*, pt. II at 7–9.

39. *Id.*, pt. I at 62–63.

40. *Id.*, at 65.

41. §2(b), *supra* note 18. CEQ Chairman Train is generally credited with having this language included in the executive order.

42. See note 18 *supra*.

43. *Id.*, at 66.

44. *Id.*, at 67.

45. See S.1075 Report, *supra* note 2, at 24.

46. §3(d), *supra* note 3.

47. "Hearing on S. 1075, S. 237 and S. 1752 before the Senate

Comm. on Interior and Insular Affairs," 92d Cong., 1st Sess. 120 (1969) [hereafter cited as S.1075 Hearings].

48. *Id.*, at 66–67.

49. Dingell 1970 Oversight Hearings, *supra* note 11, pt. I, at 56.

50. *Id.*, at 150.

51. House Comm. on Merchant Marine and Fisheries, "Administration of The National Environmental Policy Act," H. Rep. No. 92–316, 92d Cong., 2d Sess. 18 (1972) [hereafter cited as Dingell Oversight Report].

52. August 9, 1971. Original in the files of the Dingell subcommittee.

53. Wilderness Society v. Hickel, 325 F. Supp. 422, 1 ELR 20042 (D.D.C. 1970).

54. Undersecretary of Interior William Pecora declared at a news conference that hearings would be a "circus" and "would interfere with a more thoughtful and rational analysis." See the *Washington Post*, March 21, 1972.

55. Many young, liberal, freshmen Democrats were elected to the 94th Congress, and they succeeded in deposing two committee chairmen. Whitten was reportedly one of their potential targets because of his anticonsumer and anti-environmental views. He "voluntarily" relinquished his CEQ-EPA appropriations role before he was formally challenged.

56. (Toronto: D. Van Nostrand and Company, 1966.)

57. Printed text at 12. Speech was delivered on February 15, 1972.

58. "Hearings on Agriculture-Environmental and Consumer Protection Appropriations for 1972 before a Subcomm. of the House Comm. on Appropriations," 92d Cong., 1st Sess. pt. V, 512 (1971).

59. House Comm. on Appropriations, "Department of Agriculture— Environmental and Consumer Protection Appropriation Bill, 1972," H. Rep. No. 92–289, 92d Cong., 1st Sess. (1971).

60. House Comm. on Appropriations, "Department of Agriculture— Environmental and Consumer Protection Appropriation Bill, 1973," H. Rep. No. 92–1175, 92d Cong., 2d Sess. (1972). For OMB action, see 38 Fed. Reg. 12138 (May 9, 1973).

61. House Comm. on Appropriations, "Department of Agriculture— Environmental and Consumer Protection Appropriations Bill, 1974," H. Rep. No. 93–275, 93d Cong., 1st Sess. 49 (1973).

62. 119 Cong. Rec. H4784 (daily ed. June 15, 1973).

63. H. Rep. No. 93–253, 93d Cong., 1st Sess. 41 (1973).

64. *New York Times*, September 6, 1972.

65. (1965), at 292, 313.

66. *Id.*, at 314.

67. *Id.*

68. Heller, "Economic Policy Advisers," in *The Presidential Advisory System* 33 (T. Cronin and S. Greenberg eds. 1969).

69. Sax, *Defending the Environment*, 92–93 (Consumers Union ed., 1971).

70. Letter to Cong. John Dingell, reprinted in "Hearings on H. R. 14103 before the Subcomm. on Fisheries and Wildlife Conservation of the House Comm. on Merchant Marine and Fisheries," 92d Cong., 2d Sess. 110 (1972).

71. "Decision-Making in the White House," in *Nixon and the Environment* 267 (J. Rathlesberger ed. 1972).

72. Interview with the author.

73. Interview with the author.

74. Reprinted in Council on Environmental Quality, *Environmental Quality—The First Annual Report of the Council on Environmental Quality* 254 (1972) [hereafter cited as CEQ First Annual Report].

75. *Id.*, at v.

76. During the Council's first year of operation, its appropriation was contained in a bill vetoed by the President, so the CEQ did not obtain its appropriation until a revised bill was enacted in December 1970. For the first part of the year, it operated with a large number of personnel borrowed from other agencies; and the principal concern of these individuals was production of the first annual CEQ report.

77. *Christian Science Monitor*, January 13, 1971.

78. Blackwelder, "Water Resources Development," in Rathlesberger, *supra* note 71, at 59–60.

79. See discussion in *Sierra Club Bulletin*, July–August 1971 at 27.

80. For executive initiatives, see the CEQ's annual reports *supra* notes 31 and 74.

81. CEQ Second Annual Report, *supra* note 31, at xi.

82. For additional details, see "Hearings on Annual Reports of Council on Environmental Quality before the Subcomm. on Fisheries and Wildlife Conservation of the House Comm. on Merchant Marine and Fisheries," 92d Cong., 2d Sess. (1972). See also *New York Times*, August 11, 1972 and *Washington Post*, August 11, 1972.

83. House Comm. on Merchant Marine and Fisheries, "Council on Environmental Quality," H. Rep. No. 91–378, 91st Cong., 1st Sess. 10 (1969).

84. The controversy is described in detail in "White House Spikes Plan on Wetlands," *Washington Star*, February 19, 1972, from which this account is drawn.

85. The account below is drawn from newspaper reports and from interviews with CEQ staff. See the *Washington Star*, January 14, 1972; *New York Times*, January 11, 1972; and *Wall Street Journal*, January 14, 1972.

86. *Wall Street Journal*, *supra* note 85.

87. CEQ First Annual Report, *supra* note 74, at 212. CEQ's stress here on public participation now seems ironic in light of its dispute with Dingell over release of draft impact statements.

88. CEQ Second Annual Report, *supra* note 31, at 155–56.

89. *Environmental Quality—The Third Annual Report of the Council on Environmental Quality* 248 (1972).

90. *Id.*, at 256.

91. See "Hearings on S. 1032 before the Subcomm. on the Environment of the Senate Comm. on Commerce," 92d Cong., 1st Sess. pt. I, 36–42 (1971).

92. Staff of the Senate Comm. on Interior and Insular Affairs, 91st Cong., 2d Sess., "Law and the Environment" 5 (Comm. Print 1970).

93. The CEQ's defense of the public interest law firms was noted in two *New York Times* editorials that supported retention of the tax privileges. See the *New York Times*, October 15, 1970 and October 18, 1970.

94. See Int. Rev. Code of 1954, §501.

95. Statement of the Honorable Russell E. Train, Chairman, Council on Environmental Quality, before the House Committee on Ways and Means, May 3, 1972. Printed text at 2.

96. See cases cited in Anderson, "The National Environmental Policy Act," in *Federal Environmental Law* 254 (Dolgin and Guilbert eds. 1974).

97. *Supra* note 19.

98. Calvert Cliffs Coordinating Committee v. AEC, *id.*, 1 ELR 20346 at 20349.

99. The §103 statement was the report mandated by §103 of NEPA on the AEC's statutory ability to comply with NEPA. The §103 statements of all agencies are reprinted in pt. II of the Dingell 1970 Oversight Hearings, *supra* note 11.

100. *Id.*, pt. I at 5.

101. *Id.*, at 59.

102. Quoted *id.*, at 176.

103. Information on CEQ's attitude derived from interviews with CEQ staff.

104. 5 U.S.C. §§551 *et seq.*

105. Interview with CEQ staff.

106. Daniel R. Muller, an AEC representative discussing NEPA implementation at the December 1972 convention of the American Association for the Advancement of Science stated that, as of December 1972, the AEC had 200 personnel working on NEPA implementation. In commenting on the AEC's pre-Calvert Cliffs efforts to implement NEPA, he noted that the total staff involved in the preparation of environmental impact statements prior to the Calvert Cliffs decision was a mere handful of people, and they were simply rephrasing and restating the material submitted by the applicants.

107. Interview with the author.

108. "Hearing on Environmental Constraints and the Generation of Nuclear Electric Power: The Aftermath of the Court Decision on Calvert Cliffs before the Senate Comm. on Interior and Insular Affairs," 92d Cong., 1st Sess., pt. I, 27–28 (1971).

109. *Id.*, pt. I, at 36, and pt. II, at 387.

110. 455 F.2d 412, 2 ELR 20017 (2d Cir.), *cert. denied*, 41 U.S.L.W. 3184 (October 10, 1972).

111. *Id.*, 3 ELR at 20020.

112. At 1–2. Memo in file of the author.

113. Information from interviews with CEQ staff.

114. The inserted language is in §7 of the guidelines, 36 Fed. Reg. 7724 (April 23, 1971): "A Federal agency considering an action requiring an environmental statement, on the basis of: (i) A draft environmental statement for which it takes responsibility, *or (ii) comparable information followed by a hearing subject to to the provisions of the Administrative Procedure Act*, should consult with, and obtain the comment on the environmental impact of the action of, Federal agencies . . . ." [emphasis added].

115. 321 F.Supp. 1088, 1 ELR 20082 (E.D. Va.), *rev'd*, 451 F.2d 1130, 1 ELR 20612 (4th Cir. 1971).

116. Dingell 1970 Oversight Hearings, *supra* note 11, pt. II.

117. Information from staff interviews with the author.

118. Interview with CEQ staff.

119. 335 F.Supp. 1258, 2 ELR 20003 (D.N.M. 1971), *rev'd*, 469 F.2d 593, 2 ELR 20758 (10th Cir. 1972).

120. Interview with the author.

121. The concept of the "effectiveness dilemma" derives from Nadel, *The Politics of Consumer Protection* 57 (1971).

122. When Train left CEQ in the summer of 1973, to become EPA Administrator, a number of CEQ staff members moved with him. The summer and fall of 1973 saw considerable staff turnover, as many staff

members completed a three year "hitch" with CEQ and moved elsewhere.

123. By 1974, the environmental program appears to have been deemphasized. No environmental message was delivered by the President that year. The Council in 1974 appeared to be placing great emphasis on policy research by its staff and its contractors.

124. In 1974, CEQ's review comments played an important role in a ruling in the Warm Springs Dam case, Warm Springs Dam Task Force v. Gribble, No. A-1146 (U. S. June 17, 1974), 4 ELR 20669. Supreme Court Justice Douglas, in his capacity as Circuit Justice for the Ninth Circuit, stayed further work on the Corps of Engineers' Warm Springs Dam, pending the plaintiffs' appeal of an adverse lower court decision. In his opinion, Justice Douglas attached great weight to CEQ's written determination that the project's impact statement was deficient even though the Corps and a lower court thought it was adequate. Justice Douglas' reliance on the CEQ assessment suggested that, in the future, when CEQ's views were committed to print, they might have considerable impact on public controversies concerning agency activities. See Comment, "Supreme Court Ushers in New Era for CEQ in *Warm Springs* Case, *Environmental Law Reporter* 4 ELR 10130 (1974).

Chapter 4

1. L. Jaffe, *Judicial Control of Administrative Action* 49 (Abridged student ed. 1965).

2. *Id.*, at 35–38.

3. Lawrence and Lorsch, "Differentiation and Integration in Complex Organization," 12 *Admin. Sci. Qtrly.* 3 (1967); J. Thompson, *Organizations in Action* 6 (1967).

4. D. Katz and R. Kahn, *The Social Psychology of Organizations* 37 (1967).

5. *Id.*, at 225.

6. J. March and H. Simon, *Organizations* 168 (1958); R. Cyert and J. March, *A Behavioral Theory of the Firm* 102 (1963).

7. Cyert and March, *supra* note 6, at 27.

8. Thompson, *supra* note 3, at 133.

9. *Id.*, at 6.

10. Cyert and March, *supra* note 6, at 102, 119.

11. Holden, "Imperialism in Bureaucracy," 60 *Am. Pol. Sci. Rev.* 943 (1966).

12. *Id.*; P. Selznick, *Leadership in Administration* 66 (1957).

13. L. Gawthrop, *Bureaucratic Behavior in the Executive Branch* 79 (1969).

14. March and Simon, *supra* note 6, at 136.

15. *Id.*, at 154–55.

16. *Id.*

17. Katz and Kahn, *supra* note 4, at 277.

18. Selznick, *supra* note 12, at 36 *et seq.*

19. March and Simon, *supra* note 6, at 141.

20. H. Simon, *Administrative Behavior* xxvi (2d ed. 1957).

21. C. Lindblom, *The Intelligence of Democracy* 144 *et seq.* (1965).

22. For a list of some of these, see 115 Cong. Rec. 40417 (December 20, 1969).

23. 115 Cong. Rec. 40425 (December 20, 1969).

24. 115 Cong. Rec. 40419–40420 (December 20, 1969).

25. 115 Cong. Rec. 40420 (December 20, 1969).

26. *Id.*

27. S. Comm. on Interior and Insular Affairs, 90th Cong., 2d Sess., "A National Policy for the Environment" (Comm. Print 1968), cited in "Hearing on S. 1075, S. 237 and S. 1752 before the Senate Comm. on Interior and Insular Affairs," 91st Cong., 1st Sess. 30 (1969).

28. This discussion of change derives principally from H. Kaufman, *The Limits of Organizational Change* (1971).

29. *Id.*, at 10 *et seq.*

30. *Id.*, at 23 *et seq.*

31. *Id.*, at 15 *et seq.*

32. *Id.*, at 41 *et seq.*

33. *Id.*, at 45.

34. *Id.*, at 56.

35. *Id.*, at 3. March and Simon, *supra* note 6, at 174 provide an example of such a semantic quagmire. They speak of organizational innovation requiring the devising of new "performance programs" that have not previously been a part of an organization's repertoire and which cannot be introduced by a "simple application of programmed switching rules."

36. §101(b).

37. Rather than speaking of agency "change" in response to NEPA, one might refer to NEPA's "impact," NEPA's "implementation," and agency "compliance" with NEPA. These terms are used throughout the discussion above, although they are not rigorously defined. For discussion of these concepts, and problems associated with their use, see S. Wasby, *The Impact of the United States Supreme Court* 28–32 (1970), and J. Pressman and A. Wildavsky, *Implementation* 166 (1973).

38. See Comment, "Agencies' Revised NEPA Procedural Compliance Guidelines Near Completion, Months After Deadline for Submission to CEQ," *Environmental Law Reporter* 1 ELR 10167–68 (1971).

39. The August 1970 summary is printed in "Hearings on Organizational Plans of the Council on Environmental Quality before the Subcomm. on Fisheries and Wildlife Conservation of the House Comm. on Merchant Marine and Fisheries," 91st Cong., 2d Sess. 69–163 (1970). The listings for 1971 and 1972 are printed in the *Federal Register*: 36 Fed. Reg. 32666 (December 11, 1971) and 37 Fed. Reg. 22668 (October 20, 1972).

40. Delays in agency procedural compliance may have stemmed from the April 1971 revision of the CEQ guidelines and from a series of 1971 court opinions having implications for agency procedural compliance. See ELR Comment, *supra* note 38.

41. 36 Fed. Reg. 19343 (October 2, 1971). Promulgation dates for bureau procedures can be found in the 1972 CEQ list of procedures, *supra* note 39.

42. Interview with the author.

43. Engineering Circular 1120-2-56 (September 25, 1970). Reprinted in "Hearings on Federal Agency Compliances with Section 102(2)(C) and Section 103 of the National Environmental Policy Act of 1969 before the Subcomm. on Fisheries and Wildlife of the House Comm. on Merchant Marine and Fisheries," 91st Cong., 2d Sess. pt. II, at 453 [hereafter cited as Dingell Oversight Hearings].

44. Engineering Circular 1120-2-56, *supra* note 43, §4(a).

45. *Id.*, §5(a).

46. See §2 of CEQ's 1971 guidelines, 36 Fed. Reg. 7724 (April 23, 1971).

47. Engineering Circular 1120-2-56, *supra* note 43, §4(d).

48. *Id.*

49. *Id.*, §4(e).

50. *Id.*, Appendix B, §5(e).

51. DOT Order 5610.1 (October 7, 1970). Reprinted in Dingell Oversight Hearings, *supra* note 43, pt. II, at 487.

52. DOT Order 5610.1, *supra* note 51 §7(a).

53. *Id.*, §7(i)(7).

54. *Id.*, §6(a).

55. *Id.*, Attachment 1, §1.

56. See discussion in Comptroller-General of the United States, "Report to the Subcomm. on Fisheries and Wildlife Conservation, House Comm. on Merchant Marine and Fisheries, Improvements Needed in Federal Efforts to Implement the National Environmental

Policy Act of 1969," (May 18, 1972) at 17–18 [hereafter cited as GAO Report].

57. See the memorandum from HUD Secretary George Romney to HUD personnel entitled "Responsibilities and Interim Procedures for Environmental Matters by HUD Officers under P.L. 91-190," June 19, 1970. Reprinted in Dingell Oversight Hearings, *supra* note 43, pt. II, at 348. See also the testimony of HUD Deputy Undersecretary Charles J. Orlebeke in Dingell Oversight Hearings, pt. I, at 1053.

58. The Corps estimated its backlog at 2,400 statements and expected to complete them by FY74. See GAO Report, *supra* note 56, at 26.

59. Release 516 DM 1-3 of the Environmental Quality subseries of the Departmental manual, §2.6(A)(1). Reprinted in Dingell Oversight Hearings, *supra* note 43, pt. II, at 233.

60. Engineering Circular 1120-2-56, *supra* note 43, §4(b).

61. DOT Order 5610.1, *supra* note 51, at Attachment 1, §4(b).

62. Reprinted in "Hearings on Red Tape—Inquiring into Delays and Excessive Paperwork in Administration of Public Works Programs, before the Subcomm. on Investigations and Oversight of the House Comm. on Public Works," 92d Cong., 1st Sess. 42 (1971) [hereafter cited as Red Tape Hearings].

63. Sullivan and Montgomery, "Surveying Highway Impact," *Environment*, November 1972, at 12.

64. *Id.*, at 15.

65. *Id.*

66. *Id.*, at 13–14. Emphasis in the original.

67. "Hearings on H.R. 14103 before the Subcomm. on Fisheries and Wildlife Conservation of the House Subcomm. on Merchant Marine and Fisheries," 92d Cong., 2d Sess. 23 (1972).

68. Interview with CEQ staff member.

69. The source of these figures is a CEQ compilation in the author's files. An examination of CEQ's *102 Monitor* for this period reveals that virtually no draft highway statements were prepared in 1970, while 66 percent of them were prepared in 1971.

70. 36 Fed. Reg. 23696 (December 11, 1971).

71. 37 Fed. Reg. 879 (January 20, 1972).

72. *Id.*, §6.7(b)(1).

73. For 4,900 grants totalling $5.3 billion, EPA prepared only 44 statements. Reported in the *Washington Post*, November 18, 1973.

74. Council on Environmental Quality, *102 Monitor*, November 1973, at 148.

75. Memorandum reprinted in "Hearings on Agriculture, Environ-

mental and Consumer Protection Appropriations for 1973 before a Subcomm. of the House Comm. on Appropriations," 92d Cong., 2d Sess. pt. V, at 258 [hereafter cited as Whitten Hearings].

76. Copy in author's files.

77. 115 Cong. Rec. 40418 (December 20, 1969).

78. 115 Cong. Rec. 40423 (December 20, 1969). Language similar to the understanding between Senators Muskie and Jackson was inserted by Representative Dingell into the House debate over NEPA. See 115 Cong. Rec. 40925 (December 23, 1969).

79. Environmental Policy Division, Congressional Research Service, Library of Congress, 93d Cong., 1st Sess., "A Legislative History of the Water Pollution Control Act Amendments of 1972" pt. I, at 201 (Senate Public Works Comm. Print, 1973). In its guidelines, CEQ construed the Muskie-Jackson agreement to exempt FWPCA and NAPCA from the impact statement requirement, and extended the exemption to EPA following the amalgamation of the FWPCA and NAPCA into the fledgling agency. See §4(d) of the Interim CEQ guidelines at 35 Fed. Reg. 7390 (May 12, 1970), and §5(d) of the guidelines at 36 Fed. Reg. 7724 (April 24, 1971).

80. 335 F. Supp. 1, 1 ELR 20637 (D.D.C. 1971). The suit was brought because some environmentalists felt that the permits would be lax and would constitute "licenses to pollute."

81. Pub. L. No. 92-500, 86 Stat. 816, 33 U.S.C. §§1251 *et seq.*

82. Reports in 1972 of OMB involvement in EPA decision making served to buttress these contentions. See the *New York Times*, February 17, 1972.

83. Two court decisions, in 1972 and 1973, appeared to lend credence to this fear. See Essex Chemical v. Ruckelshaus, 486 F.2d 427, 3 ELR 20732 (D.C. Cir. 1973), and the district court decision in Anaconda v. Ruckelshaus, 352 F. Supp. 697, 3 ELR 20024 (D. Colo. 1972), *rev'd*, 482 F.2d 1301, 3 ELR 20719 (10th Cir. 1973).

84. See Table 4-7. The suits had many causes of action besides NEPA, but it is nevertheless important that NEPA was perceived by industry as an added weapon in its legal arsenal.

85. These cases are listed at 3 ELR 10022, 10090, and 10133 (1973).

86. Getty Oil v. Ruckelshaus, 467 F.2d 349, 2 ELR 20683 (3rd Cir. 1972); Duquesne Light Co. v. EPA, 481 F.2d 1, 3 ELR 20483 (3rd Cir. 1973); Buckeye Power, Inc. v. EPA, 481 F.2d 162, 3 ELR 20634 (6th Cir. 1973); Appalachian Power Co. v. EPA, 477 F.2d 495, 3 ELR 20310 (4th Cir. 1973); Anaconda v. Ruckelshaus, 482 F.2d 1301, 3 ELR 20719 (10th Cir. 1973); International Harvester v. Ruckelshaus, 478 F.2d 615, 3 ELR 20133 (D.C. Cir. 1973). However, only the D.C. Circuit bothered, in

Portland Cement Association v. Ruckelshaus, 486 F.2d 375, 3 ELR 20642 (1973), to examine closely NEPA's legislative history and the policy objectives to be served or undercut by application of the impact statement requirement to EPA's regulatory actions.

87. §7(c), Pub. L. No. 93-319, 88 Stat. 246 (1974).

88. *Environmental Policy and Impact Analysis* (1973).

89. *Id.*, at 36.

90. Memorandum from EPA Deputy Administrator Robert Fri to EPA regional administrators and others, entitled "Release of EPA Comments on Environmental Impact Statements," October 18, 1971. Reprinted in Whitten Hearings, *supra* note 75, pt. V, at 225. This coding scheme was revised in November 1972.

91. *Supra*, note 88, at 37.

92. Interviews were conducted by the author in three EPA regional offices and at EPA's Washington headquarters.

93. 5 U.S.C. Reorg. Plan of 1970 No. 3.

94. Clean Air Act Amendments of 1970, Pub. L. No. 91-604, 84 Stat. 1713, 42 U.S.C. §§1857 *et seq.*

95. 42 U.S.C. §1857 h-7. For a detailed discussion of §309 and EPA's oversight of NEPA, see Healy, "The Environmental Protection Agency's Duty to Oversee NEPA's Implementation: Section 309 of the Clean Air Act," *Environmental Law Reporter* 3 ELR 50071 (1973).

96. The SST controversy is referred to in discussion of §309 at 116 Cong. Rec. 42386 (December 18, 1970).

97. Memorandum from George Marienthal, acting director, EPA Office of Federal Activities, to regional administrators and others, entitled "Environmental Impact Statements," August 24, 1971. Reprinted in Whitten Hearings, *supra* note 75, pt. V, at 215. Despite the effort to decentralize review activity, the problem of review delay persisted through 1973. The Office of Federal Activities set as one of its FY74 goals an average overdue comment frequency of less than 25 percent of the review requests received per month, with no comments to be more than thirty days past due.

98. Reprinted in Whitten Hearings, *supra* note 75, pt. V, at 236, 253 and 256.

99. *Id.*, at 238.

100. Conference on EPA Review and Preparation of Environmental Impact Statements, San Francisco (July 10 to 11, 1972), New York (July 17 to 18, 1972). A second conference was convened in March 1973. Copies of agendas in author's files.

101. Interview with OFA staff.

102. The EPA comments listed in Table 4-6 are for a time period which overlaps the time period represented in Table 4-5.

103. The length of EPA's review comments on nuclear power plants tended to be much greater than the length of its review comments on other agency actions.

104. That observation is based on a nonsystematic comparison by the author of large numbers of SCS and AEC impact statements. The lack of detailed EPA comments on SCS projects may have been attributable to the influence exerted by Representative Jamie Whitten over EPA's budget. See Richard N. L. Andrews, "Environmental Policy and Administrative Change: The National Environmental Policy Act of 1969 (1970–71)" 373 (Unpublished Ph.D. dissertation, Department of City and Regional Planning, University of North Carolina, 1972).

105. Whitten relinquished control over the EPA appropriations in early 1975, probably in anticipation of a challenge to this control from newly elected liberal Democrats.

106. House Comm. on Appropriations, "Department of Agriculture —Environmental and Consumer Protection Bill, 1973," H. Rep. No. 92-1175, 92d Cong., 2d Sess. 67 (1972).

107. See EPA comment in Corps of Engineers, *Environmental Statement—March 1971—Tennessee-Tombigbee Waterway—Alabama and Mississippi—Navigation* C-22 (1971).

108. Red Tape Hearings, *supra* note 62, at 353.

109. Interview with the author.

110. U.S. Atomic Energy Commission, *Final Environmental Statement Related to Operation of the Maine Yankee Atomic Power Station*, A-16 (1972).

111. 37 Fed. Reg. 13207 (July 4, 1972).

112. L. Ortolano *et al.*, "An Analysis of Environmental Statements for Corps of Engineers Water Projects," 114 (NTIS # AD-747-374, June 1972).

113. *Id.*, at 92.

114. *Id.*, at 79.

115. *Id.*, at 109–10.

116. Interview with the author. The Corps circulated in September 1971 a list of its personnel engaged in impact statement work. There were 280 persons listed, most of whom were engineers. The many district and division offices of the Corps varied considerably in their NEPA manpower allocations. Copy of list in author's files.

117. Andrews, *supra* note 104, at 347.

118. The pre–Calvert Cliffs AEC figure is derived from a comment by an AEC official at the 1972 annual meeting of the American

Association for the Advancement of Science. See chapter 3, note 106. The post–Calvert Cliffs AEC figure is taken from testimony by AEC Chairman Dr. James Schlesinger, in "Hearings on H.R. 13752 before the Subcomm. on Fisheries and Wildlife Conservation of the House Comm. on Merchant Marine and Fisheries," 92d Cong., 2d Sess. 25 (1972). The funding level for FY72 impact statement preparation was $5.8 million, compared to less than $1 million for pre–Calvert Cliffs FY71. The pre–Greene County FPC figures derive from "Hearings on Public Works for Water and Power Development and AEC Appropriations Bill, 1973, before a Subcomm. of the House Comm. on Appropriations," 92d Cong., 2d Sess. pt. III, at 1018 (1972). The post–Greene County FPC figure derives from "Hearings on Public Works and Power Development and AEC Appropriations Bill, 1974, before a Subcomm. of the House Comm. on Appropriations," 93d Cong., 1st Sess. pt. III, at 942 (1973).

119. See Dingell Oversight Hearings, *supra* note 43, pt. II, at 597 *et seq.*

120. House Comm. on Merchant Marine and Fisheries, "Administration of the National Environmental Policy Act," H. Rep. No. 92–316, 92d Cong., 2d Sess. 34 *et seq.* (1972) [hereafter cited as Dingell Oversight Report].

121. *Id.*, at 38.

122. Most of the §103 reports were brief and undetailed, although there were some exceptions. BSFW and the Park Service stressed ways in which their environmental protection/preservation authority could be enhanced, and BLM and the Defense Department agencies listed specific regulatory changes that were in order. The Bureau of Reclamation, in its report, sought greater stream channelization authority.

123. 430 F.2d 199, 1 ELR 20023 (5th Cir. 1970), *cert. denied*, 401 U.S. 910 (1971).

124. "The National Energy Crisis—Revisited," speech delivered April 10, 1973. Printed text at 17. Copy in author's files.

125. August 15, 1973.

126. Testimony of Chairman John Nassikas and Commissioner Albert Brooke, Jr. in "Hearings on H.R. 5277 before the Subcomm. on Communications and Power of the House Comm. on Interstate and Foreign Commerce," 92d Cong., 1st Sess. 414 (1971), cited in statement by Chairman Nassikas in "Hearings on S.1684, S.1915, and S.3631 before the Senate Comm. on Commerce," 92d Cong., 2d Sess. 339, n.3 (1972).

127. "Hearings on S.1684, S.1915, and S.3631," *supra* note 126, at 399.

128. 38 Fed. Reg. 33356 (December 3, 1973).

129. "Hearings on H.R. 13752," *supra* note 118, at 21.

130. The Dingell committee, in a June 1971 report based on its December 1970 oversight hearings, noted that through December 31, 1970, only seven impact statements had been prepared for agency legislative proposals. The committee report estimated that the impact statement workload for environmental legislation should probably involve at least eight hundred or more bills in each congressional session. See Dingell Oversight Report, *supra* note 120, at 23. CEQ figures show that through November 30, 1972, only 118 draft and 45 final impact statements had been prepared for legislative proposals. See F. Anderson, *NEPA in the Courts* 126 (1973).

131. §3(c), 35 Fed. Reg. 7390 (May 12, 1970).

132. Reprinted in Dingell Oversight Hearings, *supra* note 43, pt. II, at 42.

133. Dingell Oversight Report, *supra* note 120, at 26.

134. 36 Fed. Reg. 23710 (December 11, 1971).

135. GAO Report, *supra* note 56, at 52–53.

136. *Id.*, at 55.

137. Interview with CEQ staff member.

138. The letter is reprinted in Anderson, *supra* note 130, at 131, n. 325.

139. Environmental Policy Division, Congressional Research Service, Library of Congress, 93d Cong., 1st Sess., "National Environmental Policy Act of 1969—An Analysis of Proposed Legislative Modifications —First Session, 93d Congress" 46–47 (Senate Interior Comm. Print, 1973).

140. See, *e.g.*, sources cited in notes 39, 43, and 56, *supra*.

141. "Hearing on the Implementation of the National Environmental Policy Act as it Relates to the Planning and Construction of Highways, before the Subcomm. on Roads of the Senate Comm. on Public Works," 91st Cong., 2d Sess. (1970); "Hearing on the Report of the Council on Environmental Quality, before the Subcomm. on Air and Water Pollution of the Senate Comm. on Public Works," 91st Cong., 2d Sess. (1970).

142. Cramton and Berg, "On Leading a Horse to Water: NEPA and the Federal Bureaucracy," 71 *Mich. L. Rev.* 522 (1973). Cramton and Berg attribute the absence of congressional interest to the unavailability of an effective enforcement mechanism; the courts cannot enjoin congressional actions as readily as they can those of agencies.

143. See Council on Environmental Quality, *102 Monitor*, January 1972, at 34. At hearings on its FY72 budget request, held in March 1971

NPS estimated it would be submitting nine wilderness plans to Congress through the end of FY71. See "Hearings on Department of Interior and Related Agencies Appropriations, 1972, before a Subcomm. of the House Comm. on Appropriations," 92d Cong., 1st Sess. pt. III, at 798 (1971).

144. See Council on Environmental Quality, *102 Monitor*, September 1971, at 90. The figure on the number of master plans can be found in "Hearings on Department of Interior and Related Agencies Appropriations, 1973, before a Subcomm. of the House Comm. on Appropriations," 92d Cong., 2d Sess. pt. II, at 685 (1972).

145. See "Hearings on Department of Interior and Related Agencies Appropriations, 1972," *supra* note 143, pt. III, at 798–99.

146. For statistics on BSFW's wilderness designations, see "Hearings on Department of the Interior and Related Agencies Appropriations before a Subcomm. of the House Comm. on Appropriations," pt. II, at 16; pt. II, at 6; and pt. II, at 894, for Fiscal Years 1971, 1972 and 1973, respectively.

147. See CEQ list of statements received, 37 Fed. Reg. 12340 (June 22, 1972).

148. Interview with the author.

149. Interview with the author.

150. Through August 1972, HUD had produced only forty-one statements. See Council on Environmental Quality, *102 Monitor*, September 1972, at 83.

151. Letter dated August 18, 1972. Copy in author's files.

152. Housing Act of 1949, 42 U.S.C. §1441.

153. Green, "Nuclear Power Licensing and Regulation," in *Annals*, March 1972, at 124. Green, a recognized expert in nuclear energy law, had earlier developed this view in H. P. Green and A. Rosenthal, *Government of the Atom: The Integration of Powers* (1963).

154. New Hampshire v. AEC, 406 F.2d 170 (1st Cir.) *cert. denied*, 395 U.S. 962 (1969).

155. See Andrews, *supra* note 104, at 405.

156. See Table 4-7.

157. *New York Times*, September 27, 1973.

158. *Washington Post*, October 6, 1973.

159. Daniel R. Muller, in a discussion of NEPA's implementation before a panel at the December 1972 convention of the American Association for the Advancement of Science.

160. *New York Times*, August 20, 1971.

161. *Id.*

162. Atomic Industrial Forum, "Nuclear Industry," cited in R. Lewis *Citizens vs. The Atomic Industrial Establishment* (1972).

163. Reported in the *Christian Science Monitor*, October 28, 1971.

164. *Id.*

165. *New York Times*, October 21, 1971.

166. *Washington Star*, July 13, 1972.

167. *Washington Post*, May 16, 1973. See also Gillette, "Nuclear Safety (III): Critics Charge Conflicts of Interest," 177 *Science* 970 (September 15, 1972).

168. *Washington Post*, July 4, 1973.

169. See Gillette, "Nuclear Safety (I): The Roots of Dissent," 177 *Science* 771 (September 1, 1972).

170. *New York Times*, June 15, 1973.

171. *Washington Post*, July 4, 1973.

172. CBS Evening News, June 11, 1973 (Printed transcript at 8).

173. *Id.*

174. *Washington Star News*, June 26, 1973.

175. In 1972, long-time member Senator Clinton Anderson retired and Representative Aspinall was defeated. Two new members of the committee, Senators Symington and Baker, took a more detached view of atomic energy than that of these old committee stalwarts.

176. John Ferejohn, "Congressional Influences on Water Politics," (Unpublished Ph.D. dissertation, Department of Political Science, Stanford University, 1972) at 399.

177. *New York Times*, February 20, 1972.

178. For details, see Mazmanian and Lee, "Tradition be Damned! The Corps of Engineers is Changing!" *Pub. Admin. Rev.*, March–April 1975, at 166.

179. Andrews, *supra* note 104, at 254–55.

180. *Id.*, at 236 *et seq.*

181. EC 1165-2-85, April 22, 1970, "Water Resource Policies and Authorities; Budget Material in Response to the National Environmental Policy Act of 1969 for Authorized Projects."

182. EC 1165-2-86, April 30, 1970, "National Environmental Policy Act of 1969."

183. Memorandum entitled "Utilization of Attorneys in the Implementation of Section 102(2)(C) of the National Environmental Policy Act of 1969 (Public Law 91-190)." Copy in author's files.

184. Association of Northwest Steelheaders v. Corps of Engineers, Civil No. 3362 (E.D. Wash., filed March 11, 1971); Environmental Defense Fund v. Corps of Engineers, Civil No. 2655-69 (D.D.C., amended complaint filed April 9, 1970); Akers v. Resor, Civil Action No.

C-70-349 (M.D. Tenn., filed April 23, 1970); Sierra Club v. Laird, Civil No. 70–78 (D. Ariz., filed May 25, 1970).

185. A preliminary injunction was entered in Sierra Club v. Laird, 1 ELR 20085 (June 23, 1970). It should be noted, however, that beginning with the Cross-Florida Barge Canal opinion in January 1971 and the Gillham I opinion in February 1971, a series of decisions was delivered in federal courts which was to have a significant impact on Corps response to NEPA. This litigation is discussed in chapter 5, *infra*.

186. Brooks v. Volpe, 319 F. Supp. 90, 1 ELR 20045 (W.D. Wash., Sept. 25, 1970), preliminary injunction against highway construction denied; Pennsylvania Environmental Council v. Bartlett, 315 F. Supp. 238, 2 ELR 20752 (M.D. Pa., April 30, 1970), injunction against highway construction denied; Wilderness Society v. Hickel, 325 F. Supp. 422, 1 ELR 20042 (D.D.C., April 30, 1970), trans-Alaskan pipeline construction enjoined; Texas Committee on Natural Resources v. U.S., 2 ELR 20574 (W.D. Tex., February 5, 1970), golf course construction stayed pending appeal.

187. See "Omnibus Bill Bypasses Crucial Step," *Environmental Action*, October 31, 1970, at 3.

188. House Comm. on Public Works, "Rivers and Harbors and Flood Control Acts of 1970," H. Rep. No. 91-1665, 91st Cong., 2d Sess. 3 (1970). The House committee further demonstrated its lack of concern for proper evaluation of projects by authorizing many that had not been reviewed by the Secretary of the Army or OMB. See Love, "The Failures of an Act That Once Sparked Hope," *Environmental Action*, January 9, 1971, at 4.

189. There was some indication, from interviews conducted by Daniel Mazmanian, that the committees had, as of 1974, begun to take environmentalist witnesses more seriously than they had in the past.

190. The committees continued, however, to freeze the discount rate at which projects' economic viability was adjudged, thereby sustaining the non-economical "pork barrel" aspects of the Corps program. Corps benefit-cost analyses are discussed in chapter 5, *infra*.

191. *New York Times*, February 20, 1972.

192. Similarly, Daniel Mazmanian and Jeanne Nienaber found variations in District Engineers' participation in "citizen participation" programs. See Mazmanian and Nienaber, "Bureaucracy and the Public: A Case of Citizen Participation in the Corps of Engineers," paper presented at the Midwest Political Science Association Annual Meeting, 1974.

193. Engineering Circular EC 1120-2-62, November 18, 1970, at 2.

194. Red Tape Hearings, *supra* note 62, at 322.
195. Interview with former Corps official.

Chapter 5

1. (Cambridge: Harvard University Press, 1965), *passim.*
2. *Washington Post*, September 28, 1973.
3. For an excellent collection of court decisions, law review materials and testimony pertaining to the fee-shifting issue, see "Hearings on the Effect of Legal Fees on the Adequacy of Representation, before the Subcomm. on Representation of Citizen Interests of the Senate Comm. on the Judiciary," 93d Cong., 2d Sess. pts. III and IV (1973).
4. For a discussion of the three exceptions, see the testimony of J. Anthony Kline, in the Senate hearings cited *supra*, note 3, pt. III, at 788.
5. The notion of the private attorney-general suing to vindicate the public interest had been born in 1943 in Associated Industries v. Ickes, 134 F.2d 694, 704 (2d Cir., 1943). In that decision, the court noted that the attorney-general can be vested with the authority to vindicate the interest of the public or the government by bringing suit against an official acting in violation of his statutory powers. The court observed that it was also constitutional for Congress to empower individual citizens to bring suit to prevent such extrastatutory action, even if the sole purpose of such private action was to vindicate the public interest. It stated that "such persons, so authorized, are, so to speak, private Attorneys-General."
6. See, *e.g.*, La Raza Unida v. Volpe, 2 ELR 20691 (N.D. Cal., October 19, 1972), wherein Olson's discussion of the economics of public interest representation is cited.
7. 495 F.2d 1026, 4 ELR 20279 (D.C. Cir., April 4, 1974).
8. 325 F.Supp. 422, 1 ELR 20042 (D.D.C. 1970).
9. 479 F.2d 842, 3 ELR 20085 (D.C. Cir., February 9, 1973).
10. Pub. L. No. 93-153, 87 Stat. 584 (1973), amending 30 U.S.C. §185.
11. Wilderness Society v. Morton, *supra* note 7.
12. 28 U.S.C. §2412.
13. Wilderness Society v. Morton, *supra* note 7, at 20280.
14. *Id.*, at 20284, n.9.
15. *Id.*, at 20286.
16. *Id.*, at 20287.
17. *Id.*
18. *Id.*, at 20288.

19. Alyeska Pipeline Service Co. v. Wilderness Society, 5 ELR 20286 (U.S., May 12, 1975).

20. Rules 56(c) and 65(c). Of course, issuance of a preliminary injunction is contingent upon satisfying requirements pertaining to the merits of the action and the need for injunctive relief. See, e.g., Ohio *ex rel.* Brown v. Calloway, 3 ELR 20892, 20893 (S.D. Ohio, August 24, 1973).

21. 337 F.Supp. 167, 2 ELR 20089 (D.D.C. December 17, 1971).

22. *Id.*

23. The early decision was Sierra Club v. Laird, 1 ELR 20085 (D. Ariz. 1970), in which bond was reduced from $75,000 to $20,000. The court provided no explanation in its published opinion for the original figure or for the reduction.

24. J. Sax, *Defending the Environment* 59 (Consumers Union ed. 1971).

25. M. Nadel, *The Politics of Consumer Protection* 211–12 (1971).

26. Grossman, "A Model for Judicial Policy Analysis: The Supreme Court and the Sit-in Cases," in *Frontiers of Judicial Research* 412 (Grossman and Tannenhaus eds. 1969).

27. Philip Bereano, "Courts as Institutions for Assessing Technology," Paper delivered at 1972 Annual Meeting of the American Association for the Advancement of Science, Washington, D. C., at 1. See also Sax, *supra* note 24, at xxii.

28. Scenic Hudson Preservation Conference v. F.P.C., 354 F.2d 608, 1 ELR 20292 (2d Cir. 1965).

29. Interview with the author. The project was still tied up in the courts in 1974.

30. This formulation is borrowed, in modified form, from K.C. Davis, *Administrative Law Treatise* §22.01 (1958). The question "where" is substituted here for Davis' "whether."

31. The "how" and "how much" considerations are not considered at length here. The "how" question pertains to the type of relief that will be granted (preliminary injunction, remand to lower court or to agency, *etc.*) while the "how much" question pertains to the scope of review, *i.e.*, the scope of the record that will be reviewed and the evidentiary tests applied to the record selected for review. The scope of review was a key question in some of the NEPA cases discussed later in this chapter.

32. Northeast Area Welfare Rights Organization v. Volpe, 1 ELR 20186 (E.D. Wash., Dec. 3, 1970).

33. Lloyd Harbor Study Group v. Seaborg, 1 ELR 20188 (E.D. N.Y., April 2, 1971); Thermal Ecology Must Be Preserved v. AEC, 433 F.2d

524, 1 ELR 20078 (D.C. Cir. July 20, 1970). In both opinions the AEC was warned that its actions might be later reversed by the courts.

34. Sierra Club v. Hardin, 325 F.Supp. 99, 1 ELR 20161 (D. Alas., March 25, 1971); Clark v. Volpe, 461 F.2d 1266, 2 ELR 20459 (5th Cir., July 10, 1972).

35. 458 F.2d 1323, 2 ELR 20162 (4th Cir., April 4, 1972).

36. *Id.*, 2 ELR at 20163. Emphasis in the original. Footnotes omitted.

37. "Venue" is considered as a "whether" question in Davis, *supra* note 30, along with the matters of whether the issue raised was "federal" and whether the "case and controversy" clause of the Constitution was satisfied.

38. Dolbeare, "The Federal District Courts and Urban Public Policy," in Grossman and Tannenhaus, *supra* note 26.

39. The district court denied a petition for change of venue but was reversed by the 2d Circuit. NRDC v. TVA, 340 F.Supp. 400, 1 ELR 20634 (S.D. N.Y. 1971), *rev'd*, 459 F.2d 255, 2 ELR 20152 (2d Cir. 1972).

40. "Hearings on H.R. 14103 before the Subcomm. on Fisheries and Wildlife Conservation of the House Comm. on Merchant Marine and Fisheries," 92d Cong., 2d Sess. 218 (1972).

41. That rumor is reported here only because it suggests the intensity of the lawyers' feelings concerning the treatment of federal agencies in the D.C. Circuit. The source of this report is a professional acquaintance of the author who formerly served in the Justice Department.

42. EDF v. Corps of Engineers, 331 F.Supp. 925, 1 ELR 20466 (D.D.C. 1971), 348 F.Supp. 916, 2 ELR 20536 (N.D. Miss. 1972).

43. Canal Authority of Florida v. Calloway, 4 ELR 20164, 20168 (5th Cir., February 15, 1974). The reasoning of the U.S. District Court for the Middle District of Florida can be found in its January 31, 1974, opinion in the case at 4 ELR 20259. For the earliest opinion in the canal controversy, see EDF v. Corps of Engineers, 324 F.Supp. 878, 1 ELR 20079 (D.D.C. 1971).

44. For example, in 1967, a church group was granted standing as a private attorney general to challenge FCC renewal of a broadcasting license for an antiblack, southern television station. See Office of Communications, United Church of Christ v. FCC, 359 F.2d 994 (D.C. Cir. 1966). From the time of this landmark decision, perhaps one hundred stations were monitored by civic activists, and many stations sought to escape legal action by agreeing to improve minority programming and to hire minority workers. See the *New York Times*, July 16, 1973.

45. Scenic Hudson Preservation Conference v. FPC, *supra* note 28.

46. 5 U.S.C. §702.

47. See, *e.g.*, Citizens Committee for the Hudson Valley v. Volpe, 302 F.Supp. 1083, 1 ELR 20001 (S.D. N.Y. 1969), *aff'd*, 425 F.2d 97, 1 ELR 20006 (2d Cir. 1970); Parker v. U.S., 307 F.Supp. 685, 1 ELR 20588 (D. Colo. 1969).

48. 397 U.S. 150 (1970).

49. 397 U.S. 159 (1970).

50. *Data Processing, supra* note 48, at 152–53.

51. Sierra Club v. Hickel, *aff'd sub nom.* Sierra Club v. Morton, 405 U.S. 345, 2 ELR 20192 (1972).

52. 1 ELR 20097 (9th Cir., January 19, 1971).

53. 433 F.2d 24, 1 ELR 20015 (9th Cir. 1970).

54. Sierra Club v. Morton, *supra* note 51.

55. U.S. v. SCRAP, 412 U.S. 669, 3 ELR 20536 (U.S. June 18, 1973).

56. *Id.*, 3 ELR at 20549.

57. *Discretionary Justice* 20 (1971).

58. *Id.*

59. Davis, *supra* note 57, at 4.

60. Bereano, *supra* note 27, at 6. Private interests whose claims are presently recognized by an agency suffer losses when competing claims are even put on an agency's agenda for decision. Opening the decision-making arena can only reduce the former claims' impact and increase the possibility that decision-making outcomes will be less favorable to them. Bachrach and Baratz, "Two Faces of Power," 56 *Am. Pol. Sci. Rev.* 947 (1962), cited in Nadel, *supra* note 25, at 214–15.

61. Davis, *supra* note 57, at 5.

62. *Id.*, at 55.

63. 439 F.2d 584, 1 ELR 20059 (D.C. Cir., January 7, 1971).

64. *Id.*, 1 ELR at 20064.

65. *Id.*

66. 3 ELR 20127 (D.C. Cir., February 6, 1973).

67. *Id.*, at 20128–29.

68. *Id.*

69. Sierra Club v. Laird, *supra* note 23.

70. Texas Committee on Natural Resources v. U.S., 2 ELR 20574, *vacated*, 430 F.2d 1315 (5th Cir. 1970).

71. In Brooks v. Volpe, 319 F.Supp. 90, 1 ELR 20045 (W.D. Wash., September 25, 1970), Judge Beeks contended that NEPA was not "retrospective" and could not be applied to a road project on whose location a decision had been made in 1967. Application of NEPA to the road was impermissible without clear indication by Congress that the statute was to be so applied. Judge Beeks did not cite NEPA's

legislative history in reaching this conclusion. Bucklein v. Volpe, 1 ELR 20043 (N.D. Cal., October 29, 1970) was a challenge to expenditure of federal emergency relief funds for road repairs. The decision was quite brief; the comments concerning NEPA were placed in brackets, suggesting they were a hastily drafted aside. Without referring to NEPA's legislative history, the judge stated that NEPA is simply a declaration of congressional policy and as such it does not seem to create any rights or impose any duties of which a court could take cognizance. The decision in Investment Syndicates v. Richmond, 318 F.Supp. 1038, 1 ELR 20044 (D. Ore., October 27, 1970) resulted from a challenge to the Bonneville Power Administration's routing of a power line across some private property. NEPA was raised as a defense to condemnation. The project was first funded in 1967, the government had acquired a portion of the easement prior to 1970 and had let some clearing and construction contracts after 1970. Judge Belloni, citing Brooks, said that to apply NEPA to the project would mean to give the statute retrospective effect. The decision in Brooks was appealed and was reversed by the 9th Circuit.

72. Calvert Cliffs' Coordinating Committee v. AEC, 449 F.2d 1109, 1 ELR 20346, 20347 (D.C. Cir. 1971).

73. *Id.*, 1 ELR at 20348–50.

74. *Id.*, 1 ELR at 20349. Judge Wright also suggested in dicta that courts could review agency decisions for their substantive compliance, as well as for their procedural compliance, with NEPA.

75. 401 U.S. 402, 1 ELR 20110 (U.S. 1971).

76. §4(f) of the Department of Transportation Act permitted the secretary of transportation to approve construction through parkland only after he had decided that there was no feasible and prudent alternative to the use of the land, and only if the construction program included all possible planning to minimize harm to the park.

77. This evidentiary test is embodied in a provision of the Administrative Procedure Act, 5 U.S.C. §706(2)(A).

78. Citizens to Preserve Overton Park, *supra* note 75, 1 ELR at 20113.

79. *Id.*, 1 ELR at 20114.

80. See the cases cited in F. Anderson, *NEPA in the Courts* 64–66 (1973).

81. E.g., Named Members of the San Antonio Conservation Society v. Texas Highway Department, 446 F.2d 1013, 1 ELR 20379 (5th Cir. 1971).

82. Anderson, *supra* note 80, at 74.

83. See, e.g., McQuery v. Laird, 449 F.2d 608, 1 ELR 20607 (10th Cir.

1971); Port of New York Authority v. Interstate Commerce Commission, 451 F.2d 783, 2 ELR 20105 (2d Cir. 1971).

84. These were the Price Commission and the Pacific Islands Trust Territory Commission. See Cohen v. Price Commission, 337 F.Supp. 1236, 2 ELR 20178 (S.D. N.Y. 1972) and People of Saipan, by Guerrero v. Department of the Interior, 356 F.Supp. 645, 3 ELR 20298 (D. Ha. 1973).

85. Hanly v. Mitchell, 2 ELR 20181 (S.D. N.Y.), *rev'd*, (Hanly I), 460 F.2d 640, 2 ELR 20216 (2d Cir.), *cert. denied*, 41 U.S.L.W. 3247 (November 7, 1972), *sub nom.* Hanly v. Kleindeinst, 3 ELR 20016 (S.D. N.Y.), *rev'd* (Hanly II), 471 F.2d 823, 2 ELR 20717 (2d Cir. 1972).

86. Hanly I, *id.*, 2 ELR 20216 at 20220.

87. Hanly II, *supra* note 85, 2 ELR 20717 at 20723.

88. See discussion in chapter 3.

89. The initial language cited here was borrowed from the Gillham I decision; the second phrase is CEQ's.

90. This language is from Ely v. Velde, 451 F.2d 1130, 1 ELR 20612 (4th Cir. 1971).

91. EDF v. Corps of Engineers, *supra* note 42, 2 ELR 20536 at 20540.

92. EDF v. Corps of Engineers, 342 F.Supp. 1211, 2 ELR 20260 and 2 ELR 20353, 20355 (E.D. Ark. 1972).

93. 458 F.2d 827, 2 ELR 20029 (D.C. Cir. 1972).

94. 325 F.Supp. 728, 1 ELR 20130 (E.D. Ark. 1971).

95. 463 F.2d 783, 1 ELR 20469 (D.C. Cir. 1971).

96. NRDC v. Morton, *supra* note 93, 2 ELR at 20034.

97. *Id.*, 2 ELR at 20033.

98. *Id.*, 2 ELR at 20032.

99. *Id.*, 2 ELR at 20038.

100. EDF v. Corps of Engineers, *supra* note 94, 1 ELR at 20142.

101. *Id.*, 1 ELR at 20134.

102. *Id.*, 1 ELR at 20142.

103. *Id.*, 1 ELR at 20141.

104. Citizens Committee for Nuclear Responsibility v. Seaborg, *supra* note 95, 1 ELR at 20470.

105. Anderson, *supra* note 80, at 179.

106. Calvert Cliffs, *supra* note 72, 1 ELR at 20350.

107. Daly v. Volpe, 350 F.Supp. 252, 2 ELR 20443, 20444 (W.D. Wash. 1972).

108. Citizens for Clean Air v. Corps of Engineers, 349 F.Supp. 696, 2 ELR 20650, 20655 (S.D. N.Y. 1972).

109. Anderson, *supra* note 80, at 290.

110. The details of the CEQ memos are discussed in chapter 3.

111. 481 F.2d 1079, 3 ELR 20525 (D.C. Cir., June 12, 1973).

112. Sierra Club v. Froehlke, 359 F.Supp. 1289, 3 ELR 20248, 20269–70 (S.D. Tex. 1973). This was an unusual decision, as is noted in the text *infra*.

113. The generalization about the representativeness of water resource development litigation must be modified by two caveats. First, the benefit-cost review question as discussed in the text *infra* is unique to water resource development litigation. Second, the cases discussed here do not touch very heavily on questions central to NEPA litigation in other substantive areas; *e.g.*, the segmentation and impact statement delegation problems characteristic of highway NEPA litigation. See Anderson, *supra* note 80, at 64–70 and 186–96.

114. Among the projects challenged were one on the East Fork of the Little Miami River, the Cross-Florida Barge Canal, the Tennessee-Tombigbee Waterway, and channelization of the Obion and Forked Deer Rivers. These projects were authorized in 1938, 1942, 1946, and 1948, respectively.

115. A Corps evaluation of 578 projects found 440 economically justified at $5\frac{3}{8}$ percent, 295 at 7 percent, and 143 at 10 percent. For a good description of interagency disputes over the discount rate, see National Water Commission *Water Policies for the Future* 383–87 (1973); and Blackwelder, "Water Resources Development," in *Nixon and the Environment* 78 (J. Rathlesberger, ed. 1972). See also §80 of the Water Resources Development Act of 1974, Pub. L. No. 93-251, 88 Stat. 12 (March 7, 1974).

116. Sierra Club v. Laird, 1 ELR 20085 (D. Ariz., June 23, 1970).

117. EDF v. Corps of Engineers, 324 F.Supp. 878, 1 ELR 20079 (D.D.C., January 27, 1971).

118. EDF v. Corps of Engineers, *supra* note 94.

119. Texas Committee on Natural Resources v. Resor, 1 ELR 20466 (E.D. Tex., June 29, 1971).

120. U.S. v. 247.37 Acres of Land, 1 ELR 20513 (S.D. Ohio, September 9, 1971). In this case, NEPA compliance was raised as an issue by landowners challenging Corps condemnation of their land. A preliminary injunction was not issued, but the court vacated the writ of possession until such time as the Corps complied with NEPA.

121. EDF v. Corps of Engineers, 331 F.Supp. 925, 1 ELR 20466 (D.D.C., September 21, 1971).

122. Sierra Club v. Resor, 1 ELR 20366 (W.D. Wis., July 9, 1971).

123. EDF v. TVA, 339 F.Supp. 806, 2 ELR 20044 (E.D. Tenn., January 11, 1972).

124. NRDC v. Grant, 341 F.Supp. 356, 2 ELR 20185 (E.D. N.C., March 16, 1972).

125. Akers v. Resor, 339 F.Supp. 1375, 2 ELR 20221 (W.D. Tenn., March 23, 1972).

126. EDF v. Froehlke, 473 F.2d 346, 3 ELR 20001 (8th Cir., December 14, 1972).

127. EDF v. Froehlke, 348 F.Supp. 338, 2 ELR 20620 (W.D. Mo., September 13, 1972).

128. Allison v. Froehlke, 2 ELR 20357 (W.D. Texas, June 18, 1972).

129. EDF v. Armstrong, 352 F.Supp. 50, 2 ELR 20735 (N.D. Cal., November 14, 1972).

130. Sierra Club v. Froehlke, 345 F.Supp. 440, 2 ELR 20307 (W.D. Wis., June 2, 1972).

131. Conservation Council of North Carolina v. Froehlke, 340 F.Supp. 222, 2 ELR 20155 (M.D. N.C., February 14, 1972).

132. EDF v. Corps of Engineers (Gillham II), 342 F.Supp. 1211, 2 ELR 20260 (E.D. Ark., March 22, 1972), 2 ELR 20353 (E.D. Ark., May 5, 1972).

133. EDF v. Corps of Engineers, 348 F.Supp. 916, 2 ELR 20536 (N.D. Miss., August 4, 1972).

134. EDF v. Corps of Engineers, 470 F.2d 289, 2 ELR 20740 (8th Cir., November 28, 1972).

135. EDF v. TVA, 468 F.2d 1164, 2 ELR 20726 (6th Cir., December 13, 1972).

136. EDF v. Froehlke, *supra* note 126.

137. *Id.*, 3 ELR at 20005.

138. EDF v. Corps of Engineers (Gillham II), *supra* note 132, 2 ELR at 20355; EDF v. Froehlke, *supra* note 127, 2 ELR at 20627.

139. Conservation Council of North Carolina v. Froehlke, 473 F.2d 664, 3 ELR 20132 (4th Cir., February 8, 1973).

140. Sierra Club v. Froehlke, *supra* note 112.

141. Montgomery v. Ellis, 364 F.Supp. 517, 3 ELR 20845 (M.D. Ala., September 11, 1973).

142. NRDC v. Grant, 335 F.Supp. 280, 3 ELR 20176 (E.D. N.C., February 15, 1973).

143. EDF v. Armstrong, 356 F.Supp. 131, 3 ELR 20294 (N.D. Cal., March 16, 1973).

144. EDF v. Froehlke, 368 F.Supp. 231, 4 ELR 20062 (W.D. Mo., November 8, 1973).

145. Cape Henry Bird Club v. Laird, 359 F.Supp. 404, 3 ELR 20571 (E.D. Va., April 2, 1973).

146. EDF v. TVA, 4 ELR 20120 (E.D. Tenn., October 25, 1973).

147. Sierra Club v. Froehlke, *supra* note 112.

148. See discussion in text *supra*, at note 101.

149. *Supra*, note 141.

150. Cape Henry Bird Club v. Laird, *supra* note 145.

151. Sierra Club v. Froehlke, *supra* note 112, 3 ELR at 20285.

152. EDF v. Corps of Engineers (Gillham II), *supra* note 92, 2 ELR at 20355.

153. Sierra Club v. Froehlke, *supra* note 112, 3 ELR at 20266.

154. EDF v. TVA, 4 ELR 20225 (6th Cir., February 22, 1974), at note 1.

155. EDF v. Froehlke, *supra* note 144, 4 ELR at 20065.

Chapter 6

1. The Quad Cities decision is Izaak Walton League v. Schlesinger, 337 F. Supp. 287, 2 ELR 20039 (D.D.C.), court-approved settlement, 2 ELR 20388 (D.D.C. 1971).

2. The excerpts quoted here from the transcript were reported in Jack Anderson's "Washington Merry Go Round" column, March 17, 1972; *New York Times*, April 30, 1972; and *Washington Post*, May 2, 1972.

3. S.3939, 92d Cong., 1st Sess. §147; H.R.16656, §113.

4. Named Individual Members of the San Antonio Conservation Society v. Texas Highway Department, 446 F.2d 1013, 1 ELR 20379 (5th Cir. 1971).

5. 118 Cong. Rec. H9276 (daily ed. October 5, 1972).

6. See the letters from EPA Administrator Ruckelshaus and CEQ member Dr. Gordon J. McDonald inserted in the Congressional Record at 118 Cong. Rec. E8350 (daily ed. October 4, 1972) and 118 Cong. Rec. E8195 (daily ed. September 27, 1972).

7. The San Antonio North Expressway provision was retained by voice vote, 118 Cong. Rec. H9279 (daily ed. October 5, 1972).

8. 118 Cong. Rec. S14840–41 (daily ed. September 13, 1972).

9. The vote was 24-49-27, with Senator Jackson voting to retain the provision. 118 Cong. Rec. S14846 (daily ed. September 13, 1972).

10. 118 Cong. Rec. H10409 (daily ed. October 18, 1972).

11. Pub. L. No. 93-87, 87 Stat. 250.

12. For an analysis of affected projects, see Environmental Policy Division, Congressional Research Service, Library of Congress, 93d Cong., 1st Sess., "National Environmental Policy Act of 1969—An Analysis of Proposed Legislative Modifications—First Session, 93d Congress," 43–44 (Senate Interior Comm. Print 1973).

13. H.R.943, 93d Cong. 1st Sess. (1973).

14. S.3381, 92d Cong., 2d Sess. introduced by Senator Montoya; H.R.16092, introduced by Congressman Mizell.

15. S. 3381, §103(b)(1).

16. S. 3381, §103(b)(2).

17. S. 232, 93d Cong., 1st Sess., introduced by Senator Randolph for Senator Montoya (1973); H.R.7234, introduced by Congressman Mizell.

18. H.R.11066, 92d Cong., 1st Sess., introduced by Congressman MacDonald (1971); S.1684, introduced by Senator Magnuson (1971).

19. Council on Environmental Quality, *The President's 1971 Environmental Program* 241 (1971).

20. *Id.*, at 258.

21. "Hearings on S. 1684, S. 1915, and S. 3631 before the Senate Comm. on Commerce," 92d Cong., 2d Sess. (1972). See testimony of Sierra Club President Michael McCloskey at 143, Washington Environmental Council President Jack Robertson at 147, and Sierra Club Consultant Richard Lahn at 274.

22. Interview with the author.

23. Council on Environmental Quality, *The President's 1973 Environmental Program* 284 (1973). Introduced as S.935, 93d Cong., 1st Sess. by Senator Jackson (1974) and as H.R.4874 by Congressmen Staggers and Devine.

24. Izaak Walton League v. Schlesinger, *supra* note 1.

25. Kalur v. Resor, 335 F.Supp. 1, 1 ELR 20637 (D.D.C. 1971).

26. 117 Cong. Rec. 38857 (1971). Jackson's support is indicated at 118 Cong. Rec. S16888 (daily ed. October 4, 1972).

27. The vote was 267-125, in favor of retaining the provision. 118 Cong. Rec. H2621 (daily ed. March 28, 1972).

28. 117 Cong. Rec. 38857 (1971).

29. Barfield and Corrigan, "Environment Report/White House Seeks to Restrict Scope of Environmental Law," 4 *Nat'l. Jn'l.* 336, 343 (1972).

30. The entire controversy is discussed in detail in Barfield and Corrigan, *id.*

31. *Id.*, at 346.

32. The Dingell bill suspended the impact statement requirement for a three year period and provided that permits issued pursuant to its provisions, if for effluent discharges that would otherwise require impact statements, would not remain in effect past December 31, 1977. The temporary suspension of the statement requirement did not apply to permits issued for facilities constructed after April 1, 1972.

33. "Hearings on H.R. 14103 before the Subcomm. on Fisheries and

Wildlife Conservation of the House Comm. on Merchant Marine and Fisheries," 92d Cong., 2d Sess. 77 (1972) [hereafter cited as H.R.14103 Hearings].

34. Memo to EPA Administrator William Ruckelshaus reprinted *id.*, at 102.

35. Quarles memo, reprinted *id.*, at 100.

36. See, *e.g.*, *Environmental Action*, April 15, 1972, at 3; *The Living Wilderness*, Winter 1971–72 (Special Alaska Issue) at 3; *Sierra Club Bulletin*, May 1972, at 17; *Wilderness Society Wilderness Report*, May 1972, at 6; *Not Man Apart*, June 1972, at 4.

37. See sources cited *supra*, notes 29 and 36.

38. See, *e.g.*, comments in *National Wildlife Federation Conservation Report*, May 5, 1972, at 157.

39. See, *e.g.*, testimony of Robert Rauch, assistant legislative director of Friends of the Earth, in H.R.14103 Hearings, *supra* note 33, at 149–50.

40. *Id.*

41. H.R.14103 Hearings, *supra* note 33, at 199–200.

42. *Id.*, at 110.

43. Dingell's fears for NEPA are described in Barfield, "Environment Report/Exemptions from NEPA Requirements Sought for Nuclear Plants, Pollution Permits," 4 *Nat'l. Jn'l.* 1025, 1028 (1972).

44. H.R.14013 Hearings, *supra* note 33, at 152–53.

45. Barfield, "Environment Report/Water Pollution Act Forces Showdown in 1973 Over Best Way to Protect Environment," 4 *Nat'l. Jn'l.* 1971, 1978 (1972).

46. 118 Cong. Rec. H8884 (daily ed. September 28, 1972). See §§511(c)(1) and 511(c)(2).

47. Muskie argued this point of view on the Senate floor, 118 Cong. Rec. S16885–86 (daily ed. October 4, 1972).

48. Muskie further argued that §511(c), in requiring impact statements for some of EPA's actions, imposed some alternative NEPA obligations where none had existed previously. Senator Jackson, for his part, refused to concede in 1972 that he had agreed in 1969 to an exemption for EPA.

49. See 118 Cong. Rec. H9126–27 (daily ed. October 4, 1972) for Representative Dingell's comments and 118 Cong. Rec. S16887–88 (daily ed. October 4, 1972) for Senator Jackson's. More details of the dispute can be found in Barfield, "Environment Report/Pollution Law May Produce Delays In Nuclear Power Plant Licensing Process," 5 *Nat'l. Jn'l.* 128 (1973).

50. See Barfield, *supra* note 45.

51. The FPC figures are discussed in a letter from AEC Chairman James Schlesinger to Senator Jackson. See "Hearing on Environmental Constraints and the Generation of Nuclear Electric Power: The Aftermath of the Court Decision on Calvert Cliffs before the Senate Comm. on Interior and Insular Affairs," 92d Cong., 1st Sess. pt. II, 447 (1971).

52. The Schlesinger letter, *id.*, was dated January 28, 1972.

53. The legislation, H.R.13731, was introduced by Congressman Price, 118 Cong. Rec. H1954 (daily ed. March 9, 1972).

54. The Council, while it supported the legislation, suggested some clarifying amendments. See Russell Train's statement in "Hearings on H.R. 13731 and H.R. 13732 before the Joint Committee on Atomic Energy," 92d Cong., 2d Sess. pt. I, 111 (1972) [hereafter cited as JCAE Hearings].

55. Both bills would have exempted the AEC from some of the requirements of the Administrative Procedure Act and would have reduced the AEC's obligation to hold public adjudicatory hearings.

56. See, e.g., testimony of Joseph Karaganis, JCAE Hearings, *supra* note 54, pt. I, at 195.

57. See testimony of Robert Rauch, JCAE Hearings, *supra* note 54, pt. I, at 285.

58. Karaganis testimony, JCAE Hearings, *supra* note 54, pt. I, at 194.

59. *Id.*

60. *Id.*, at 196.

61. E.g., all reference to the Administrative Procedure Act was deleted. The reported bill was designated H.R.14655.

62. See Barfield, *supra* note 43, at 1027.

63. *Id.*

64. 118 Cong. Rec. H4038 (daily ed. May 3, 1972).

65. Pub. L. No. 92-307, 86 Stat. 191 (1972).

66. In Barfield, *supra* note 43, at 1028, Dingell is reported to have said that "the enemies of NEPA are gathering around" and that "we haven't seen anything yet—none of the real jackals have come out of their lairs."

67. H.R. 13752, §§106(a)–(c).

68. "Hearings on H.R. 13752 before the Subcomm. on Fisheries and Wildlife Conservation of the House Comm. on Merchant Marine and Fisheries," 92d Cong., 2d Sess. 16 (1972).

69. *Id.*, at 29.

70. 118 Cong. Rec. H3087 *et seq.* (daily ed. April 17, 1972).

71. 42 U.S.C. §1857h-2.

72. *The President's 1971 Environmental Program, supra* note 19, at 120.

73. 117 Cong. Rec. 40026 (1971).

74. 117 Cong. Rec. 40063 (1971). The effort to restore the "adversely affected" standing test was defeated by a vote of 209-167-55.

75. See Noone, "Environment Report/Dispute between Senate Committees Threatens Pesticide Control Bill," 4 *Nat'l. Jn'l.* 1394, 1396 (1972).

76. *Id.*, at 1397.

77. *Id.*

78. 118 Cong. Rec. S15895 (daily ed. September 26, 1972).

79. Pub. L. No. 92–516, 86 Stat. 973, 7 U.S.C. 136 *et seq.*

80. See §505(g) of H.R.11896, in H. Rep. No. 92-911, 92d Cong., 2d Sess. 56 (1972) [hereafter cited as H.R. 11896 Report].

81. H. Rep. No. 92-911, *id.*, at 393 *et seq.*

82. *Id.*, at 408–09.

83. *Id.*, at 409. Citizen suit provisions similar to those of the Clean Air Act could be found in S.1478 and S.2770, the toxic substances and water pollution control acts passed by the Senate.

84. H.R.11896 Report, *supra* note 80, at 134.

85. See 118 Cong. Rec. D326 (daily ed. March 28, 1972).

86. Quoted in 30 *Cong. Qtr'ly* 814 (1972).

87. 118 Cong. Rec. H8883 (daily ed. September 28, 1972).

88. 118 Cong. Rec. H8900 (daily ed. September 28, 1972).

Chapter 7

1. Daniel Dreyfus, Professional Staff Member, U.S. Senate Committee on Interior and Insular Affairs, Remarks at the 1972 Annual Convention of the American Association for the Advancement of Science, Washington, D.C.

2. Gillette, "National Environmental Policy Act: How Well is it Working?", 176 *Science* 146 (1972).

3. ". . . A Little Rebellion Now and Then," Forest Service document cited in Borelli, "Facelift for the Forest Service," *Sierra Club Bull.*, February 1973, at 22.

4. Remarks at the 1972 AAAS Convention, *supra* note 1.

5. "Hearings on H.R. 14103 before the Subcomm. on Fisheries and Wildlife Conservation of the House Comm. on Merchant Marine and Fisheries," 92d Cong., 2d Sess. 127 (1972).

6. Address to the ALI-ABA Conference on Environmental Law, San Francisco, February 9, 1974, *passim*.

7. Yarrington, "The National Environmental Policy Act," *BNA Environment Reporter* Monograph #17, January 4, 1974, at 11.

8. For a summary, see Yost, "NEPA's Progeny: State Environmental Policy Acts," 3 ELR 50090 (1973).

9. Senate Comm. on Commerce, "Energy Policy Act of 1973," S. Rep. No. 93-114, 93d Cong., 1st Sess. (1973).

10. *Id.*, at 19.

11. The discussion of the Commission's view draws on a story in the *Washington Post*, February 10, 1973.

12. The landmark decision in the broadcasting area is discussed in Chapter 5 *supra*, at note 44. As for the field of education, in November 1972, Judge Pratt of the D.C. District Court ruled that the Department of HEW violated the congressional intent embodied in the 1964 Civil Rights Act by failing to use its powers to withdraw federal funds from segregated school systems and public colleges. HEW had, in effect, practiced a policy of "benign neglect." See the *Washington Post*, November 17, 1972.

13. Press release, March 14, 1975. Copy in author's file.

14. Friesema and Culhane, "Social Impacts, Politics, and the Environmental Impact Statement Process," *Nat'l. Res. J.* (forthcoming, 1976).

15. Sierra Club v. Morton, 5 ELR 20383 (D.D.C., June 6, 1975).

16. See 40 Fed. Reg. 16662 and 16708 (April 14, 1975).

17. EDF v. Weinberger, No. 75-1444 (D.C. Cir.) (Petition for review filed May 5, 1975).

18. *Final Environmental Statement—China Meadows Dam and Reservoir—Lyman Project—Wyoming*, Appendix H (1972).

19. Friesema and Culhane, *supra* note 14.

20. *Id.*

Index

Abzug, Bella, 205–6

access to judicial review, 62–63, 154–60

action-forcing provisions of NEPA, 16–17

administrative behavior theory, 75–85, 187

Administrative Procedure Act, 158

administrative response to NEPA. *See* agencies, federal

AEC (Atomic Energy Commission): Calvert Cliffs case, 40, 64–67, 164; CEQ comments on, 65, 66; exemption from NEPA, 195–96, 200–3; impact statement review by NEPA, 113; licensing by, 129–30; LMFBR program, 174–75; personnel actions, 117; response to NEPA, 121, 129–33; rules and regulations on NEPA, 95–96

agencies, federal: administrative behavior of, 75–85, 187; attacks on NEPA, 119–21; CEQ as NEPA overseer for, 37–48; change in, 82–85, 139; constituencies as affecting NEPA response, 122–25; decision making in, 77–82, 85–89, 211–16; discretion of, 160–65; goals of, 125–26; impact statement preparation by, 97–107; impact statements reviewed, 107–17; implementation procedures, 89–97; intra-agency rivalry, 126–29; injunctions against, 134; judicial impact on, 141, 186–88; lawsuits against, 134; measurement of administrative change in, 82–85;

personnel actions of, 116–17; response to civil rights law, 211; response to NEPA, 74–141, 211–16; as systems, 76–78; theory of, 75–82

agencies, state, 98–102, 194–95

agricultural interests, and pesticides, 203–4, 207

Alameda Conservation Assn. v. California, 159

Alaska pipeline case, 50, 145–48

Allott, Gordon, 20, 26–27, 31

alternatives: evaluation of, 17–18, 182; in impact statements, 169–72

Alyeska Pipeline Co., 146

ambiguities of NEPA, 85–89, 165–76, 209–10

Amchitka, 168, 172, 182

APA (Administrative Procedure Act), 158

Arlington Coalition on Transportation v. Volpe, 154–55

Aspinall, Wayne, 11, 24–31, 208

Association of Data Processing Service Organizations v. Camp, 158

Atkeson, Timothy, 41, 68

Atomic Energy Commission. *See* AEC

attorneys-general, private, 145

Bagge, Carl, 132

Baker, Howard H., Jr., 196, 199, 201

Barlow v. Collins, 158

Bazelon, David, 162–63

benefit-cost, 171, 177–80, 183–86

BEQA (Board of Environmental Quality Advisors), 19, 20

266